THE CHALLENGE
OF EFFECTIVE SPEAKING

**THE CHALLENGE
OF EFFECTIVE SPEAKING
Third Edition**

Rudolph F. Verderber
University of Cincinnati

Wadsworth Publishing Company, Inc.
Belmont, California

TO GREG AND RANDY

CREDITS

Designer: Dare Porter
Communications Editor: Rebecca Hayden
Production Editor: Larry Olsen
Technical Illustrator: John Foster

PREFACE

When we see the new edition of a book, we are inclined to ask why. I think the best reason I can give for writing the third edition of *The Challenge of Effective Speaking* is consistent with the thinking of any good teacher, "I'm going to do it over until I get it right!"

In each edition an author realizes a great sense of satisfaction when he sees portions of his book doing what they are intended to do. But along with that sense of satisfaction comes that sense of frustration when colleagues and students alike agree that some portions, however small or large they may be, are not yet working. I do not know if "I've got it right" in this edition, but I have made the effort. For those who are trying to learn how to give effective speeches, everything in this book is directed toward helping you achieve that goal in the easiest, most understandable, and most interesting way possible.

Challenge continues to differ from most books in its assumption that learning best occurs when specific principles are presented in units and are applied in assignments that stress those principles. Thus, Fundamental Principles are discussed as a background for preparing a first speech assignment, and remaining chapters then focus on such skills as using visual aids, explaining processes, describing, defining, lecturing, reasoning, motivating, and refuting. Each chapter contains an assignment, a student outline, and a student speech illustrating the assignment.

Part One, Orientation, reflects only minor changes. This part shows the relationship between public speaking and the communication process and stresses the importance of listening.

Part Two, Fundamental Principles, considers the steps of speech preparation in four chapters relating to content, organization, style, and delivery. The nine exercises included within the unit lead to the preparation and delivery of a first speech, and the assignment for the speech serves as a culmination. In addition to updating all illustrative material, I have tried to build greater depth of analysis without altering the basic strengths of the chapters.

Parts Three and Four, the units on informative and persuasive speaking, have been significantly strengthened. The changes were primarily directed to those courses in which only one informative and/or one persuasive speech can be assigned within the term. The student can approach his or her one speech with considerably more confidence as a result. In Part Three, Informative Speaking, the introductory chapter has been completely revised to give the student a better idea of what is required of successful information exchange in any context. The speech assignment chapters preserve the basic content that has made them so popular. Part Four, Persuasive Speaking, has received the greatest revision. The introductory chapter was completely revised to give the student a complete overview of the persuasive speaking process. The chapter on motivation now offers a more complete analysis of psychological and emotional development.

In Part Five, Alternate Forms, a chapter on speeches for special occasions has been added to the group discussion chapter, so that a course of greater length can have greater variety of procedure.

Special thanks are due all the students who have evaluated materials in the second edition and who contributed speeches and outlines appearing in the text. Likewise I owe a debt of gratitude to the many instructors who commented specifically and helpfully about their experience in using the earlier edition, especially Gerard J. Bevan, County College of Morris; M. Eugene Bierbaum, State University of New York, College at Cortland; Phyllis Selby Dabbs, Bakersfield College; Harvey Dubin, Catonsville Community College; Michael W. Fedo, North Hennepin Community College; James Glann, State University of New York, College of A & S at Oswego; Hazel Heiman, University of North Dakota; and Sherwood Snyder III, Chicago State University. I also wish to express appreciation to my colleagues, faculty, and graduate students who read portions of the revised text; to Nicholas M. Cripe, Butler University, and Gary L. Miller, West Valley College, who read the complete manuscript for this edition and offered excellent suggestions; and to Rebecca Hayden, who I am convinced is the most helpful speech editor a person could ever want to work with. Finally, a special thanks to my wife, Kathleen, for her careful editing and sound advice in weighing many diverse suggestions for improvement, as well as for her tender prodding when the creative juices were not flowing very well and complete understanding when creative juices were flowing so well that she had cause to wonder whether she were wife or editor.

R. F. V.

CONTENTS

APPENDIX

THREE CONTEMPORARY SPEECHES

THE CHALLENGE
OF EFFECTIVE SPEAKING

ORIENTATION

PART ONE

EFFECTIVE SPEAKING AND THE COMMUNICATION PROCESS

Whether we are talking with a person next to us before class begins, discussing things at a student-union board meeting, or giving instructions to a karate class, we are involved in *communication*. This book is about one type of communication: effective speaking. However, to become an effective speaker, we should understand the parts or variables of the communication process.

What is communication? An analysis of more than fifty different definitions leads me to suggest this working definition: *Communication is the process of sending and receiving messages. A source stimulates meaning in the mind of a receiver by means of a message conveyed by symbols. The receiver responds either mentally or physically to the message.* In this definition the communication process involves at least six variables: *source, message, channel, receiver, feedback,* and *noise.* Let us look at how these six variables operate when you are delivering a speech.

THE SOURCE

originator

The source is the *originator* of the communication message. The source is usually an individual; however, it may be a group of people —a committee, a company, or even a nation. As the author of this book, I am the source of the communication you are reading. In speeches you prepare and deliver, you will be the source. As the source, what you say in speeches is affected by your past experiences, moods, feelings, attitudes, beliefs, values, unbringing, sex, occupation, religion, even climate and weather. In this book, we will discuss how the nature of the source, the speaker, affects the informational or persuasive value of the message being communicated.

THE MESSAGE

i dea or feeling

The message is the idea or feeling that the source communicates. In this book, my message is information about how to prepare speeches. The content of your speeches will be your message. Messages have three components: *meaning, symbols* expressing the meaning, and *form or organization.*

Meaning is the ideas and feelings within us. Each of us knows what it feels like to be hungry, tired, in love. To communicate meaning, we must stimulate the same or analogous meaning in the mind of someone else. To do this, we turn the ideas and feelings we have into symbols—that is, words or actions that stand for or represent something.

The process of turning ideas and feelings into symbols is called *encoding.* Generally, we do not consciously think about the encoding process. When our stomach begins to gnaw, we say, "I'm hungry," not "I wonder what symbols I can use to best express what I am feeling." Sometimes we come close to realizing we are encoding when we grope for words, when we have an idea and stutter and stammer to find the word that "is on the tip of our tongue." In encoding, we select verbal symbols—words—to represent our meaning. At the same time, our facial expressions, gestures, tone of voice, and attitudes—all nonverbal cues—accompany our words and affect the meaning of our message.

Messages may be intentional or unintentional. By intentional, we mean that the speaker makes a conscious effort to select the symbols used in the communication; the message being sent has a deliberate purpose. Yet, at the same time, messages may be sent unintentionally. For instance, if you ask a person how things are going and the reply is "Great," whether you interpret the message as honest or sarcastic will depend on whether "Great" was accompanied by a smile or a growl. Both intentional and unintentional messages are important in stimulating meaning.

The third component of the message is the form or organization for the many facets of the message you wish to send. Again, part of this organization is intentional and part of it is unintentional, influenced by our years of cultural experience as well as trial and error. Good intentional communication requires message preparation. Although some people look upon message preparation as something that relates only to formal speaking, the process is much the same even when the message is to be sent in conversation on the spur of the moment. For instance, if someone asks you how to get to the post office, even though you would be expected to answer nearly instantaneously, your mind would still take time to prepare an answer. In fact, if the route were complicated you might even reply, "Let me think . . . ," to give yourself a few more seconds to prepare your answer. So whether you must speak virtually instantaneously or whether you have considerable time, your mind must still consider idea selection and development, message organization, and the verbal and nonverbal symbols that will convey the message.

At first, putting carefully prepared statements together coherently so that they meet all the tests of effective communication will take time and will appear to be quite difficult. Later, as you improve with practice, you will find yourself speaking more effectively, even when message preparation time is nearly instantaneous. Nearly all of Part 2, Fundamental Principles, is devoted to message preparation. The remainder of the book deals with the preparation of particular kinds of informative and persuasive messages.

THE CHANNEL

The channel is the *means* by which you convey the symbols. Words are delivered from one person to another by air waves; facial expressions are delivered by light waves. Usually the more channels that can be used to carry a message, the more likely the successful communication of that message. Although our everyday interpersonal communication is carried intentionally and unintentionally by any of the sensory channels—a fragrant scent and a firm handshake are both forms of communication—effective speaking is basically two channel; that is, carried by sound and sight.

THE RECEIVER

The receiver is the destination of the message, the listener or reader. Like the source, it may be an individual or a group. You are one of the receivers of the message of this book; in your speeches, the members of the audience will be your receivers. The message is received in the form of symbols by means of sound waves and light waves. The receiver then turns these symbols back into meaning. This process of turning symbols back into meaning is called *decoding*. In the case of receiving most communication, your decoder is your brain.

Just as the source's experience affects the character of the message being sent, so does the receiver's experience affect the way it is received. As a result, the meaning that is stimulated in the receiver may not be the same as that of the source. Much depends upon how the receiver's field of experience affects the decoding process. Most of the time we just are not conscious of the complexity of the decoding process. When a speaker says, "The water level dropped 2 feet," our perception is that we have an instant mental picture of the meaning being communicated. We do not consciously think, "Let's see, *water level* means the height of the water, *dropped* means went down, and *2 feet* is a distance of 24 inches—so the water is 24 inches lower than it was." Our mind goes through this process instantaneously. Moreover, we are seldom aware of the potential for misunderstanding within the decoding process. As a receiver, we may not pay too much attention to whether our mental picture of "dropped" is necessarily the same as that of the source. From the complexity of the encoding-decoding process, we can see that we are very lucky to be able to communicate at all.

At this point, some theorists would say that our analysis of communication between two persons is complete. Communication theorists used to say communication operated on a SMCR model— that is, a source (S) sends a message (M), by means of one or more channels (C), to a receiver (R). Such a model depicts communication as one-directional. But modern theorists argue that feedback is fundamental to the communication process.

FEEDBACK

Whether communication really takes place is determined by the verbal and nonverbal *response* of the receiver. This response, called feedback, tells the source whether his message was heard, seen, or understood. If feedback indicates that the communication was not received, or was received incorrectly, or was misinterpreted, the source can send the message again, perhaps in a different way.

Different kinds of communication situations provide for different amounts of feedback. A zero feedback situation is said to exist when it is virtually impossible for the sender to be aware of a receiver's response. Suppose that right now I stated in this book: "Stop what you are doing and draw an equilateral triangle resting on one of its sides." I would have no way of knowing whether you understood what I was talking about, whether you actually drew the triangle, or, if you drew it, whether you drew it correctly. As the source of that message—as well as the other messages in this textbook—I cannot know for sure whether I am really communicating. The lack of direct feedback is one of the weaknesses of any of the forms of mass communication. The source has little or no immediate opportunity to test the impact of his message.

Suppose, however, that instead of being the author of a book I am your instructor in a class of fifty students. Now suppose that I asked you to draw an equilateral triangle resting on one of its sides. Even if you said nothing, my presence would enable me to monitor your nonverbal feedback directly. If you drew the triangle, I could see it; if you refused, I would know; in some cases I could see exactly what you were drawing. Now suppose that in this classroom, as I asked you to draw the triangle, you were free to ask me any direct questions and I was free and willing to respond. The free flow of interacting communication that would take place represents the highest level of feedback.

How important is feedback to effective communication? Leavitt and Mueller[1] conducted an experiment similar to the one described above. They reported that communication improved markedly as the situation moved from zero feedback to complete interaction. In our communication, whether conversation or public speaking, we want to stimulate as much feedback as the situation will allow. In various places in this book we will be concerned with monitoring feedback and responding to it. Although many of your speaking assignments will not allow direct verbal feedback during the regular speaking time, you should learn to take advantage of any non-verbal feedback you get.

NOISE

Our ability to interpret, understand, or respond to symbols is often inhibited by the amount of "noise" accompanying the communication. Noise can consist of both *external* interference in the channels and the *internal* perceptions and experiences that affect communication. Much of your success as a communicator will depend on how you avoid, lessen, or deal with noise. For instance, if, while I am giving the verbal instructions for drawing a triangle, a jack hammer is going full blast outside the window of our classroom, you would not hear the message because of the physical noise; and communication could not take place until the noise was eliminated. If, while giving the directions, I exhibit certain annoying mannerisms or speak with a severe speech impediment, these noise factors could intrude enough so that communication could not take place unless the source lessened the noise or the receiver determined not to let the noise bother him. In each of these cases, actual physical noise would be clogging the channels of communication.

More often the noise that provides a barrier to communication is not physical but semantic noise that grows from our perceptions and experiences—and semantic noises may cause us to misinterpret or misunderstand without our even knowing it. For instance, suppose I asked you to meet me at the greenhouse. You may perceive a greenhouse as a place where plants are grown under glass; if I perceived a greenhouse as a house painted green, we might never

[1] H. J. Leavitt and Ronald A. H. Mueller, "Some Effects of Feedback on Communication," *Human Relations*, Vol. 4 (1951), p. 403.

meet. Suppose a speaker talks of the benefits of democracy in ensuring personal freedom. If the speaker and all the listeners had the
same middle-class experiences, then communication would probably
take place. But if listeners had experienced a good deal of social
injustice, the concept of "democracy ensuring personal freedom"
might well sound like hypocrisy. Communication cannot take place
if semantic noise causes the source and the receiver to perceive the
symbols of communication differently. Because we view language
in terms of our own experiences, the semantic noise factor may be
the most important barrier to the communication process and the
most difficult one to deal with. Especially in Chapter 5, on style, we
will discuss the use of language to convey ideas and feelings clearly,
vividly, emphatically, and appropriately.

**SUMMARY OF
COMMUNICATION
PROCESS**

Now let us look at these six variables in model form. Through
a pictorial representation we may be able to see how these variables
interrelate. Figure 1.1 represents the communication process in
terms of a one-to-one relationship. Figure 1.2 illustrates the process
in a public speaking setting.

Now to summarize, let us relate a simple communication act and
trace the six variables in operation. As the professor looks at his
watch he sees he has only five minutes left. He frowns because he
still has one more major point, but, aware that time is too short to

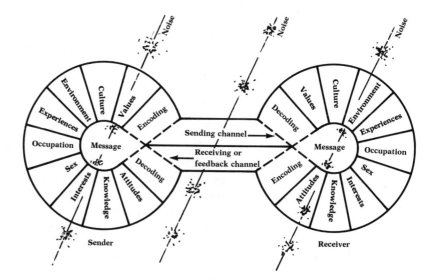

Figure 1.1   A model of communication between two individuals.

cover it, he says, "That's enough for today." Members of the class gather books, pencils, paper, and coats, and begin filing out.

The professor, the *source*, conveys his *message* in verbal and nonverbal symbols. His language "That's enough for today" is the verbal representation of his thoughts; his frown and his dejected tone are the nonverbal representation of his frustration at not having more time. In this case, the nonverbal symbols say more than the words about the professor's feelings. His words and the tone of voice are carried by air waves and facial expression and bodily action by light waves (the *channel*) to each member of the class. Each member of the class, the *receiver*, records the sound and light waves and then interprets (decodes) the verbal and nonverbal symbols that carried the message. As a result of their interpretation of the message, the class responds, by *feedback*, by gathering materials and leaving. In this example there were no barriers (*noise*) to the satisfactory completion of the communication.

The variables of source, message, receiver, channel, feedback, and noise are used to analyze the nature of any communication act whether it is accidental or intentional. As we have discussed

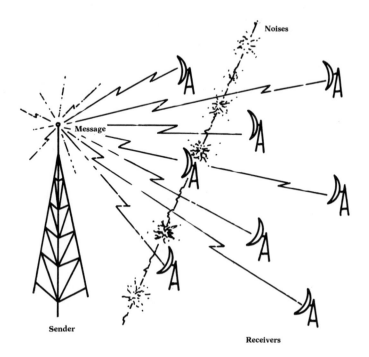

Figure 1.2 A model of communication between a public speaker and audience.

these variables we have tried to show how each of them may be considered in the context of effective speaking. We should note that, first, effective speaking is message oriented; it deals with transmission of information. Second, the meaning of the message is source selected; a speaker intends to get some point across with his communication, and he makes an effort to prepare the message so that it will communicate that point. Third, effective speaking is basically verbal and nonverbal.

The ultimate value of effective speaking arises from the fact that we live in a society that requires comprehensive and accurate information to function. Our role in that society is furthered by our ability to prepare and to send messages effectively, by our sensitivity to the barriers of effective communication, and by our understanding of the importance of meaningful listening. How we meet these goals is the concern of the rest of this book.

LISTENING TO SPEECHES

2

talk 140-180 wpm
hear over 400/min

Your goal in this course is to become a better speaker. And, curiously enough, becoming a better speaker is a product of becoming a better listener. Why is that so?

First, being a better listener will help you make the most from the speeches of others. Everyone in class, including your professor, is attempting to model characteristics of effective speaking in classroom speeches and lectures. In contrast to the five to ten speeches you will be giving in this class, you can expect to hear somewhere between one hundred and two hundred—probably more than you will hear during the next several years outside the classroom. Because you will see a much wider selection of methods and techniques in operation than you could hope to try out yourself in your comparatively few classroom speeches, you can use the experience of others to help you. By learning to listen effectively, you can identify those elements of effectiveness that you want to incorporate in your speaking and the mistakes of others that you can try to avoid.

In addition, through good listening you can help your classmates (as they in turn can help you) by evaluating their effectiveness. Although your instructor will discuss the speeches in terms of his standard of speech effectiveness, it will be up to you as part of a sympathetic but critical audience to describe the effect the speech had on you. Effective criticism—honest, accurate appraisal—is invaluable to learning. But to be able to make more than superficial, obvious comments, you must listen carefully.

As a bonus, your careful listening will enable you to learn about more subjects in this course than in any other course you are taking. Remember, much of what your classmates say will be new information or will give new insights to you. You will find that your speech class is truly a liberal arts course, and you will want to make the most of your opportunity to learn. Moreover, you may find the information you take in as a listener today may well be of use to you as a speaker some other time.

WHAT KIND OF LISTENER ARE YOU?

Perhaps you believe you are already a good listener. Unfortunately, most college students are not. Studies indicate that listening proficiency among college students is only about 50 percent—and with a short period of delay between time of utterance and testing, average listening efficiency drops to near 25 percent. Ralph Nichols, a leading authority on listening, has conducted numerous studies and has reported the research of others for the last 20 years. All his work points to the same sad figures: 25 percent to 50 percent efficiency.[1] These percentages are especially important when we realize that roughly half our daily communication time is spent listening. Paul Rankin's original study of time spent communicating (a study completed more than forty years ago) showed 45 percent listening, 9 percent writing, 16 percent reading, and 30 percent speaking.[2] Nichols reports a variety of recent studies to substantiate these findings.[3] These figures refer to *listening*, not to hearing. What's the difference? Hearing is your ability to record the sound vibrations that are transmitted; listening means making sense out of what we hear.

Since listening and speaking are by far the two most important communication tools, we should try to improve them as much as we try to improve our reading and writing. Assuming that your listening efficiency is about average, what can you do about it? An average listener can almost double his listening efficiency in a few months if he wants to. In fact, by following a few simple steps, you can improve your listening immediately.

WHAT FACTORS DETERMINE YOUR LISTENING LEVEL?

Your listening is a product of many factors. Although you have only minimal control over some of them, you can change others if you want to. Let us consider three factors that are a function of your heredity and environment.

Hearing Acuity

Some people have real hearing problems. Estimates are that as many as 10 percent of any adult audience have some hearing difficulty—even a high school or college audience. If you are aware of a hearing problem, you may now wear a hearing aid or you may have learned to adapt to the problem. But if you are not aware of

[1] Ralph Nichols and Leonard A. Stevens, *Are You Listening?* (New York: McGraw-Hill Book Co., 1957), pp. 5–6.

[2] Paul Tory Rankin, "The Measurement of the Ability to Understand Spoken Language," doctoral dissertation, University of Michigan, 1926, University Microfilm, 1952, Publ. No. 4352; cited by Nichols and Stevens, *Are You Listening?*, p. 6.

[3] Nichols and Stevens, pp. 6–10.

the problem, poor hearing alone may limit your listening effectiveness.

Vocabulary

Listening and vocabulary are definitely related. If you know the meaning of all the words used by a speaker, you are likely to have a better understanding of the material and as a result have a better retention. However, if you do not know the meaning of some of the words used in a lecture or if you are not familiar with the specialized vocabulary of a particular study, you may not understand, and your listening may well be affected. Many poor students may have average or better intelligence but be handicapped by a poor vocabulary. If you have a below-average vocabulary, you may have to learn to work that much harder on listening.

An Ear for the English Language

If your family is very verbal, there's a good chance that you will have a natural ear for language, that you will have a grasp of good structure, and that you will have a great deal of experience in a variety of kinds and levels of listening. If you have not developed an ear for language at home, then your ear may not be tuned in to the more difficult kinds of listening that you may encounter at school. Although a student of college age cannot suddenly make up for years of lack of practice with language, you can use your classroom experiences to help you improve, even if your former environment has been a source of your listening problems.

WHAT CAN YOU DO TO IMPROVE?

A key factor in listening is your own attitude and behavior. Each of the following recommendations can be put into practice *now*.

Get Ready to Listen

The first step to improved listening is to get yourself ready to listen. Good listening takes time, effort, and energy; and, to be frank, many of us just are not willing to work at it. But what is acceptable listening effort for sitting in on a bull session with friends may not help you in listening to your physics professor, and the listening you are accustomed to doing while watching television may not help when you are listening to information needed to help you solve a problem, evaluate quality, or determine right from wrong. You have to know when it is appropriate to go into high gear; and you have to know what it means to be in high gear.

What is characteristic of being ready to work at listening? An outward sign is whether you look as if you are listening. Poor listeners often slouch in their chairs. Their eyes wander from place to place. They appear to be bored by what is going on. In contrast, good listeners sit upright—sometimes almost on the edge of their chairs. They rivet their eyes on the speaker. These physical signs of attention are indicative of mental alertness.

At first look these recommendations may seem shallow or over-drawn. But test these ideas for yourself. When I discuss listening in class, I precede short comprehension tests by saying "For the next five minutes, I want you to listen as hard as you can. Then I'm going to give a test on what you heard." What happens when the class realizes it has an investment in what will take place? Eyes come forward, people straighten up, and extraneous noises—coughing, clearing throats, rustling—drop to near zero.

By sitting upright and looking at the speaker you may be able to resist distractions and keep from thinking about lunch, about your date for that evening, or about how you feel. Even though you may not be able to listen at peak efficiency for long periods (at-tention lags of a split second just do occur whether we want them to or not), you can help keep distracting thoughts from capturing your attention and you can improve your listening—if you main-tain a listening posture.

Listen Actively

get involved

The second step you can take immediately is to become an active listener. Effective communication involves feedback; the source sends a message and the receiver responds to that message. Research on learning psychology indicates that a listener learns better and faster and makes sounder judgments about what he hears when he is mentally and physically active—when he is in-volved. Let us explore the thinking behind such a generalization.

A speaker talks about 140 to 180 words per minute. We think at between 300 and 600 words per minute. Whether we are listening effectively or not depends a lot on what we are doing during that time difference. Some listeners do nothing; others think about eat-ing, sleeping, a test the next hour, and other things that eventually capture all of their attention. Active listeners use the extra time to weigh and consider what the speaker has said. They may attempt to repeat key ideas, to ask questions related to the topic, or to test the accuracy of the speaker's assertions.

When the speaker says, "The first major election reform bill was passed in England in 1832," active listeners might mentally repeat "reform bill," "England, 1832." When the speaker says, "Napoleon's battle plans were masterpieces of strategy," active listeners might ask themselves, "What were the characteristics of his strategy?" When the speaker says, "An activity that provides exercise of almost every muscle is swimming," active listeners might inwardly question the point, examining the supporting material the speaker offers. Each of these forms of involvement helps the listener to master the ideas.

Active listening can also mean taking notes. Whereas poor listeners fidget, doodle, or look about the room, good listeners often make notes on what the speaker is saying. Perhaps they write down words or phrases denoting key ideas; perhaps they write the most important ideas in complete sentences. The physical activity reinforces the mental activity. If, as the speaker says, "The first artificial orbiting satellite was launched by Russia in 1957," we write that down, the act of writing, coordinated with thinking the country and the year, will provide both a better chance of mental recall and the written record to refer to later.

Withhold Evaluation

be objective

A third step to improved listening is to keep an open mind and to withhold evaluation of what we hear until comprehension is complete. This recommendation involves both the control of arbitrary judgments about a subject and control of emotional responses to content. It is a human reaction to listen attentively only to what we like or what we want to hear. Yet, such an attitude is self-limiting and self-defeating. Let us remind ourselves of why we listen in the first place—to learn and to gather data for evaluation. Neither of these goals is possible if we refuse to listen to anything outside our immediate interests. For instance, if a classroom speaker indicates that he or she will talk about the history of unions, you may say you are neither interested in history in general nor in unions in particular. But if during the first sentence or two of the speech you find yourself saying "I don't think I am going to be interested in this topic," you should remind yourself that judgment must follow and not precede the presentation of information. Poor listeners make value judgments about the content after the first few words; good listeners approach what they are listening to objectively.

But even when we show a willingness to listen to a topic, content elements may so affect us emotionally that we no longer "hear" what the speaker has to say. Ralph Nichols talks about words that "serve as red flags to some listeners." He goes on to list such words as "mother-in-law," "pervert," "income tax," and "evolution."[4] Perhaps these words evoke no emotional response from you, but what if a speaker says "liberal," "racist," "Watergate," "CIA," "big business," "policemen," or "ghetto"? Would any of these words

[4] Ralph G. Nichols, "Do We Know How to Listen? Practical Helps in a Modern Age," *Speech Teacher*, Vol. 10 (March 1961), p. 123.

—or development of them—turn you off? Often, poor listeners (and occasionally even good listeners) are given an emotional jolt by a speaker invading an area of personal sensitivity. At this point all you can do is to be wary. When the speaker trips the switch to your emotional reaction—let a warning light go on before you go off. Instead of quitting or getting ready to fight, work that much harder at being objective. Can you do it? If so, you'll improve your listening.

But in our efforts to make some changes in our behavior, we should try not to take on the characteristics of three types of listeners described by Dominick Barbara:[5] first, those who listen with a modest ear—compulsive nodders who shake their heads in agreement when they are not listening at all; second, those who listen with a rebellious ear—chatterboxes who are thinking of their next reply rather than listening to what is taking place; and, third, those who listen with a deaf ear—those who close their ears to unpleasantness.

Since it is easier to pay attention to a speech if it is well presented, the principles in this book are directed to making speeches so clear and interesting that good and poor listeners alike will pay attention. Nevertheless, some of the speeches we hear, in or out of class, will be less than good. In such instances, we will have to work to make the most of the experience. Since attitudes affect our perception of information, the more we allow our emotions to intrude into the listening process, the more distorted will be our recollection of what was said.

HOW TO LISTEN FOR IDEAS AND MEANING

When have we really listened? Some of us mistakenly think we have listened when we can feed back the words themselves or the details that were communicated. Actually, neither of these acts is necessarily characteristic of good listening. Good listeners listen for ideas more than for details. Earlier we suggested notetaking as a means of listening actively. But notetaking does not involve outlining everything a speaker said. Good notetaking refers to getting down key ideas. If all our effort is used to master each detail as it comes up, we are unable to relate detail to principle or for that matter to differentiate the important from the unimportant. Fortunately, listening for ideas is one of the easiest parts of listening to learn. The information we will discuss in Chapter 4 that deals with

[5] Dominick A. Barbara, *The Art of Listening* (Springfield, Ill.: Charles C Thomas, 1958).

organizational patterns will contribute to our ability to separate ideas from details.

Of equal importance is our ability to separate speaker intent from speaker content. When a person says, "Isn't this a beautiful day?" when it is raining like mad, we all know that the speaker is being sarcastic. In this case, we realize that intent of the message differs from the content, the ordinary meaning of the words. But much of our listening poses less obvious problems. On a personal level, friends will often say things that do not really express what they mean or how they feel. When a roommate says, "Go ahead, I don't mind," to our request to borrow something, his statement may or may not really be reflecting his attitude. Although the contradiction between content and intent is probably less frequent in public speaking than in interpersonal communication, such differences still exist. In the example in Chapter 1 of the professor looking at his watch and frowning, a good listener would be receptive to the professor's feeling of frustration at not having time to cover a major point as well as to the words "That's all for today."

A good listener, therefore, virtually absorbs all the speaker's meaning by being sensitive to tone of voice, facial expression, and bodily action as well as to the words themselves. Sincerity, depth of conviction, confidence, true understanding, and many subtle implications may well be revealed, regardless of the words used.

CRITERIA FOR EVALUATION

To review what we hope to gain from listening to a speaker: we hope (1) to gain information, (2) to evaluate the speaker's ability, and (3) to consider the speaker's method to help determine what elements we should adopt and what elements we should avoid. Improving general listening efficiency will help us meet the first goal. The other two goals require that we have a critical capacity, that we have some standard criteria we can apply.

What are the elements of speechmaking that a critic evaluates? First, the setting can help or it can hurt the speaker's cause. If a speaker faces several thousand people in a large auditorium but the public address system is bad and the seating arrangements unfavorable, the speaker will have little chance of success, even though the majority of the audience are advocates of his or her ideas.

Second, the nature of the audience is also important in determining and in predicting speaker success. The age, sex, occupation, religion, socioeconomic level, attitudes, interests, and knowledge of the audience all affect how that audience will view the speaker's ideas. For instance, an audience of conservatives is likely to be far more receptive to a speech by William F. Buckley, Jr., than to a speech by Shana Alexander.

In addition to the setting and the audience, the reputation, appearance, and demeanor of the speaker will affect his or her relative success. In the chapter on persuasion we will consider speaker credibility as the keystone of persuasive effectiveness. If the speaker is not trusted by the audience, this lack of trust will affect the speaker's prospects of success.

Yet, in the final analysis the burden of evaluation will be on the speech itself—specifically, the content, the organization, and the presentation of that speech. Thus, with each speech given in class, you should make a complete analysis of content and method.

The Speech Evaluation questions (opposite page) are applicable to all kinds of speeches. Most of them review the material covered in the next part (Chapters 3–6). Your answers will enable you to prepare a complete profile of what you have heard. When you have applied these questions, you should have a sound basis for speech criticism and an awareness of the criteria for effective speaking.

Speech Evaluation

Speech Setting: Was there anything about the room (size, lighting, heating, and the like), distribution of the audience, public address system, or any other aspect of setting that added to or detracted from the speaker's potential success?

Speech Audience: Was there anything about the audience size, age, sex, race, religion, socioeconomic level, attitude, interests, or knowledge that added to or detracted from the speaker's potential success?

The Speaker: Was there anything about the speaker's attitude, dress, demeanor, posture, and the like that added to or detracted from his potential success? (Although this section overlaps somewhat with delivery below, these questions are worth considering separately.)

The Speech:

Content:

    Was the speaker prepared?

    Was the speaker's reasoning, support, or proof logical? *verses*

    Was the speaker ethical in the handling of his material?

    Did the speaker have specific evidence to support or to explain his major statements? Or did he speak in generalities?

Organization:

    Did the introduction gain attention, gain goodwill for the speaker, and lead into the speech?

    Were the main points clear, substantive ideas?

    Did the conclusion tie the speech together?

Style:

    Was the speech in an oral style?

    Were the ideas clear?

    Was the language vivid?

    Were ideas presented emphatically?

    Was the language appropriate?

Delivery:

    Did the speaker have a positive attitude?

    Did the speaker look at his audience?

    Was the delivery spontaneous?

    Did the speaker show sufficient variety and emphasis?

    Was articulation satisfactory?

    Did the speaker show sufficient poise and have good posture?

FUNDAMENTAL PRINCIPLES

PART TWO

SELECTING TOPICS AND FINDING MATERIAL

3

Thurs 3/4

PRINCIPLE 1   Effective speaking begins with good content.

They say you cannot make a silk purse out of a sow's ear, and indeed whether it is purses, buildings, or speeches, we can get a lot farther if we have good material to work with. By using a little common sense and by proceeding systematically, you will find that determining what you will say will be much easier than you might expect it to be. Let us consider the essentials of good content: selecting your topic, determining your purpose, analyzing your audience, and finding your material.

**SELECTING
YOUR TOPIC**

In daily conversation you do not usually consider the selection of a topic as a conscious effort—often it may seem that you just start talking. What, then, determines your subject matter? In conversation you talk about subjects that concern you. Did you just see a good movie? Are you distressed over your football team? Are you concerned about the mayor's position on crime? Do you have a big test coming up tomorrow? If so, it is likely that these are among the things you will be talking about today—at lunch, while walking to class, or after dinner with a friend.

What is true of conversation is also true of public speaking: George Meany talks about labor, Betty Friedan talks about women, Jesse Jackson talks about black progress, Paul Samuelson talks about economics, William Buckley, Jr., talks about conservative principles, Billy Graham talks about God. In public speaking as in conversation, people talk about the things they are concerned with.

Where speakers sometimes have trouble is in translating their concerns into specific topics. If good topics do not often occur to you, try brainstorming. This is like the old word-association process: think of "snow," and you may also think of "sled," "cold," "shoveling," and "snowman." Likewise, when you suggest a word or idea related to your major areas of interest, you can often put thirty other related ideas and concepts down on paper.

To start, take a sheet of paper and divide it into three columns. Label column 1 "Major" or "Vocation"; column 2 "Hobby" or "Activity"; and column 3 "Current Events" or "Social Problems." Work on one column at a time. If you begin with column 2, "Hobby," you might write "chess." Then you would jot down everything that comes to mind, such as "master," "Bobby Fisher," "openings," "carving chess men." Work for at least five minutes on a column. Then begin with a second column. Although you may not finish in one sitting, don't begin an evaluation until you have noted at least twenty items in each column.

Suppose your prospective vocation is "elementary education." A five- to ten-minute session might yield the following word associations:

teachers	discipline	desks	math	supervisors
classroom	creativity	tests	science	principals
children	materials	quizzes	music	school nurse
books	financing	spelling	art	visiting teacher
learning	bulletin boards	language	friends	assemblies
interest	schedules	reading	problems	grouping
motivation	lesson plans	health	phys ed	programmed texts

After you believe you have exhausted your personal resources, look over your list and check the three or four items that "ring a bell"—that is, that best capture your concerns and interests. Now the point of this exercise is to enable you to take advantage of a basic psychological principle—it is easier to answer a multiple-choice question than it is to answer the same question without the choices. Thus, whereas you may be stumped if you saddle yourself with the question "What should I talk about for my speech?" you may find it easy to make a choice from among the twenty or more topics you yourself have listed. For instance, if you are interested in elementary education, you may find it much easier to decide that you like "programmed texts," "reading," or "motivation" from the list than it would be to come up with one of these topics cold.

You may find, however, that the words or phrases you select are still too general to give you direction. If so, start a new list with one of the general topics. For instance, a few additional minutes of brainstorming on "programmed texts" might yield: "writing programs," "principles underlying programs," "use of programmed texts," "effectiveness of programmed learning." From this list you might be inclined to select "principles underlying the construction of programmed texts." If you make a selection of this kind from each of the three columns, you may realize that you have three good topics to choose from for your first speeches.

Exercise 1

1.   Divide a sheet of paper into three columns labeled "Vocation" or "Major," "Hobby" or "Activity," and "Current Events" or "Social Problems"; complete a list of twenty to forty items in each column.

2.   Select three items from each list.

3.   If any of these three items seems too broad, continue the brainstorming process until you have limited the topic sufficiently.

4.   In order of preference, indicate the three topics that are most interesting or most important to *you*.

DETERMINING YOUR SPECIFIC PURPOSE

Your topic states the general subject area, and if you have worked carefully, it should limit the scope of the material you wish to cover as well. The topic selection process is completed by deciding what you plan to do with that topic in your speech. Although you may want to delay your final decision until you have analyzed your audience or until you have further explored the material, let us consider the concept of specific purpose now.

A specific purpose is a single statement that summarizes exactly what you want to do with the speech or exactly what response you want from your audience as a result of the speech. Although some people prefer the terms "governing idea," "central idea," "theme statement," or "proposition," they all mean about the same thing: distilling the goal of the speech into a single, specific topic statement. I suggest that the specific purpose be stated as an infinitive phrase: the infinitive indicates the intent of the speaker and the rest of the phrase contains the thesis statement. From the subject area of "elementary education" on the brainstorming sheet, we could select the topic "principles underlying programs." A specific purpose based upon that topic could be phrased: "To explain three major principles underlying construction of programmed texts." Notice that this purpose states exactly what the speaker hopes to achieve with his topic. From the subject area "health," we could select the topic "programs of disease research." "To motivate the audience to support the Easter Seals campaign" is a specific purpose based on the topic—a purpose that clearly states the response the speaker wants as a result of the speech. With any one topic a number of specific purposes are possible. You want to arrive at one clear statement that embodies a single purpose.

Let's examine two examples that illustrate the process of wording acceptable purpose statements:

Subject Area: football

Topic: screen pass

Specific Purpose:

"How to throw a screen pass." (No direction)

"How a screen pass develops." (Better)

"The steps required for execution of a screen pass." (Better)

"To show the four steps required for successful execution of a screen pass." (Acceptable)

"To explain that a successful screen pass depends upon the deception created by the players, the positioning of key players to form the 'screen,' the timing of the receiver, and the blocking after the pass is completed." (A more complete statement of the same idea; a statement that probably could not be made until after material was gathered.)

Subject Area: punishment of criminals

Topic: capital punishment

Specific Purpose:

"We should do something about capital punishment." (No direction)

"Why capital punishment is bad." (Better)

"To prove that capital punishment should be abolished." (Acceptable)

"To prove that because it does not deter crime and because it is not just, capital punishment should be abolished." (A more complete statement that probably could not be made until after material was gathered.)

After you have written a number of purpose statements, you will note that almost all of them can be loosely classified under the headings of purposes stated (1) to entertain an audience, (2) to inform an audience, or (3) to persuade an audience. Because speech is a complex act that may serve many purposes, we never want to hold slavishly to any rigid guidelines that these categories might suggest. They are useful only in showing that in any communicative act one overriding purpose is likely to predominate. For instance, Johnny Carson's opening monologue may have some informative elements and may even contain some intended or unintended persuasive message, yet his major goal is to entertain his viewers. Your history professor's discussion of the events leading up to World War I may use elements of entertainment to gain and to hold your attention, and the implication of the discussion of those events may have persuasive overtones, yet the primary goal is to explain those events in a way that will enable the class to understand them.

Procter and Gamble may seek to amuse you with their commercials, and they may well include some elements of information in their presentation, but there can be no question that their goal is to persuade you to buy their soap.

Because one common way of assigning speeches is by purpose, the assignments discussed later in this book are made by purpose: Part 3, informative speeches, and Part 4, persuasive speeches.

Why is it so important to have a clearly stated specific purpose so early in speech preparation? First, the specific purpose helps to limit your research. If you know you want to talk about "the causes of juvenile delinquency," you can limit your reading to causes, at a saving of many hours of preparation time. Second, a good specific purpose will assist you in the organization of your ideas, and you will see how this is true in the next chapter. And, third, the phrasing of a good specific purpose will put your topic in a form that will enable you to apply the necessary tests.

When you believe that your topic is clearly phrased in specific-purpose form, you should test it by asking these five questions:

1. *Am I really interested in the topic?* Although you began your selection of the topic on the basis of interest, you should make sure that you have not drifted into an area that no longer reflects that interest.

2. *Does my purpose meet the assignment?* Whether the assignment is made by purpose (to inform or to persuade), or by type of speech (expository or descriptive), or by subject (book analysis or current event), your specific purpose should reflect the nature of that assignment.

3. *Can I cover the topic in the time alloted?* "Three major causes of World War I" can be discussed in five minutes; "a history of World War I" cannot. Your time limits for classroom speeches will be relatively short; although you want your topics to have depth, avoid trying to cover too broad an area.

4. *Is this topic one that will provide new information, new insights, or reason for a change of opinion for my audience?* Usually, there is no sense taking time to talk about a subject the audience already understands or believes in. "How to hold a tennis racket" would be a waste of time for a group of tennis players; "a comparison of wooden and aluminum rackets by their ability to generate power and spin" would be much better. Likewise, "to persuade you to go to college" would be a waste of time for college students; "to persuade you to take a course in economics" would be much bet-

ter. When you have decided that your audience already knows much of what you are going to say, or already believes in or is doing what you wish, you should work for a different specific purpose within the same subject area. An audience is making a time investment; it is up to you to make that time worthwhile. Likewise, try to stay away from the superficial, the banal, and the frivolous: "how to tie shoe laces" and "my first day at camp" are just not good topics. If you have worked on your brainstorming lists, superficiality should be no problem.

5. *Are my motives for speaking legitimate?* Examination of the speech purpose is the starting point for ethical consideration. If you find yourself using the assignment as a platform for airing personal views regardless of audience reaction, you should take time to question your motives. Likewise if your only purpose is personal gain, you should reexamine your goals.

Exercise 2

1.   For each of the three topics you selected in Exercise 1, phrase one or more specific purposes.

2.   Evaluate each in terms of the five tests above.

**ANALYZING
YOUR AUDIENCE**

Before you go very far in speech preparation, you need to analyze your audience carefully, examining its members' knowledge, interests, and attitudes to develop criteria so that you can later measure whether your speech development, organization, language, and delivery are really adapted to the audience. If you can answer the following three groups of questions accurately, you should have a good idea what you will need to do to give an effective speech.

1.   What is the nature and extent of my audience's knowledge of this topic?

Is my listeners' knowledge of the subject area sufficient to allow them to understand my topic?

Will the developmental material provide new information to most of them?

What kinds of development and language will be most suitable in meeting their level of knowledge?

2.   What is the nature and the extent of my listeners' interest in this topic?

Do they already have an immediate interest?

If not, can I relate my topic to their interest?

What kinds of material are most likely to arouse or to maintain their interest?

3.   What is the nature and the intensity of my listeners' attitude toward this topic?

Will they be sympathetic? apathetic? hostile?

Can I expect them to have any preconceived biases that will affect their listening, understanding, or emotional reactions?

If sympathetic, how can I present my material so that it will take advantage of their favorable attitude?

If apathetic, how can I present my material so that I can create a favorable attitude?

If hostile, how can I present my material in a way that will lessen or at least not arouse their hostility?

If you could give your audience a comprehensive exam and an aptitude test and then if you could take an opinion poll, you could answer these questions with no difficulty. Since such methods are impracticable, you have to approach the problem more indirectly. The procedure requires that you gather as much data about the audience as you possibly can, and then use that data in making judgments about knowledge, interests, and attitudes.

Data about your listeners are gathered in a variety of ways. If you know them, if you have spoken to them before, you can gather data by direct observation and experience. Any familiar group such as your family or the group you live with, your political group, your service organization, or your speech class can be analyzed in this way.

If you are not familiar with the group, you can ask the chairman or group contact to provide information for you. If you cannot learn anything about the audience beforehand, you can make qualified guesses based upon such things as the kind of group most likely to attend a speech on this topic, the location of the meeting place, and the sponsor of the speech.

Usually, before you speak you will have a chance to observe the audience, and often you will have an opportunity to talk with a few of the members. For instance, if you are scheduled to speak after a dinner, you can observe the physical characteristics of your audience directly; your informal conversation with those around you will often reveal information that substantiates and supplements your observations.

What are the clues you are looking for in audience analysis? Judgments (guesses) about audience knowledge, interests, and attitudes can be made by gathering the following data:

Age: What is the average age? What is the age range?

Sex: Is the audience all or predominantly male? female? Or is the sex of the group reasonably evenly balanced?

Occupation: Is everyone of one occupation such as nurses? bankers? drill press operators? Is everyone of a related occupation such as professional men? educators? skilled laborers?

Income: Is average income high? low? average? Is range of income narrow? large?

Race, Religion, Nationality: Is the audience primarily of one race, religion, or nationality? Or is it mixed?

Geographic Uniqueness: Are all the people from one state? city? region?

Group Affiliation: Is the audience a member of one group such as a fraternity or sorority, professional organization, political group?

Remember, your goal is to determine how the members of the audience are alike and in what ways they differ. The more similar or homogeneous the members of the group, the easier it will be to answer questions about knowledge, interests, and attitudes. Suppose, for instance, that you are scheduled to talk to a group of Boy Scouts about the uses of plastics. The members have certain things in common: (1) they are all boys, (2) they are roughly the same age, and (3) they are all Scouts. Their total knowledge will be far more limited than that of an adult audience—especially about plastics in general; their interests will relate to scouting and other boys' activities; their attitude about plastics will unlikely be to close their minds to the subject. In your speech, then, by alluding to uses of plastics in scouting equipment and in boys' activities and by alluding to boyhood experiences, you will be able to adapt directly to them.

Yet, even when members of the audience are dissimilar or heterogeneous, you can uncover similarities that will provide a base for adaptation. Suppose the speech on the uses of plastics is to be given to a local adult community organization. If that is the only information you have available, you could still make some good guesses about similarities: (1) because the organization is an adult organization, you can assume that the audience will be mostly adult —most will be married, many will have homes and families; (2) because the organization is a local community organization, they have a geographic bond. As adults their knowledge about plastics in general can be assumed; their interest will relate in part to home, family, and neighborhood; their experience with plastics will be varied—some may regard plastics as a cheap substitute for wood, steel, or aluminum. In your speech then, by alluding to uses of plastics within the range of adult experiences, by talking about home, garden, neighborhood, and community, and by stating ideas that will show comparative strength and durability of plastics, you will be able to adapt to that audience.

Exercise 3

1.   Write an analysis of your public speaking class based upon age, sex, occupation, income, race, religion, nationality, and geographic uniqueness.

2.   Take one of your purpose statements from page 28 and answer the questions posed on pages 28–29.

**FINDING
YOUR MATERIAL:
WHERE TO LOOK**

What you say about the topic you have selected is going to determine much of your effectiveness as a speaker. Knowing where to look for material is a starting point for finding the best possible information on your topic. Most speakers find that the best way to look for material is to start from within their own experiences and work outward to other sources. Let us explore what you can expect to find from exploring your own knowledge, observation, interviewing, and reading.

Your Own Knowledge

What do you know? At times you may have questioned the extent and the accuracy of your knowledge; yet, when you test yourself, you discover that you really know quite a lot, especially about your major interests. For instance, athletes have special knowledge about their sports, coin collectors about coins, detective-fiction buffs about mystery novels, do-it-yourself advocates about house and garden, musicians about music and instruments, farmers about animals or crops and equipment, and camp counselors about camping. As a result of the special knowledge, you should be your first, if not your best, source of information for the topics you have selected. After all, first-hand knowledge of a subject enables the speaker to develop unique, imaginative, original speeches. Regardless of what topic you have selected, take the time to analyze and record your knowledge before you go to any other source.

Of course, you must not accept every item you know or remember without testing its accuracy. Our minds play tricks on us, and you may well find that some "fact" you are sure of is not really a fact at all. Nevertheless, you should not be discouraged from using your prior knowledge. Verifying a fact is far easier than discovering material in the first place.

Observation

Take advantage of one of your best resources, your power of observation. Many people are poor observers because they just do not apply their critical powers. Why are policemen better observers than most eyewitness reporters? Because they have been trained to use their powers.

You, too, can be a better observer if you try. Get in the habit of seeing and not just looking. Pay attention to everything about you. The development of nearly any topic you select can profit from the use of materials gained by observation. Are you planning to give a speech on how newspapers are printed? Before you finish your preparation, go down to your local newspaper printing plant and take a tour. The material drawn from your observation will provide excellent additions to your speech. Are you planning to evaluate the role of the city council in governing the city? Attend a couple of council meetings. Do you want to talk about the urban renewal of your downtown area? Go downtown and look around. Remember, through observation, you can add a personal dimension to your speech that will make it more imaginative and probably more interesting.

Interviewing

The time it takes to set up and conduct an interview usually multiplies itself in speaker benefits. Through the interview you get the ideas and feelings of a person involved firsthand. Although some public officials appear to be too busy to take time to talk with a student, you will be surprised to find that most people in public positions are approachable. The reason? Publicizing what they do and how they do it is an important part of their public relations. Moreover, many officials have a vested interest in keeping their constituents informed. Are you concerned with the way a recent Supreme Court ruling will affect policework in your community? Make an appointment with a local judge, the chief of police, or a precinct captain to get his views on the subject. Are you interested in more information on some aspect of your college? Make an appointment with the head of a division, the chairman of a department, or even a dean, the provost, or the president himself. Make sure, however, that you are trying to see the person who is in the best position to answer your question. The old adage "When you want to know something, go to the top" has its limitations. A better approach is "Discover who has the information you need, and go see that person."

One of the most important features of interviewing is that you have a good idea of the questions you wish to ask. People are far more likely to grant interviews when you tell them that you have three or four specific questions you would like them to answer. Moreover, the interviewee is likely to be impressed by your careful preparation, and he might be more open with you than you would expect.

A variation of the interview is the survey. When you have a topic in which you need individual comments, you can conduct a poll of students, dorm residents, commuters, or any segment of the group whose views you want. Again, if you prepare a few well-worded questions, you are more likely to get answers. You may well be surprised at how many times the answers to your questions are worth quoting in your speech. Of course, you will want to make sure that you have polled a large enough group and that you have sampled different segments of the larger group before you attempt to draw any significant conclusions from your poll.

Source Material

Experience has shown that the most effective speakers are also effective researchers. Whether your library is large or small, well equipped or poorly equipped, its contents are of little value to you unless you know how to find what you need. Here are the sources that will provide most of the developmental materials you will need for speeches.

Card Catalog   The card catalog indexes all your library's holdings by author, title, and subject. Your principal use of the card catalog will be to locate the best books on your topic.

Periodicals and Magazines   Periodicals are publications that appear at fixed periods: weekly, biweekly, monthly, quarterly, or yearly. The materials you get from weekly, biweekly, and monthly magazines are more current than you will find in books. Of course, some magazines are more accurate, more complete, and more useful than others. Since you must know where and how to find articles before you can evaluate them, you should know and use three indexes: *Readers' Guide to Periodical Literature, Education Index,* and *Index to Behavioral Sciences and Humanities.*

By far the most valuable source for topics of current interest, *Readers' Guide to Periodical Literature* is an index of articles in some 125 popular American journals. Articles, indexed by topic, come from such magazines as *The Atlantic, Ebony, Business Week, New Yorker, Newsweek, Reader's Digest, Vital Speeches,* and *Yale Review.*

If your purpose sentence is related directly or indirectly to the field of education, including such subject areas as school administration, adult education, film strips, intelligence, morale, tests and scales, Project Head Start, or ungraded schools, *Education Index*, a cumulative subject index to a selected list of some 150 educational periodicals, proceedings, and yearbooks, will lead you to the available sources.

In contrast to *Readers' Guide*, which will lead you to articles in popular journals, the *Index to Behavioral Sciences and Humanities*, a guide to some 150 periodicals, will lead you to articles in such scholarly journals as *American Journal of Sociology, Economist, Modern Language Quarterly*, and *Philosophical Review*.

Encyclopedias   Not only do encyclopedias give you an excellent overview of many subjects, but also they offer valuable bibliographies. Nevertheless, because the articles could not possibly cover every topic completely, relatively few are very detailed. In addition, because of the time lag, an encyclopedia is seldom of value for the changing facts and details needed for contemporary problems. Most libraries have a recent edition of *Encyclopaedia Britannica, Encyclopedia Americana*, or *World Book Encyclopedia*.

Biographical Sources   When you need biographical details, from thumbnail sketches to reasonably complete essays, you can turn to one of the many biographical sources available. In addition to full-length books and encyclopedia entries, you should explore such books as *Who's Who* and *Who's Who in America* (short sketches of British and American subjects, respectively) or *Dictionary of National Biography* and *Dictionary of American Biography* (rather complete essays about prominent British and American subjects, respectively).

Statistical Sources   When you need facts, details, or statistics about population, records, continents, heads of state, weather, or similar subjects, you should refer to one of the many single-volume sources that report such data. Three of the most noteworthy sources in this category are *World Almanac and Book of Facts* (1868 to date), *Statistical Abstract of the United States* (1878 to date), and *Statesman's Yearbook: Statistical and Historical Annual of the States of the World* (1867 to date).

Newspapers   Despite the relatively poor quality of reporting in many of our daily newspapers, newspaper articles should not be overlooked as sources of facts and interpretations of contemporary problems. Your library probably holds both an index of your nearest major daily and the *New York Times Index*.

Since the holdings of libraries vary so much, a detailed account of other bibliographies, indexes, and special resources is impractical.

The reference librarian will be able to lead you to special sources and indexes in your interest areas. If, however, you take full advantage of those listed above, you will find an abundance of material for your prospective topics.

Exercise 4   For one of the three purpose sentences you wrote for Exercise 2, compile a partial bibliography, including books, articles, and notations from at least three categories mentioned in the preceding section.

FINDING YOUR MATERIAL: WHAT TO LOOK FOR   Although tapping your own knowledge, observing, interviewing, and discovering useful library sources will facilitate the research process, these sources will yield speech material only if you know what you are looking for. Speech materials should amplify or prove the points you wish to make, and, if at all possible, the materials should be interesting. Keep a lookout for examples and illustrations, comparisons, anecdotes and narratives, statistics, definitions, descriptions, quotable explanations and opinions, and visual aids.

Examples and Illustrations   A common response to a generalization is "Give me an example." An example is a single instance of a generalization or an assertion; an illustration is a more detailed example. Your intellect allows you to generalize—to draw conclusions from your experiences and observations. Yet your listeners may not have had the benefit of those experiences, and they will not be impressed by the assertions or generalizations alone. The example helps to test assertions and generalizations and helps illustrate them for others. Examples make speeches easier to comprehend or more persuasive.

The examples you find will be of three kinds: *real* examples that indicate actual specifics; *fictitious* examples that allude to instances that are or have been made up to explain the point; and *hypothetical* examples that suggest what would happen in certain circumstances. For instance:

Real: Automobile companies are making some effort to make their cars safer. Disc brakes are being used more frequently. Sharp or extended pieces of chrome on the interior are being eliminated.

Fictitious: Just because a person is slow does not mean that he is or should be considered a loser. Remember the story of the tortoise and the hare: the tortoise, who was much slower, still won the race.

Hypothetical: Dogs do very poorly on simple tests of intelligence. If a 10-foot section of fence were put between a dog and a bone, he would try to paw through the fence rather than go the 5 feet or so it would take to get around that fence.

Notice in the following how the speaker makes his point that Bethelehem Steel employees are good citizens by specific, concise use of a few examples:

Equally important is personal participation, and here's the greatest opportunity I can think of for making real contributions.

One of our product sales managers is a member of the Executive Council of the Lutheran Church in America.

Our corporate art director is a Trustee of the Episcopal Theological Seminary of the Caribbean.

Our assistant medical director is on the Board of Directors of the National Council on Alcoholism.

Our San Francisco district sales manager is a director of Big Brothers of America.[1]

Because examples are such excellent aids to clarity and vividness, you should keep a constant lookout for them and employ them frequently.

Anecdotes and Narratives

Anecdotes are brief, often amusing stories; narratives are accounts, tales, or lengthier stories. In essence, each of these means about the same thing—the detailed relating of material, often in story form. Because interest is so important to any kind of communication and because our attention is always focused by a story, anecdotes and narratives are worth looking for. Actually, these forms are very closely related to examples and illustrations. Anecdotes and narratives may be thought of as extended examples or as one or more examples in story form. For instance, by adding details, dialogue, or elements of plot, each of the three examples noted above could be made into anecdotes. For a two-minute speech, you do not have the time to develop a very detailed story, so one or two examples or a very short story would be preferable. In longer speeches, however, the inclusion of at least one longer anecdote or narrative will pay dividends in audience attention. Remember the last time one of your professors said, "That reminds me of a story"? Probably more people listened to the story than to any other part of the lecture.

As an example, notice how this speaker makes his point about how devaluation of the dollar has affected the cost of European travel for Americans:

[1] Stewart S. Cort, "Changing Attitudes," *Vital Speeches*, February 15, 1974, p. 282.

There's a story making the rounds about an American businessman telling a colleague he had just spent $5,000 on a ten-day trip to Europe.

"How did you do it?" the friend asked.

"Easy," was the reply. "I skipped lunches."[2]

Comparisons

One way to discuss a new idea in terms that can be understood, is to compare the new idea with a familiar concept. Comparison involves showing the similarities between two entities. Although you will be drawing your own later in speech preparation, you should still keep your eye open for comparisons in your research.

Comparisons may be figurative or literal. A *figurative* comparison expresses one thing in terms normally denoting another. We may speak of a person who is "slow as a turtle," meaning that he or she moves extremely slowly in comparison to other persons. A *literal* comparison is an actual comparison. We may describe a ball as being about the same size as a tennis ball. In this instance, we mean that both balls are about 2½ inches in diameter.

Comparisons may be cast as metaphors or as similes. A *metaphor* is a figure of speech in which a word or phrase literally denoting one kind of object or idea is used in place of another. "Advertising is the sparkplug that makes our system work" and "Their line is a stone wall" are both metaphors. A simile is a figure of speech in which a thing or idea is likened to another. "He walks like an elephant" and "She smiles like a Cheshire cat" are both similes.

Occasionally a comparison is cast as a *contrast*, which focuses on differences rather than on similarities. "Unlike last year when we did mostly period drama, this year we are producing mostly comedies and musicals," would be a contrast. As you do your research, try to find comparisons that will help you express your ideas more meaningfully and more interestingly.

Statistics

Statistics are numerical facts. Statements such as "seven out of every ten voted in the last election" or "the cost of living rose three tenths of one percent" enable you to pack a great deal of information into a small package. When statistics are well used, they can be most impressive; when they are poorly used, they may be boring and, in some instances, downright deceiving.

Your first and most important concern should be the accuracy of the statistics you find. Taking statistics from only the most reliable sources and double-checking statistics that are startling against another source will help you avoid a great deal of difficulty.

[2] John T. Gurash, "The Year of Europe," *Vital Speeches*, January 15, 1974, p. 195.

In addition, record only the most recent statistics. Times change; what was true five or even two years ago may be significantly different today. For instance, in 1971 only 12 out of 435 members of Congress were women. If you wanted to make a point about the number of women in Congress today, you would want the most recent figures.

If you are satisfied that you have found recent, reputable statistics, you will also want to be careful with how you use them. Statistics are most meaningful when they are used for comparative purposes. To say that industry offered the nation's supermarkets about 5,200 products this year does not mean much unless we know how many products are already on the shelves.

In comparisons, we should make sure that we do not present a misleading picture. For instance, if we say that during the last six months Company A doubled its sales while its nearest competitor, Company B, improved by only 40 percent, the implication would be misleading if we did not indicate the size of the base; Company B could have more sales, even though its improvement was only 40 percent.

Although statistics may be an excellent way of supporting material, be careful of overdoing them. A few well-used statistics are far better than a battery of statistics. When you believe you must use a number of statistics, you may find that putting them on a visual aid, perhaps in the form of a chart, will help your audience understand them more readily.

The following passage, from a speech by a university vice-president, illustrates excellent use of statistics to make his point about population and consumption:

Where do the United States and Americans stand in the world picture? Our growth rate has slowed, and current birth rates place us near that zero population growth level advocated by many.

Suppose world population was compressed into a single city of 1,000 people. In this imaginary city, 55 of the 1,000 people would be American citizens, and 945 would represent all other nations. Of this 945 people, 215 would be citizens of the People's Republic of China. The 55 United States citizens would receive more than 40 percent of the town's income. These 55 people, representing 5½ percent of the population would consume almost 15 percent of the town's food supply; use, on a per capita basis, 10 times as much oil, 40 times as much steel, and 40 times as much general equipment.

Among the 1,000 people in the town, less than 300 would be Christian, and more than 700 would have some other religion or no religion at all. Of the population, about 300 would be white and 700 nonwhite. The 55

Americans and their European counterparts would have a life expectancy of 70 years compared to 45 years for the other citizens of the town.[3]

Quotable Explanations and Opinions

Whether you find that a writer's explanation or opinion is valuable either for what was said or the way it was said, you may record the material precisely as stated. If you use the material in the speech, you should remember to give credit to your source. Use of any quotation or close paraphrasing that is not documented is plagiarism, an unethical procedure that violates scholarly practice. Many of our most notable quotations are remembered because they have literary merit. Winston Churchill's "I have nothing to offer but blood, toil, tears, and sweat," included in his first speech as Prime Minister in 1940, and John F. Kennedy's "Ask not what your country can do for you—ask what you can do for your country," from his 1961 Inaugural Address, are examples from speeches that are worth remembering and repeating. At other times, you will find that the clear, concise manner in which ideas were stated is worth repeating, even if the words themselves have no literary merit. In your speeches you have an opportunity and a right to use the words of others, as long as you keep quotations to a minimum and give credit where it is due.

Definitions

A definition is a statement of what a thing is. Our entire language is built on the assumption that we, as a culture, share common meanings of words. But of course most of us can define only a fraction of the words in the English language. For instance, a standard collegiate dictionary may have more than 100,000 entries, whereas first-year students may have vocabularies ranging from 10,000 to 30,000 words. Since many of the words we want to use may not be totally understood by our audience, we need to offer definitions when they are appropriate. And, of course, the nature of the definition will determine whether the audience really understands. The types of definitions, their uses and functions, are discussed in detail in Chapter 10.

Descriptions

Description is the act of picturing verbally or giving an account in words. We think of description relating to concrete, specific materials. Thus, we try to describe a room, a city, a park, a dog, or any other object, place, person, or thing with the goal of enabling the audience to hold a mental picture that corresponds to the actual thing. The elements of description are discussed in Chapter 11.

[3] Arthur H. Doerr, "The Bounds of Earth," *Vital Speeches*, February 1, 1974, p. 229.

Visual Aids

The visual aid is a form of speech development that allows the audience to see as well as to hear about the material. A speaker will rarely try to explain complicated material without the use of visual aids, such as charts, drawings, or models. In information exchange, visual aids are especially important in showing how things work, are made, are done, or are used. Some common visual aids and their use are considered in Chapter 9.

**FINDING
YOUR MATERIAL:
HOW TO RECORD**

In your research (including observation, interviewing, and prior knowledge as well as printed sources), you may find a variety of examples, illustrations, quotations, statistics, and comparisons that you want to consider for your speech. How should you record these materials so that they will be of greatest value? You will be able to use only a fraction of the material you find. Moreover, you can never be sure of the order in which you will use the materials in the speech. Therefore, you need a method of recording that will allow you to use or select the better materials and to order the materials to meet your needs.

The note card method is probably the best. As you find materials, record each item separately on 3-by-5-inch or 4-by-6-inch cards. Although it may seem easier to record materials from one source on a single sheet of paper or on a large card, sorting and arranging

---

Topic: <u>Conviction of Politicians</u>

"In the three years that he has been the U.S. Attorney for northern Illinois, James ("Big Jim") Thompson has won convictions of 239 errant politicians, cops and other public servants. Currently another 40 are under indictment."

"Big Jim's Laws," <u>Time</u>, February 3, 1975, p. 58.

Figure 3.1 Example of a note card recording information.

material is much easier when each item of that material is re-corded on a separate card. In addition to recording each item separately, you should indicate the name of the source, the name of the author if one is given, and the page number from which it was taken. You will not necessarily need this material, but should you decide to quote directly or to reexamine a point, you will know where it came from. Figure 3.1 illustrates a useful note card form.

How much source material will you need? A rule-of-thumb an-swer is to have at least two or three times the amount of develop-mental material that you could use in the speech. If your speech is a three-minute assignment and you can read aloud all the material you have discovered in that time, the volume of material is probably sufficient.

How many sources should you use? As a rule, you should never use fewer than three sources. One-source speeches often lead to plagiarism; furthermore, a one-source or two-source speech just does not give you sufficient breadth of material. The process of selection, putting material together, adding, cutting, and revising will enable you to develop an original approach to your topic.

How you go about organizing, developing, and adapting material to your audience will be considered in the next two chapters.

Exercise 5   For one of the specific purposes you plan to use for a speech this term, gather examples of each kind of developmental material dis-cussed above: example, illustration, comparison, statistics, and quo-tation. Make sure that you draw your material from at least three and preferably from four or more sources.

ORGANIZING SPEECH MATERIALS

4

PRINCIPLE 2 Effective speaking involves organizing material so that it develops and heightens the speech purpose.

Now that you have enough material to develop a speech that will meet your time limit, your next step is to organize the material. Effective speech organization is achieved through a systematic preparation of the body, the introduction, and the conclusion of the speech, and it is tested by means of a speech outline.

PREPARING THE BODY OF THE SPEECH

Since the body of the speech contains the essence of the content and since the introduction and the conclusion relate to it directly, the body should be prepared first. Its preparation involves selecting and stating main points and selecting and adapting developmental materials.

Selecting and Stating Main Points

If you think of your prospective speech as a series of ideas, some more important than others, this may help explain the principle of subordination that underlies the theory of speech organization. The specific purpose states the goal of the speech; the main points divide the specific purpose into its key parts; and the rest of the body of the speech develops, explains, or proves the main points. Since the main points anchor the structure of the speech and since they are next in importance to the purpose of the speech, they should be carefully selected and phrased.

As a rule, main points are complete sentence statements that best develop the specific purpose. Let us consider the practical application of this rule to speech preparation. For the specific purpose "To explain that three major causes of juvenile delinquency are poverty, broken homes, and lack of discipline," what would be the main points? The answer can be expressed in complete-sentence outline form:

I. One cause of juvenile delinquency is poverty.

II. A second cause of juvenile delinquency is broken homes.

III. A third cause of juvenile delinquency is lack of discipline.

Likewise, the main points for the specific purpose "To prove that the ungraded primary system has many advantages" would be the sentence statements of each of the advantages. Remember, there is nothing mysterious, unusual, peculiar, or tricky about selecting main points. Each of the stated or implied areas of the specific purpose will be one of the main points of the speech.

Actually, the ease with which you can determine your main points may prove to be an excellent test of the soundness of your specific purpose. For if you cannot determine what your main points are, the specific purpose is probably too vague and should be revised. For instance, what would be the main points for the specific purpose "To talk about airplanes"? Since the phrase "about airplanes" gives no clue to the intended line of development, the main points cannot be determined.

Once you have selected the main points, you need to consider whether you have phrased them in clear, specific complete-sentence form. Vague, meaningless main points will have the same effect on the speech development as a vague purpose. If you do not know exactly what your main points mean, you cannot expect your audience to understand them. To illustrate careful phrasing, let us examine three different sets of main points, one composed of labels, a second composed of carelessly phrased sentences, and a third composed of complete, substantive statements:

Purpose: To explain that our clothes tell us several things about our society.

Set 1	Set 2	Set 3
I. Casual	I. They are casual.	I. Our clothes indicate our casual look.
II. Youthful	II. They are youthful.	II. Our clothes indicate our emphasis on youthfulness.
III. Similarities	III. There is a similarity between men's and women's.	III. Our clothes indicate the similarity in men's and women's roles.
IV. Little distinction	IV. There is little distinction between rich and poor.	IV. Our clothes indicate the lack of visual distinction between the rich and poor.

The labels in the first column indicate the subject areas only. Although the words "youthful," "casual," "similarities," and "little distinction" relate to the purpose and indicate the subject areas of the main points, the nature of the relationship is unknown. In the second set, the complete-sentence main points are more meaningful than the labels. Nevertheless, the use of "they" and "there" along with the verb "to be" makes the statements vague, indirect, and generally unclear. The speaker might get his point across, but any effectiveness would be a result of speech development rather than a result of clear statement of main points. The third set is considerably better. The main points include each of the classifications; moreover, they explain the relationships of the categories to the purpose sentence. If the audience remembers only the main points of Set 3, they would still know exactly what our clothes tell us about our society.

As you begin to phrase prospective main points, you may find your list growing to five, seven, or even ten that seem to be main ideas. If you will remember that every main point must be developed in some detail and that your goal is to help the audience retain the subject matter of each main point, you will see the impracticality of more than two to five main points. More than five is usually a sign that your purpose needs to be limited or that similar ideas need to be grouped under a single heading.

Stating main points is also a matter of order. Effective speakers have found that their ideas blend together better, will be more easily phrased, and will be more easily understood if they follow some identifiable order. As a beginning speaker, you will probably find that three of the basic speech patterns—*time order, space order,* or *topic order*—will meet your organizational needs quite well. On pages 180–182 we will consider variations that are especially appropriate for persuasion.

Time Order   Time order is a kind of organization in which each of the main points follows a chronological sequence of ideas or events. It tells the audience that there is a particular importance to the sequence as well as to the content of those main points. This kind of order often evolves when you are explaining how to do something, how to make something, how something works, or how something happened. For each of the following examples notice how the order is as important to the fulfillment of the purpose as the substance of the points:

Purpose: To explain the four simple steps involved in antiquing a table.

  I. Clean the table thoroughly.

  II. Paint on the base coat right over the old surface.

  III. Apply the antique finish with a stiff brush, sponge, or piece of textured material.

  IV. Apply two coats of shellac to harden the finish.

Purpose: To explain the steps involved in the course of office of the Roman citizen.

  I. Before he was eligible for office, a young Roman needed ten years' military experience.

  II. At age twenty-eight, he was eligible for the office of Quaester.

  III. The office of Aedile, next in line, could be skipped.

  IV. After serving as Aedile, or Quaester, if he skipped Aedile, a Roman could become a Praetor.

  V. Finally, at age forty-two, the Roman could obtain a Consulship.

Purpose: To indicate the major events leading to World War I.

  I. Between 1904 and 1910, a series of entangling alliances committed the major nations of Europe to the defense of almost any nation in Europe.

  II. In 1912, several Balkan wars affected relationships among Turkey, Serbia, Greece, and Bulgaria.

  III. In 1914, the assassination of Archduke Frances Ferdinand precipitated a series of ultimatums eventuating in Germany's invasion of Belgium.

  IV. Once Germany moved, nearly every nation in Europe became involved.

Space Order   Space order is a kind of organization in which each of the main points indicates a spatial relationship. If a speaker's intent is to explain a scene, place, object, or person in terms of its parts, a space order will allow him to put emphasis on the description, function, or arrangement of those parts. Because we remember best when we see a logical order of items, the speaker should proceed from top to bottom, left to right, inside to outside, or any constant direction that will enable the audience to follow visually. For each of the following examples, notice how the order proceeds spatially:

Purpose: To describe the arrangement of the tower dormitory.

  I. The first floor contains the administrative offices, meeting rooms, and student lounges.

II. The next fifteen floors contain twelve rooms with four persons in each.

III. The top floor contains two penthouse apartments for the resident counselors.

Purpose: To describe the three layers that comprise the earth's atmosphere.

I. The troposphere is the inner layer of the atmosphere.

II. The stratosphere is the middle layer of the atmosphere.

III. The ionosphere is the succession of layers that constitute the outer regions of the atmosphere.

Purpose: To describe the function of the parts of a golf club.

I. The grip allows the golfer to hold the club securely.

II. The shaft provides leverage.

III. The head affects the nature of the drive.

Topic Order Topic order is a kind of organization in which each of the main points arbitrarily develops a part of the purpose. Although the points may go from general to specific, least important to most important, or some other logical order, the order is still at the discretion of the speaker and is not a necessary part of the topic. With this kind of order, the content of the topics and not their relationship to each other is of paramount importance. The following illustrate the use of topic order in speeches:

Purpose: To indicate that telepathy, clairvoyance, and precognition are three elements of extrasensory perception.

I. Telepathy refers to the communication of an idea from one person to another without benefit of the normal senses.

II. Clairvoyance refers to seeing events and objects that take place elsewhere.

III. Precognition refers to the ability to know what is going to happen before it happens.

Purpose: To explain major duties of the Presidency.

I. The President is the chief of foreign relations.

II. The President is commander-in-chief of the armed forces.

III. The President is the head of his party.

IV. The President is the head of the executive branch.

Purpose: To prove that more stringent controls should be imposed upon government agencies gathering information about U.S. citizens.

I. The use of advanced technology to gain information is a serious invasion of U.S. citizens' rights of privacy.

II. The laws that are supposed to protect our right of privacy are ineffective or inapplicable to the use of advanced technology.

III. More stringent controls would solve the problems.

Selecting and Adapting Developmental Materials

Taken collectively, your main points outline the structure of your speech. Whether your audience understands, believes, or appreciates what you have to say will usually depend upon the nature of your development of those main points. In Chapter 3, you learned that examples, illustrations, statistics, comparisons, and quotations were the materials to look for; now you must select the best of that material, and you must think about whether it relates to the knowledge, interests, and attitudes of your audience.

If you have done adequate research, you will have plenty of material to choose from, so that as your outline evolves, you should be able to develop each main part rather completely with little difficulty. The more interesting and more challenging aspect of speech development is adapting what you have found to your audience. Since an audience responds most favorably when the material relates to its knowledge, interests, and attitudes, you should consider the potential for adaptation of every item of information you plan to use. Because audience adaptation is so important to successful speaking, we will consider it in detail next chapter.

At this stage of preparation, the following three suggestions will guide you in the evaluation and selection of your developmental material for your first speech:

1.   If you have a choice between two kinds of material, use audience adaptation as the major criterion for making the selection. If two examples are equally informative and one of them relates more directly to the audience, choose it.

2.   If you have a variety of developmental material that supports your point, but none of it relates to your audience, create an adaptation. Remember, you can invent comparisons, hypothetical examples, and narratives.

3.   If most of your developmental material is composed of statistics, detailed explanations, or elaborate quotations, make a special effort to find additional material that has built-in audience appeal. Illustrations, anecdotes, narratives, comparisons, and contrasts are inherently more interesting. Their novelty alone will often earn audience attention.

Now, let us see how these three suggestions can be applied to a typical problem of idea development. Suppose you were working on the main point "Japan is a small, densely populated nation." This sentence calls for you to show Japan's area and population. Using material from an almanac, you could say:

> Japan is a small, densely populated nation. Her 97 million people are crowded into a land area of 142,000 square miles. The density of her population is 686 persons per square mile.

The essential statistics about population and area have been given. Although the statistics are accurate and the unit is clear, the development is neither as interesting nor as meaningful as it could be. Now compare the following development, which incorporates the suggestions listed above:

> Japan is a small, densely populated nation. Her population is 97 million—only about half that of the United States. Yet the Japanese are crowded into a land area of only 142,000 square miles—roughly the same size as the single state of California. Just think of the implications of having one half of the population of the United States living in California. Moreover, Japan packs 686 persons into every square mile of land, whereas in the United States we average about 60 persons per square mile. Japan, then, is about eleven times as crowded as the United States.

This second development was built upon an invented comparison of the unknown, Japan, with the familiar, the United States and California. Even though most Americans do not have the total land area of the United States (let alone California) on the tip of their tongue, they know that the United States covers a great deal of territory and they have a mental picture of the size of California compared to the rest of the nation. It is through such detailed comparisons that the audience is able to visualize just how small and crowded Japan is.

If you were trying to explain the size and population of Japan to your class, what kinds of materials would you use to make those ideas meaningful? Suppose a Frenchman was trying to make the same point to a French audience? How could he adapt that content to his audience? When you get in the habit of asking yourself *why* you are developing ideas in a particular way, you will begin using your research material artfully. Remember, speech development is not just putting together ideas and facts you have researched. Not only must you have enough material, but also you must consider how you will adapt the material to your audience.

**PREPARING
THE INTRODUCTION**

At this stage of preparation, the substance of the speech, the body, is ready for practice. Now you must concern yourself with the strategy of getting your listeners ready for what you have to say.

What you say before you get to the body may well determine whether they will really listen to you. Although your audience is captive (few of them will get up and leave), having an audience present physically does not mean having an active, alert, listening audience. It is the introduction that brings the audience to this state.

Any introduction has at least three potential purposes: (1) to get initial attention, (2) to create a bond of goodwill between speaker and audience, and (3) to lead into the content of the speech. These three things are not necessarily synonymous. A speaker may get attention by pounding on the stand, by shouting "Listen!" or by telling a joke. The question is whether any of these approaches will prepare the audience for the body of the speech. If the attention does not relate to the speech topic, it is usually short-lived.

Let us look at each of the three potential purposes in detail.

Getting Attention

The members of the audience would not be present if they were not expecting a speech, but this presence does not ensure their attention. The sound of your voice may be enough to jolt them alert, especially if they already have a great deal of respect for you or have great interest in what you are about to say. But many audiences are like the one you will face in class: a group of people who, though they won't throw tomatoes, have little motivation for giving undivided attention. They hope they will like your speech, but if they do not, they can think their private thoughts. So, your first goal is to determine what you can do to win your listeners' undivided attention.

Creating a Bond of Goodwill

Your listeners may be totally familiar with you and what you stand for. Even before you begin, they may be thinking about your last speech and looking forward to hearing you again. On the other hand, they may not know you at all. Or they may know you but view you as a potential threat—as someone who may tell them things they do not want to hear, who may make them feel uncomfortable, or who may make them do some work. If they are going to invest time in your words, they have to be assured that you are OK. So, your second goal is to determine what you can do or say that will make the audience feel good about listening to you. Especially in an opening for a persuasive speech this goal is paramount, although for information exchange the goodwill of the audience is less crucial and occasionally may be omitted.

Leading into the Speech

Somehow you have to get attention focused on the goal of the speech. In an informative speech you need to tell your listeners what you are going to be talking about in a way that will sustain their attention. In a persuasive speech, whether or not you tell them what you are planning to do depends on audience attitudes, nature of the proposition, and other factors. Whereas an audience will appreciate a statement such as "So now let's look at the five steps in creating this gourmet's delight," it may not appreciate a statement like "So now I'm going to give you material that will persuade you to vote for Jones." If you are intending to persuade, you may want to move from attention and goodwill right to the heart of the speech. So you need to determine how you can get the attention focused on the content without alienating audience attitudes about you and the topic.

A survey of suggested introductions would produce as many as twenty different ways of beginning a speech, most of them directed to getting attention. Let me here suggest some representative approaches that will work for short and long speeches; but keep in mind that how you begin is largely up to your imagination. The only way to be sure that you have come across a winner of a speech introduction is to try out three to five different ones in practice and pick the one that seems best.

How long should the introduction be? Introductions may go from less than 7 percent to nearly 50 percent of the speech. How long should yours be? Long enough to put the audience in the frame of mind that will encourage them to hear you out. Let us look at some examples.

Startling Statement

Especially in a short speech, the kind you will be giving in your first few assignments, you must obtain your listeners' attention and focus on the topic quickly. One excellent way to do this is to make a startling statement that will penetrate various competing thoughts and get directly to the listener's mind. The following opening illustrates the attention-getting effect:

> History reveals the startling fact that twenty-two civilizations have risen and declined or disappeared during the life of man upon this earth. Nothing that I learned in college or since has intrigued me more.[1]

Question

The direct question is another way to get the audience thinking about ideas we want it to think about. Like the startling statement, this opening is also adaptable to the short speech. The question has to have enough importance to be meaningful to the audience. Notice how a student began her speech on counterfeiting with a series of short questions.

[1] Howard E. Kershner, "Why Civilizations Rise and Fall," *Vital Speeches*, January 15, 1974, p. 216.

What would you do with this ten-dollar bill if I gave it to you? Take your friend to a movie? Buy some new clothes? Treat yourself to a few beers and a pizza? Well, if you did any of those things, you could get in big trouble—this bill is counterfeit!

Quotation

In your research you may well have discovered several quotable statements that are appropriate to your speech. If a particular quotation is especially vivid or thought provoking, you may decide to use it to open your speech. A quotation is best suited to a speech introduction when it is short, concise, and attention getting. The speaker then usually works from the quotation itself to the subject of the speech.

Notice how the following three quotations lead directly into a speech on politics and politicians:

A few decades back it was considered a great joke when the humorist Artemas Ward declared: "I am not a politician, and my other habits are good." Boise Penrose, the editor of *Collier's* magazine claimed that, "Public office is the last refuge of the scoundrel."
Even as learned an observer as Walter Lippmann said politicians are ". . . insecure and intimidated men who advance politically only as they placate, appraise, bribe, seduce, bamboozle, and otherwise manage to manipulate the views and opinions of the people who elect them."
Recent events make these jokes especially amusing. They are more timely than ever. They are equally erroneous.
Obviously, I am here to talk about politics and politicians.[2]

Anecdote, Narrative, Illustration

Nearly everyone enjoys a good story. However, anecdotes, narratives, and illustrations can be the best or the worst ways of beginning a speech, depending upon how they relate to the topic. Some speakers who are so taken with the notion that a story is worth telling may begin with one whether it relates to the topic or not, with the result that the audience enjoys the story and ignores the speech. Since most good stories take time to tell, they are usually more appropriate for speeches of eight to ten minutes or longer.

The following illustrates the use of a story to begin a speech on changing attitudes:

A year or so ago an investment banker found out that his daughter was going steady with a young man of very modest means. The banker called the young fellow in and said, "I want to warn you that my daughter is accustomed to a luxurious standard of living. As a matter of fact, she's a very extravagant young lady. So I won't give you permission to marry her until you've got $10,000 in the bank."

[2] James M. Thomas, "Politics and Politicians," *Vital Speeches*, September 15, 1974, p. 731.

As time went by, the young couple appeared to be getting more serious, the girl kept spending money like water, and the stock market took a nose dive. So the banker called the young man into his office and said, "Well, it's been a year now. How much money have you saved?"

The fellow hemmed and hawed, and said, "Twelve dollars and eighteen cents." And the banker said, "That's close enough." I'm sure you see the moral—we older people are willing to change our attitudes if you give us a good reason.[3]

Personal Reference

Since the audience is the object of all communication, a direct reference to the audience or occasion may help achieve your goals. Actually, any good opening has an element of audience adaptation to it. The personal reference is directed solely to that end. Although we have learned to be suspect of insincere use of this method made by individuals who are only after our votes, proper use of the personal reference is particularly effective.

The following is a good example of the personal reference opening used by Laurence H. Silberman, Under Secretary, U.S. Department of Labor, before the Conference of the National Foundation of Health, Welfare, and Pension Plans in Honolulu:

Good morning, members of the National Foundation. As a one-time resident of Hawaii, I still tend to think of it as home. If you think of Hawaii as Heaven—and some people do—then I have one foot in Washington and one foot in heaven. This is not quite the same as having one foot in heaven and one foot in hell—but sometimes it comes pretty close.

Anyhow, as an old Hawaii hand, I think it's appropriate for me to welcome you here today and to sympathize with you over the fact that, for some of you, your first exposure to the Islands should come in the form of an early morning speech. It's more than a man should be asked to bear. But if we must have a speech, this is the right place to be talking about retirement and pensions. It's a good place to retire—and you'll want a healthy pension if you have the idea of doing it here yourselves.[4]

Suspense

An extremely effective way of gaining attention is through suspense. If you can start your speech in a way that gets the audience to ask, "What is he leading up to?" you may well get it hooked for the entire speech. The suspense opening is especially valuable when the topic is one that the audience might not ordinarily be willing to listen to if started in a less dramatic way.

Consider the attention-getting value of the following:

[3] Stewart S. Cort, "Changing Attitudes," *Vital Speeches*, February 15, 1974, p. 280.

[4] Laurence H. Silberman, "Proposed Pension Legislation," *Vital Speeches*, January 15, 1971, p. 197.

It cost the U.S. $20 billion in *one* year. It has caused the loss of more jobs than a recession. It caused the death of more than 35,000 Americans. No, I'm not talking about a war; but it is a problem just as deadly. The problem is alcoholism.

Compliment

It feels good to be complimented. We like to believe we are important. Although politicians often overdo the compliment, it is still a powerful opening when it is well used. Consider the following opening on tax credits:

Congratulations to the Minnesota Federation of Citizens for Educational Freedom. Congratulations to all the people of Minnesota. You have achieved what no other state has achieved—substantial tax credits for parents who send their children to church-related schools. You have won an overwhelming victory in the legislature in defense of the right of parents to educate their children in the school of their choice. You convinced your lawmakers that parents who choose God-centered education should not be penalized, that they should give them financial assistance for the secular education of their children.[5]

Although each has been discussed individually, the various types of introductions may be used alone or in combination, depending upon the time you have available and the interest of your audience. The introduction is not going to make your speech an instant success, but an effective introduction will get an audience to look at you and listen to you. That is about as much as you have a right to ask of an audience during the first minute of your speech.

Exercise 6

For any topic that you might use during this term, prepare three separate introductions that would be appropriate for your classroom audience. Which is the better one? Why?

PREPARING THE CONCLUSION

Shakespeare said, "All's well that ends well," and nothing could be more true of a good speech. As you complete the body of your speech you are suddenly seized with the notion that you have got only one last chance to hit home with your point. And although a poor speech certainly is not going to be saved by a good conclusion, a good speech can be lost for lack of a good conclusion, and any speech can be enhanced by the presence of an outstanding conclusion. Unfortunately, all too many speakers, knowing that they have only this one last chance, ramble on incessantly as they try to find

[5] Virgil C. Blum, "The Supreme Court and Religion," *Vital Speeches*, March 15, 1974, p. 337.

those words that will save the day. But, like a good introduction, a good conclusion is not a matter of accident; it is a carefully planned occurrence.

What is a conclusion supposed to do and how can you do it? A conclusion has two major goals: (1) wrapping the speech up in a way that reminds the audience of what you have said and (2) hitting home in such a way that the audience will remember your words or consider your appeal. Here are conclusions that will work for both short and long speeches.

The Summary

By far the easiest way to end a speech is to summarize the main points. Thus, the shortest appropriate ending for a speech on the causes of juvenile delinquency would be, "In conclusion, the three major causes of juvenile delinquency are poverty, broken homes, and lack of discipline." The virtue of such an ending is that it restates the main points, the ideas that are the three main ideas of the speech. Although such a conclusion is appropriate, easy, and generally satisfactory, it is not very stimulating. A better one would lead up to the summary more interestingly. Notice how the following conclusion improves the overall effect:

Each of us is concerned with the problem of juvenile delinquency; likewise, each of us realizes that no real dent can be made in the problem until and unless we know the causes. I hope that as a result of what I've said you have a better understanding of the three major causes of juvenile delinquency: poverty, broken homes, and lack of discipline.

Because the conclusion may be so important to heightening the emotional impact of the speech, even when you are using a summary, you may want to supplement it in some way so that your message is impressed upon the audience. Speakers have found numerous ways to supplement and occasionally supplant the summary. Let us look at a few.

The Appeal

The appeal is a frequently used conclusion for a persuasive speech. It is as though you tell your listeners that now that they have heard all the arguments you will describe the behavior you would like them to follow.

Notice how this speaker blends a short quotation with a direct appeal for internationalism:

The global economy will not drop into our laps, no more than the Year of Europe dropped into our laps in 1973. We are simply going to have to come out from behind our desks and work for it.

The Year of Europe may have been a fable. It may have been a dream.

But Carl Sandburg has written, "Nothing happens unless first a dream."

I suggest we dream a larger dream. "The Year of the World."

Then let's go out and make it happen.[6]

The Challenge

Similar to the appeal, the challenge calls for an audience to try something new. But rather than touching an emotional chord, the challenge takes the "I dare you" approach.

In this speech to the Poultry Council, Dr. L. M. Skamser was appealing to his audience to adopt a program of radicalism to boost profits. Notice the way he wraps his speech up in a challenge:

As a research man, I know that radicalism brings forth new products and new technology.

As a marketing man, I know that radicalism can carve out for you a solid, profitable market.

As a businessman, I know that radicalism can ruin you, or make you rich.

Radicalism: movement away from the usual or the ordinary.

Try it.[7]

Humor

Whether in the beginning, the middle, or the end of a speech, humor is always effective, if it is appropriate to the material. By and large, a humorous conclusion will leave you in good standing with your audience—and perhaps because they feel good about you, they may well adopt your message.

The following conclusion of a speech about humor is an excellent illustration:

As I now glance at the hour, I am reminded of a poem:

"The coffee's cold, the sherbet wanes,

The speech drones on and on . . .

Oh Speaker, heed the ancient rule:

Be brief. Be gay. Be gone!"[8]

Emotional Appeal

Of all the conclusions possible, none is more impressive than one that truly affects the emotions of the audience.

The ending to General Douglas MacArthur's famed Address to Congress in 1951 is a classic in the use of emotional impact.

I am closing my 52 years of military service. When I joined the Army even before the turn of the century, it was the fulfillment of all my boyish hopes and dreams. The world has turned over many times since I took

---

[6] John T. Gurash, "The Year of Europe," *Vital Speeches*, January 15, 1974, p. 197.

[7] L. M. Skamser, "Radicalism," *Vital Speeches*, January 1, 1974, p. 190.

[8] Ross Smyth, "Humour (or Humor) in Public Speaking," *Vital Speeches*, September 1, 1974, p. 693.

the oath on the plain at West Point, and the hopes and dreams have long since vanished. But I still remember the refrain of one of the most popular barrack ballads of that day, which proclaimed most proudly that—

"Old soldiers never die; they just fade away."

And like the old soldier of that ballad, I now close my military career and just fade away—an old soldier who tried to do his duty as God gave him the light to see that duty.

Good-bye.[9]

Exercise 7   For the same topic used in Exercise 6, prepare a short summary conclusion. Is there any way that you can supplement the summary to give the conclusion greater impact?

EVALUATING SPEECH STRUCTURE: THE COMPLETE OUTLINE

A speech outline is a short, complete-sentence representation of the speech that is used to test the logic, organization, development, and overall strength of the structure before any practice takes place.

Does a speaker really need an outline? Most of us do. Of course, there are some speakers who do not prepare outlines, who have learned, through trial and error, alternate means of planning speeches and testing structure that work for them. Some accomplish the entire process in their head and never put a word on paper— but they are few indeed. As a beginner, you can save yourself a lot of trouble if you learn to outline ideas as suggested. Then you will *know* the speech has a solid, logical structure and that the speech really fulfills the intended purpose.

Does a speaker need to pay attention to the rules of outlining? The rules have real purpose. If you get used to complying with the six rules stated here, you will see that they will help you test your thinking and produce a *better* speech. My years of experience working with beginning speakers has definitely supported the generalization that there is a direct relationship between outlining and quality of speech content. Let us look at the rules and then at a sample outline that illustrates the rules in practice.

1. Use a standard set of symbols. Main points are usually indicated with Roman numerals (I, II, III), major subdivisions with capital letters (A, B, C), minor subheadings with Arabic numerals (1, 2, 3), and further subdivisions with small letters (a, b, c). Although greater breakdown can be shown, an outline will rarely be subdivided further.

[9] Douglas MacArthur, "Address to Congress," in William Linsley, *Speech Criticism: Methods and Materials* (Dubuque, Iowa: Wm. C. Brown, 1968), p. 344.

2. *Use complete sentences for major headings and major subdivisions*. We already noted the reason for this rule on page 45. Although a phrase or key-word outline is best when the outline is to be used as a speaker's notes, for the planning stage, the blueprint for the speech, complete sentences are best. Unless you write key ideas out in full, you'll have difficulty guaranteeing accomplishment of the next two rules.

3. *Each main point and major subdivision should contain a single idea.* By following this rule you will assure yourself that development will be relevant to the point. Let us examine a correct and an incorrect example of this rule:

Incorrect	Correct
I. The park is beautiful and easy to get to.	I. The park is beautiful. II. The park is easy to get to.

Development of the incorrect example will lead to confusion, for the development cannot relate to both the ideas at once. If your outline follows the correct procedure, you will be able to line up your supporting material confident that the audience will see and understand the relationship.

4. *Minor points should relate to or support major points*. This principle is called *subordination*. Consider the following example:

I. Proper equipment is necessary for successful play.
   A. Good gym shoes are needed for maneuverability.
   B. Padded gloves will help protect your hands.
   C. A lively ball provides sufficient bounce.
   D. And a good attitude doesn't hurt.

Notice that the main point deals with equipment. A, B, and C (shoes, gloves, and ball) relate to the main point. But D, attitude, is not equipment, and should appear somewhere else, if at all.

5. *Main points should be limited to a maximum of five*. A speech will usually contain from two to five main points. Regardless of the length of time available, an audience has difficulty really assimilating a speech with more than five points. When a speech appears to have more than five points, you usually can find a way to group points under headings in such a way that they will appear as fewer. It is a simple psychological fact that audiences will better remember two main points with four divisions each than eight main points.

6. The total words in the outline should equal no more than one third to one half the total number anticipated in the speech. An outline is a skeleton, a representation of a speech—not a manuscript with letters and numbers. One way of testing the length of an outline is by computing the total number of words that you could speak during the time limit and then limiting your outline to one third of that total. Since approximate figures are all that are needed, you can assume that your speaking rate is about average—160 words per minute. Thus, for a two- to three-minute speech, which would include roughly 320 to 480 words, the outline should be limited to 110 to 160 words. The outline for an eight- to ten-minute speech, which will contain roughly 1,200 to 1,500 words, should be limited to 400 to 500 words.

Now let us look at an example. The following outline illustrates the principles in practice. In the analysis I have tried to emphasize each of the rules, as well as to make suggestions about some other facets of outlining procedure.

Outline for a Speech (4–6 minutes)

Analysis

Outline

Specific Purpose: To explain the three major pressures that determine the selection of our clothing.

Writing the specific purpose at the top of the page before the outline of the speech reminds the speaker of his goal and should be used to test whether everything in the outline is relevant. The substance of the specific purpose will probably appear as a part of the speech introduction.

The word "Introduction" sets this section apart as a separate unit. The content of the introduction (1) is devoted to getting attention, (2) may be used to gain goodwill, and (3) leads into the content of the speech.

The introduction may be modified considerably before the speaker is ready to give his speech.

Introduction

I. Do you know what compels you to buy the clothing you wear?

II. We are not aware of it at the time, but many pressures are busily at work when we purchase clothing.

Analysis

Outline

The word "Body" sets this section apart as a separate unit.

Body

Main point I reflects a topical relationship of main ideas. It is stated as a complete, substantive sentence.

I. Clothing is selected for physical comfort.

The main point could be developed in many ways. These two subdivisions, shown by consistent symbols (A and B) indicating the equal weight of the points, consider the type and the amount of clothing that will yield physical comfort. Each of the subdivisions of B relates directly to the subject of B, the amount of clothing needed.

A. Temperature changes ranging from hot to cold dictate the type of garment that needs to be worn at that particular time.

B. Weather conditions such as snow or rain decide for us how much or how little clothing is needed for our comfort.

1. A trench coat seems fitting enough for damp, rainy days.

2. Then naturally we consider ear muffs for snow and ice in January.

3. On a hot, muggy day in July, we try to wear as little as we can.

Main point II continues the topical relationship. The sentence is a complete, substantive statement paralleling the wording of main point I. Furthermore, notice that each of the main points considers one major idea.

II. Clothing is selected to conform to our attitudes about modesty.

Since main point II considers the determinants of "modesty," the major subdivisions are related to those terms. The degree of subordination is at the discretion of the speaker. After the first two stages of subordination, words and phrases may be used in place of complete sentences in further subdivisions.

A. Our dress is in accordance with our Puritan heritage.

B. Certain religious precepts influence some people as to what is modest and what is not.

C. Our culture influences our standards of modesty.

1. In the early 1900s, a bare calf was considered indecent.

2. Today, two-piece bathing suits have become standard.

Main point III continues the topical relationship, is parallel to the other two in phrasing, and is a complete, substantive sentence.

III. Clothing is selected to make us more appealing.

Analysis

In this case the sub-divisions classify on the basis of men's motives and women's motives, as opposed to direct topical development of all the motives that are present. Throughout the outline, notice that each statement is an explanation, definition, or development of the statement to which it is subordinate.

Outline

    A. Women take great pride, expend energy, and spend money in their clothing decisions.

       1. They dress to please and to attract members of the opposite sex.

       2. They dress to get group approval from their contemporaries.

       3. Yet at the same time, they wish to remain distinctive and individualistic.

    B. Men also take pride in their appearance when dressed.

       1. They want to look appealing and distinctive.

       2. They put less emphasis on status.

The word "Conclusion" sets this apart as a separate unit.

The content of the conclusion is a form of summary tying the key ideas together. Although there are many types of conclusions, a summary is always acceptable for an informative speech.

Conclusion

    I. The next time you are driven to making a clothing decision, ask yourself honestly what has determined your decision.

    II. It may be physical comfort, it may be an attitude about modesty, or it may be to make you more appealing.

Exercise 8

Complete an outline for your first speech assignment. Test the outline to make sure that it conforms to the assignment.

PRACTICING SPEECH WORDING

PRINCIPLE 3 Effective speaking is a product of clear, vivid, emphatic, and appropriate wording adapted to audience knowledge and interests.

Unlike written communication, where wording evolves through editing and finally appears on the printed page, wording in speech communication develops through oral practice. Unless the speech is to be delivered from a manuscript, it never really becomes final until it is presented to the audience.

Think of the process of wording this way. Through careful outlining of your speech you have produced a skeleton that includes anywhere from 20 percent to 50 percent of the words that could be used in the speech. During the first practice you fill out the outline to speech length. Then through several practice periods you sample various wordings: your mind retains wordings that seem especially effective and seeks to modify awkward, hesitant, or otherwise ineffective phrasings. You continue until you are confident that the speech itself will do what you intended.

The steps of speech practice—including a discussion of how this practice is handled *without resulting in memorization*—will be discussed next chapter. Our question in this chapter is what criteria can we use to measure whether or not the words we are using in practice will result in an effective oral style? Let us begin by examining that goal of wording, oral style.

Oral style is language that is instantly intelligible to the *ear*. Although good speech and good writing have many things in common, a comparison of your own conversation with your themes, essays, and term papers can show that certain differences do exist. When we set about composing our speeches, we should think of speechmaking as an extension of the conversational process rather than as a written essay that will be spoken. Charles James Fox, a great British Parliamentary debater, once remarked: "Does it read well? Then it's not a good speech." What he said contains a great deal of truth.

Speech is for the ear; writing is for the eye. Every rule governing writing has to do with perception by the eye; but as a speaker, you must affect the ear.

Take sentences, for instance. If a written sentence is too long for comprehension, the reader can go back to reread it. A speaker knows his audience cannot go back—it must grasp all meaning as it is communicated. In writing, the compound and complex sentence is commonplace; in speaking, the simple sentence is the principle sentence form. Whereas the eye can pick up subtle relationships, the ear may not.

Moreover, you must affect the ear of a *specific* audience. Language that is instantly intelligible to the ear of an English-speaking audience may not be so to a foreign-speaking audience. Language that is intelligible to adults may not be to children; language that is intelligible to a college audience may not be to high schoolers.

To help us achieve an oral style, we need to test our language for clarity, vividness, emphasis, and appropriateness.

CLARITY

Clarity contributes to achieving instant intelligibility by eliminating ambiguity and confusion. Suppose a person describing a near accident said, "Some nut almost got me." The receiver would have only a vague idea of what happened—the communication would not be very clear. Suppose instead he said, "Some guy in a banged-up yellow Vega crashed the light and almost nailed me crossing the street." Phrased this way, the wording eliminates ambiguity and confusion. We would have an instant mental picture of exactly what happened.

What are the components of clarity? Accuracy, specificity and concreteness, and lack of clutter. Let us consider each of these separately.

Accuracy

Accuracy of style refers to the ability to select precisely the word that best represents the idea. Have you ever found yourself in the situation where a person says something like "He's a grouch"? And when you reply, "I never thought of him as grouchy," the person says, "I didn't really mean grouchy, I meant he loses his temper so quickly." Words are an imperfect way of communicating an idea intact from one mind to another. The process is made even more difficult by the shades of meaning that so many words represent. Take the simple verb "said." Notice the changes in meaning when a person uses such words as "stated," "averred," "growled," "indicated," "intoned," "suggested," "pleaded," "shouted," "purred," "answered," or "asked." Successful communication requires an understanding of words, not only what they mean in general but also how they relate to each other.

When the elder William Pitt, regarded by some as one of England's greatest speakers, was a teenager he gained an understanding and an appreciation of the language by reading Bailey's dictionary, a famous work of the day, *twice*. Even today, dictionary reading is not a bad way to sharpen your understanding of words. An interesting method of practice is to play "synonyms." Think of a word, then list as many words as you can that mean about the same thing. When you have completed your list, refer to a book of synonyms, like Roget's *Thesaurus*, to see which words you have omitted; then try to determine the shades of difference among the words. Refer to a dictionary for help—it is useful to look up words even when you are sure you know their meaning. You may be surprised to find how many times a subtle meaning of a familiar word escapes you. Now the goal of this exercise is not to get you to select the rarest word to project an idea—the goal is to encourage you to select the word that *best* represents the idea you wish to communicate.

Specificity and Concreteness

Specificity and concreteness go hand in hand in sharpening meaning by reducing choice on the part of the listener. In ordinary conversation, under the pressure of having to talk with little or no previous planning, we tend to use general and abstract words, words that allow the listener the choice of many possible images rather than with a single intended image. The more the receiver is called upon to provide his own image, the more likelihood the meaning he or she sees will be different from the meaning the speaker intended.

Let us now look at *general* versus *specific* language. "Car" is a general word. When someone says "car" to you, what do you see? You may see a large car or a small one, a sedan or a coupe, a Buick or a Datsun. If someone says "new Pinto" the number of choices you can picture are reduced. If it is "new red Pinto station wagon," the likelihood of you and the speaker picturing the same thing is considerably better.

Whereas general versus specific deals with object language, *abstract* versus *concrete* deals with ideas or values. When people say they are "loyal," for instance, you may think of the dictionary definition of faithful to idea, person, company, and so on. But what that really means is hard to say. What is an act of loyalty to me may not be an act of loyalty to you. Thus, to avoid ambiguity and confusion, we should try to state abstract ideas in concrete terms. If, however, you were to say "he always buys the products made by his employer," you would have a concrete picture of behavior.

The time to test whether or not your language is specific and concrete is during the practice periods before actual delivery. While you are going over your speech, listen critically to yourself to see whether your language is more like the examples under the headings *specific* and *concrete* or more like those under the headings *general* and *abstract*. A good exercise is to dictate into a tape recorder a portion or all of a practice and determine the ratio between general and specific or abstract and concrete. The higher the ratio of specific and concrete words you find the greater the likelihood of instant intelligibility.

General	*Specific*
Cereal	Oats, barley, wheat, rye
House	Ranch, bungalow, Cape Cod
Things	Objects or characteristics
Trees	Elms, or oaks, or redwoods
Fruit	Apples, or oranges, or pears

Abstract	*Concrete*
Honesty	Returning a five dollar bill to some one who dropped it in the street
Equality	Being able to buy a home in the suburbs if you can afford it
Justice	Equal application of the law regardless of your color, whether you have long hair, or whether you are poor

Lack of Clutter

To be instantly intelligible, language also needs to be uncluttered: it should be free from extraneous words and excessive qualification and detail.

Some people clutter their speech with extraneous words. On the printed page, breaks in thought are noted by commas, periods, and other punctuation. While speaking, you can punctuate effectively with pauses of varying lengths. An unacceptable way is with meaningless words and sounds used to fill the pauses: "uh," "er," "well," "OK," "you know." Although we accept these irritating expressions from our friends, we do not accept them from public speakers. The speaker who turns the extraneous words and sounds on, turns the audience off. If your professor calls such uses to your attention, you must learn to listen to your speech. Once you hear what you are doing, correction of the habit is rather easy. Of course, you should not be too hard on yourself for a few lapses. Not many speakers can talk for five to ten minutes without using an occasional extraneous filler —the test is whether you can keep these to a minimum.

Another enemy of simplicity is to use more words than necessary to make your point. The sentence "Yesterday about 3:00 P.M. I was almost run over by a very large, red Cadillac sedan, license AB34456, turning right at the corner of Center and Main, while I was approximately two fifths of the way across the street" is ludicrous, because it is so cluttered with excessive detail. Excessive detail, use of endless qualifiers, and reliance on that overused admission of lack of clarity, "in other words," all hinder effective communication. Examine your communication to make sure that you say all that is necessary—but only what is necessary. Once you learn selectivity, the ability to tell what is important enough to say and what should be left out, you will increase your clarity.

In the following example, note how John Cunningham, author and historian, uses accurate word selection and specific, concrete language to sharpen the clarity of his point that the good old days were not really so good:

I could take you through a full century, chick by chick, onion by onion, Irish potato by Irish potato. I could read some poetry from William Cullen Bryant and a stanza or two from Longfellow to prove in lyrics that for farmers those long-ago times were the good old days.

I will spare you that, for in truth those were NOT the good old days, regardless of poetry and Currier and Ives Lithographs. Those were days of backbreaking toil, or horrible farm failures brought on by unknown natural killers of plants and animals. Those were days when farmers stayed down on the farm chiefly because they were born down on the farm and knew no way out. It was much easier for William Cullen Bryant to catch the charm of farming on a weekend visit down from Boston than it was for the farmer's wife who toiled in the farm house 365 days a year. And Currier and Ives never seemed to be around when disease felled a half-dozen cattle.[1]

VIVIDNESS

Clear language helps the audience see the meaning; vivid language paints meaning in living color. Vividness means full of life, vigorous, bright, and intense. If your language is vivid, your audience will picture your meanings in striking detail. Consider the following two sentences:

A man in a yellow Vega went through the red light and almost hit me while I was crossing the street.

Some guy in a banged-up yellow Vega crashed the red light and almost nailed me crossing the street.

The first sentence is clear; the second is vivid. Vividness gives language staying power—it makes it memorable. How many lines can

[1] John Cunningham, "How Are You Going to Keep Them Down on the Farm?" *Vital Speeches*, March 15, 1971, p. 346.

you remember from the many Presidential speeches you've heard the last four years? Any? But there is a good chance that you have heard and remember the following lines.

Speak softly, but carry a big stick.

All we have to fear is fear itself.

The buck stops here.

Ask not what your country can do for you—ask what you can do for your country.

Each of these statements by Theodore Roosevelt, Franklin Roosevelt, Harry Truman, and John Kennedy is memorable; each is a vivid statement of the idea it represents. Of course, every sentence in a speech is not going to be remembered for all time, but there is no reason why some of the statements you make cannot be truly vivid.

Vivid speech begins with vivid thought. You must have a striking mental picture before you can communicate one to your audience. If you cannot feel the bite of the wind and the sting of the nearly freezing rain, if you cannot hear the thick, juicy T-bone steaks sizzling on the grill, if you cannot feel that empty yet exhilarating feeling as the jet climbs from takeoff, you will not be able to describe these sensations vividly. The more imaginatively you can think about your ideas, the more likely you can state them vividly.

A common means of vividness is through the verbal image. Consider the following:

This roller coaster pattern of the fertility curve has already had an impact on all facets of our national life—and will have an even greater impact on the coming years.[2]

Just think—every civilization on this earth that has collapsed and disappeared has done so when its people lost their anchors and rudders, their steering wheels and brakes . . .[3]

I especially like this one, in which putting everyone through twelve years of school is likened to cramming everyone into the same bus:

But mostly the bus creeps erratically forward, weaving rather badly from side to side, and not quite certain of its destination.[4]

[2] Fabian Linden, "Demographic Changes" *Vital Speeches*, July 15, 1974, p. 591.
[3] Theodore L. Sendak, "Anchors and Rudders," *Vital Speeches*, August 1, 1974, p. 635.
[4] James D. Koerner, "Changing Education," *Vital Speeches*, January 1, 1974, p. 178.

Another means of developing vividness is through using familiar ideas in fresh, exciting ways. Note how this speaker uses a play on the words of the Yale University *Whiffenpoof* song to make her ideas that women are not as interested in access to exclusive men's clubs as to equality of opportunity:

If the boys at Yale want to hang onto the principle of sexual segregation round "The table down at Mory's," I say "God have mercy on such as they." I'm not concerned about opening the doors to a bar, but we must be concerned about the bars to the doors of opportunity.[5]

EMPHASIS

Instant intelligibility is also a product of emphasis. In a 500-word speech, all 500 words are not of equal importance. We neither expect nor necessarily want an audience to retain the memory of every word uttered. Thus, throughout your speech preparation you are concerned with ways of emphasizing those words and ideas that are more important than others and should therefore be remembered. Emphasis may be made through organization by idea subordination, through delivery by voice and bodily action, and through language itself. Consider three elements of language that will enable you to make ideas stand out: proportion, transition, and repetition.

Proportion

One way of emphasizing points is through proportion, the amount of time spent on each of the ideas in the speech. The psychological importance of proportion can be illustrated by a hypothetical example. Assuming for a moment that proportion can be considered independently, if in a ten-minute speech on the causes of juvenile delinquency, the three main points (poverty, broken homes, and permissiveness) were discussed for about three minutes each, the audience might perceive the ideas as having equal weight. If, however, the speaker spent five minutes on poverty and only two minutes on each of the other two causes, the audience would perceive poverty, the five-minute point, as the most important one in the speech. Now, if poverty was indeed the most important cause, proportion would emphasize the point; if, however, broken homes were really a more important cause of juvenile delinquency, audience perception would differ from speaker intent.

You will probably find that your ideas have the greatest effect if proportion is correlated with position. Thus, in a ten-minute speech, if you put the most important point first, it should be the one you

[5] Mary Lou Thibeault, "The Hazards of Equality," *Vital Speeches*, July 15, 1974, p. 589.

spend four or five minutes on. If you put the second most important point last, spend three or four minutes on it. The remainder of the time should be divided among the points you put in the middle. Since audiences are likely to remember best those points that were discussed in greater detail, the artful speaker takes care that the most important points receive the greatest amount of discussion.

Proportion is brought about by amplification. If a point is important but is not receiving proper development, you should add a few examples or illustrations to build its strength. Remember, do not add words for the sake of words. If a point really is important, you should have valuable information to include. If you find that you have to invent "padding," you might want to reevaluate the importance of that particular point.

Transition

A second kind of emphasis is the carefully phrased transition. Transitions are the words, phrases, and sentences that show idea relationships. Transitions summarize, clarify, forecast, and in almost every case emphasize. Of the three methods of emphasis discussed here, phrasing good transitions is perhaps the most effective, yet the least used. We will look at two important types of transitions.

Internal Transition   Internal transitions grow from the relationships between the ideas themselves. Our flexible language provides us with numerous words that show relationships. Although the following list is not complete, it indicates many of the common transition words and phrases that are appropriate for speech.[6]

Transitions	**Uses**
also and likewise again in addition moreover	You will use these words to add material.
therefore and so so finally all in all on the whole in short	You will use these expressions to add up consequences, to summarize, or to show results.

[6] After Sheridan Baker, *The Complete Stylist* (New York: Thomas Y. Crowell Co., 1966), pp. 73–74.

Transitions	Uses
but however yet on the other hand still although while no doubt	You will use these expressions to indicate changes in direction, concessions, or a return to a previous position.
because for	You will use these words to indicate reasons for a statement.
then since as	You will use these words to show causal or time relationships.
in other words in fact for example that is to say more specifically	You will use these expressions to explain, exemplify, or limit.

Because these particular words and phrases give the oral clues needed to perceive idea relationships, you should accustom yourself to their use.

External Transition   External transitions call special attention to words and ideas. Since internal transitions can be missed if the audience is not paying close attention, both for the sake of variety and for additional emphasis you can utilize direct statements to call attention to shifts in meaning, degree of emphasis, and movement from one idea to another. These statements tell the audience exactly how they should respond.

First, external transitions tell the audience where you are in a speech. As listeners we range from very good to very bad. As a speaker you do not want to take a chance that we have missed something just because we are not very good listeners. As listeners we always want to know the relationship between the idea presently being expressed and the rest of the speech. Thus, an effective speaker spends at least a part of his time acting like a tour guide, showing us exactly where we are in the progress of the speech. Speakers will make use of the following kinds of statements:

This speech will have three major headings.

Now that we see what the ingredients are, let's move on to the second step, stripping the surface.

We'll start by showing the nature of the problem, then we'll consider some of the suggested solutions.

Second, external transitions tell the audience the importance of the particular point that is being made. As the speaker you know which ideas are most important, most difficult to understand, most significant. If you will level with the audience and state such opinions, they will know how they are supposed to be reacting to those points. Thus, speakers should make use of the following kinds of statements:

Now I come to the most important idea in the speech.

If you haven't remembered anything so far, make sure you remember this.

Pay particular attention to this idea.

Are you sure you have this point? It is the most important one.

But maybe I should say this again, because it is so significant.

These examples represent only a few of the possible expressions that leave the flow of ideas and interject subjective keys, clues, and directions to stimulate audience memory or understanding. Although these are not very subtle, experimental studies have indicated that they are effective in helping emphasize points.[7]

Repetition

The third and perhaps most common means of emphasis is by repetition. Repetition may be an exact duplication of idea or it may be a restatement. If you want the audience to remember the exact words, you should use repetition. If you want the audience to remember the idea, restatement is probably preferable. For instance, the explanation "Even a three hundred hitter only gets three hits in every ten times at bat—That means for every three hits he gets, there are seven times he is put out" reiterates the idea and not the words.

APPROPRIATENESS

The final way of achieving instant intelligibility is through appropriateness. Appropriateness means using language that adapts to the needs, interests, knowledge, and attitudes of the audience without offending, angering, or in some way turning it off. Appropriate language helps to cement the bond of trust between the speaker and the audience. Let us see how you can learn to adapt your language to your audience and how you can avoid usage that will alienate audiences.

[7] Ronald Stingley, "An Experimental Study of Transition as a Means of Emphasis in Organized Speeches," unpublished master's thesis, University of Cincinnati, Cincinnati, Ohio, 1968, p. 36.

**Adapt Your Language
to the Audience**

A question that should be foremost in your mind when you are working on the style of the speech is, "What can I do to get each member of the audience to feel that the speech is meant for him?" Although no device will give the impression of adaptation if you do not have a sincere interest in your audience, the following suggestions will help you to phrase your audience concern more directly.

**Use Personal
Pronouns**

Personal pronouns by themselves are a form of direct audience adaptation. Saying "you," "us," "we," "our," whenever possible will give the audience a verbal clue to your interest in them. Too often, speakers ignore this simplest of devices by stating ideas impersonally. Suppose you wanted the audience to consider buying a house. You could say, "When an individual eventually gets enough money for a down payment on a house, he needs to ask himself some very serious questions." Notice the psychological difference if you were to phrase the same idea this way: "When you eventually get enough money for a down payment on a house, you need to ask yourself some very serious questions." In one sentence you would be able to show *three* times that you are thinking about your audience. Although this may seem a very small matter, it may make the difference between audience attention and audience indifference. You will notice that each of the three speeches in the Appendix illustrates this form of adaptation.

**Use Audience
Questions**

One of the secrets of audience adaptation is inducing audience involvement. Public speaking is not direct conversation; your audience is not going to respond vocally to each of your ideas. How, then, can you create the impression of direct conversation? How can you generate some sense of personal involvement? One way is by asking audience questions.

In her classroom speech explaining people's reasons for wearing clothing, a woman said: "There are certain decisions you must make and there are factors affecting these decisions. One reason we wear clothing is to protect our body from any visible harm." Although she included personal pronouns, she might have augmented the directness of the statement and improved the adaptation by saying:

There are certain decisions you must make and there are factors affecting these decisions. Why do we wear clothes at all? What is a motivation for anyone to wear clothes? One reason we wear clothing is to protect our body from any visible harm.

Audience questions generate audience participation; and, of course, once an audience is participating, the content will be even more meaningful to them. Because direct audience questions seeking verbal audience responses may disrupt your flow of thought (and sometimes yield unexpected answers), the rhetorical question, a question seeking a mental rather than a verbal response, is usually safer. Rhetorical questions encourage the same degree of involvement and they are easier to handle. Moreover, questions are appropriate at any place in the speech where special emphasis is needed.

Notice how this woman speaker uses audience questions to get her largely male audience thinking with her:

> You may even know the anguish—the very real, the very understandable anguish—that men are now suffering as they take up The Problem of Women in Business Today, or, as someone suggested for these remarks, Business and the New Woman.
> What's wrong? Why this real pain? Why this soul-searching? Why all this brow-beating and brain-wrinkling?[8]

Despite their value, one caution about the use of questions is in order: Unless the speaker is really interested in asking a question, his delivery will sound artificial. Get used to asking questions naturally and sincerely.

Allude to Common Experience

Alluding to common experience also brings about audience involvement. Earlier we were talking about giving a speech to a group of Boy Scouts. If you were a Scout, your job of adapting to the audience would be much easier because you could refer to common experiences. You can often adapt directly by relating an anecdote, narrative, or illustration that will be common to the speaker and the audience alike. For instance, if you were expressing the idea that a store in a shopping center often does not have a person's size or color, you might say:

> I'm sure we've all had the experience of going to a shopping center for some item that we had particularly in mind only to find when we got there that either the store didn't have the color we wanted or they didn't have our size.

You want the audience to identify with the common experience. Identification stimulates thought. If an audience is thinking with you, they will be listening to you. The following example shows how this method can be built into the speech unobtrusively and effectively. The speaker is himself a businessman, so he can discuss the problem as common to speaker and audience:

[8] Jean Way Schoonover, "Why Corporate America Fears Women," *Vital Speeches*, April 15, 1974, p. 415.

The deterioration of costly service is partly our fault, Gentlemen. We experience the consumer's service problems every day. As businessmen, we know that the same kind of treatment is being given to our customers. Still, we don't do much about it. We tolerate the terrible, when it comes to service.[9]

Build Hypothetical Situations

Since audience involvement is so important to audience attention, you can often simulate involvement by placing the audience into a hypothetical situation. The hypothetical situation can incorporate the entire framework for the speech, or it can be used to reinforce a single item of information. Suppose you wanted to show the audience how they could turn a cast-off table or chair into a fine piece of refinished furniture. You could start the speech by placing the audience into the following hypothetical situation:

Many times we relegate our cast-off end tables, a desk, a record cabinet to the land of the lost—the storage room of our basement. We know the piece of furniture is worth saving—but we don't know why. That cast-off is probably a lot heavier and a lot more solid than most furniture being made today. So, what are we going to do with it? Why not refinish it? Let's assume for this evening that you have just such a piece of furniture in your basement. Let's take it out of that storage room and go to work on it. Where do we start? Well, first of all, we have to gather the right material to do the job.

Whether members of the audience actually have such pieces of furniture is somewhat irrelevant. Because of the hypothetical situation, they can involve themselves in the procedure.

The hypothetical situation can also be used to illustrate a single portion of the speech. In your speech on the same topic, refinishing furniture, you might explain the final step, putting on the varnish, by saying:

The final step in the process is to varnish the piece of furniture. Now, varnishing appears to be a very simple task—and it is if you do it the right way. Let's assume that you've got a good-quality 2-inch brush in your hand, with a good quality of transparent varnish open and ready to go. Now, how are you going to apply that varnish? Many of you may be used to the paintbrush method, you know, back and forth until the piece is covered. But in varnishing, this may well lead to a very poor finish. Instead, start about 4 inches from the edge with the grain, and move your brush to the edge. Now, don't go back the other way. Pick the brush up and make another stroke adjacent to the first—always keep the stroke in the same direction. After you've covered the width go back another 4 inches (now 8 inches from the edge). Move the brush in

---

[9] Edward Reavey, Jr., "The Critical Consumer Need," *Vital Speeches*, October 15, 1971, pp. 25–26.

one direction and continue right over the part you did first. If you will continue doing it in this way you will leave no brush marks in your work and you will have a smooth, even finish.

Whether you used a visual aid or not to visualize the procedure, the hypothetical example would involve each member of the audience in the actual varnishing. The hypothetical situation is just another way of inducing audience involvement.

Avoid Inappropriate Language

Appropriate language has the positive value of cementing the bond of trust between the speaker and his audience. During the last two decades or so of experimentation with the principles of speaking, we have learned a great deal about what makes people behave as they do. One concept proven to be at the base of effective communication is the effect of speaker personality on an audience. If members of an audience like you as a speaker, they often believe you. Through appropriate language you can help yourself achieve this goal. The more hostile the audience is likely to be to our person or to our ideas, the more care we need to take to use language that will be accepted by that audience. Under strain we can and we often do lose our temper. When we lose our temper, we often say things we do not really mean or we express our feelings in language that is unlikely to be accepted by strangers. If we do that, we may lose all we have gained.

Almost everyone at one time or another in his childhood replied to a particularly scathing remark, "Sticks and stones may break my bones, but words will never hurt me." I think this little rhyme is so popular among children because they know it is a lie, but they do not know how else to react. Whether we are willing to admit it or not, words do hurt—sometimes permanently. Think of the great personal damage done to the individual throughout our history as a result of being called a "hillbilly," "nigger," "wop," "yid." Think of the fights started by one person calling another's mother, sister, or a girlfriend a "slut." We all know, however, that it is not the words alone that are so powerful, it is the context of the words, the situation, the feelings about the participants, the time, the place, or the tone of voice. Recall how under one set of circumstances someone called you a name or used any four-letter word to describe you and you did not even flinch; yet under another set of circumstances someone else calls you something far less antagonistic and you become enraged.

As a result, we must always be aware that our language may have accidental repercussions. When the sender does not understand the frame of reference of his audience, he may send messages in language that distorts the intended communication. And it does not take a whole speech to ruin a speaker's effect—a single inappropriate sentence may be enough to wreak havoc with his total message. For instance, the speaker who says, "And we all know the problem originates downtown," may be referring to the city government. But if the audience is composed of people who see downtown not as the seat of government but as the home of an ethnic or a social group, the sentence takes on an entirely different meaning. Being specific can help to avoid problems of appropriateness; recognizing that some words communicate far more than their dictionary meanings will help even more.

In addition to accidental repercussions of our language, we should caution against using words for their shock value. The entire fabric of protest rhetoric is imbued with shock language; yet shock language often backfires on the user. The goal of arousing anger and hostility toward an issue often results in anger and hostility toward the speaker.

PRACTICING SPEECH DELIVERY

PRINCIPLE 4   Effective speaking requires good delivery.

When Demosthenes, the famous Athenian orator, was asked, "What is the single most important element of speaking?" he answered, "Delivery." Delivery is the source of our contact with the speaker's mind. It is what we see and hear.

Why is delivery so important? Think of delivery as a window: when it is cracked, clouded over, or dirty, it will obscure the most beautiful of scenes; when it is clean, it will allow us to more fully appreciate the scene. Although delivery cannot improve the ideas of a speech, it can provide a physical medium through which ideas are perceived.

If delivery is monotonous, harsh to the ear, or in any way unpleasant, content will lose effectiveness. If, on the other hand, the delivery of the speech is vibrant, inspiring to listen to, or generally pleasant, the speaker will gain maximum value from his words and ideas.

Now, because most of us have been getting our ideas across to people reasonably well for many years, we are seldom willing to admit that any success we have had in communicating may be in spite of and not because of our oral ability. Even Demosthenes had weaknesses of delivery that he had to work for years to overcome in order to develop his powers fully. Whether or not he really did speak with pebbles in his mouth or run up and down the hills of Greece declaiming at the greatest volume he could achieve, it is well documented that he did spend several hours every week on improving delivery.

In the last chapter we focused on wording; in this chapter we will focus on the elements of speech delivery that can be improved or perfected with practice. Then we will consider how we can go about practicing both the wording and the delivery of the speech itself.

WHAT TO PRACTICE: STANDARDS OF DELIVERY

Delivery is the use of voice and body to help convey the message of the speech. Although the best delivery will not save the poorly prepared speech, particularly poor delivery may well harm your speech so much that even exceptional content and organization are negated. Speech delivery may be the deciding factor in the audience's estimation of your effectiveness.

As you begin the speech practice, what are the qualities and characteristics you should be seeking? You are trying to develop a conversational quality that is characterized by a *desire to communicate, eye contact,* and *spontaneity;* and you are trying to maximize effectiveness of *voice, articulation,* and *bodily action.* Let us examine these six topics.

Desire to Communicate

Have you ever listened to a man whose convictions were stated so strongly that you found yourself saying, "He's got to be right—no one could speak with such strength of conviction unless he were." Likewise, have you ever heard a speaker who so bubbled with enthusiasm that you were caught up in his every word? One such spellbinder today is Billy Graham. Regardless of your religious persuasion, you can hardly escape the force of Graham's delivery. Speakers like Graham and Jesse Jackson today and Henry Clay, William Jennings Bryan, Franklin Delano Roosevelt, and Martin Luther King, Jr., in the past all have had a deep and overpowering desire to communicate. They have wanted to speak; they have wanted people to listen.

If you really want to communicate, your voice will have a quality in it that audiences will recognize and respond to. If you really care about your topic and your audience, your voice will usually reflect that attitude. And if you really want to communicate, your audience will usually listen.

Of course, you might be saying, "It's easy enough to talk about wanting to communicate, but I'm scared stiff." This nervousness or stage fright is a very real thing that has to be faced by everyone, beginner and experienced speaker alike. If before your speech, your palms perspire, your stomach feels queasy, and your mouth gets dry, remember that, like it or not, such reactions are normal. In fact, it would be quite abnormal if you did not show some nervousness. You are being observed, your ideas are being weighed and considered, your every movement and word is a matter of public record—of course, you are going to be nervous.

The question, then, is not whether you will be nervous but what you can do about it. Speakers past and present have learned to cope with and have often lessened their nervousness by recognizing the following three realities. First, if you are really well prepared, you will be less nervous than if you are only partly prepared. Nervousness is based in part on expected audience reaction. If you know you have nothing of value to say or that you have not prepared fully enough, you will and should be nervous. If you have prepared and practiced five to ten hours for a five-minute speech, there is no need to be nervous. Second, if you will try to think about communicating the subject and not about yourself, you will be less nervous. Speakers who become an active part of the communication process do not have the time to worry about themselves. Third, and perhaps most important, once you realize that you can succeed (and you can), you will be less likely to be concerned about your nervousness. Success breeds confidence. You will begin with easy speaking tasks; as you succeed with them you will build confidence for the next task. Eventually, you will have enough confidence to attempt and accomplish very complex speaking assignments. So even if you are rather nervous about your first speech, as long as you are well prepared and as long as you think about the speech and not yourself, you will be amazed to find that each time you speak you will be better able to control your nervousness.

Nervousness is related to self-concept. Some of us have a high opinion of ourselves. If we fail (and everyone fails at something at some time), we know that our failure is only temporary. We think of ourselves as winners and, of course, winners succeed. Likewise, some of us have a low opinion of ourselves and our abilities. We expect to fail and we usually do; in fact, when we succeed we are surprised. One of the goals of an effective speaking course is to strengthen the self-concept. Low self-esteem is often a matter of how we think about ourselves and may have no relationship to our actual abilities. Research shows that in most classes a high percentage of individuals reinforce a good self-concept or strengthen a weak one. All we can ask you to do is to try. In trying, you will probably be surprised with the results. Still, do not expect miracles overnight. You may see only a little improvement in the first two or three speeches—by the end of the term, however, chances are the improvement will be considerable.

Aside from being inhibited by nervousness or by low self-esteem, some of us may be inhibited by our natural tendency to be less demonstrative than is needed for effective delivery. As individuals, each of us exhibits personality traits that make him distinct. These traits combine to make some of us more outgoing than our neighbors and some of us more reserved. The relationship to speechmaking is that if you are outgoing, you may find it easier to project your attitude about your topic. If, however, you are rather reserved, the audience may not be able to pick up the cues showing your attitude so readily. If you seldom show much overt responsiveness to your feelings, you must do a little more than "what comes naturally." Whereas the extrovert shows emotional responsiveness even when his feeling is not very strong, the introvert registers the same level of expressiveness only when he has reached a high degree of emotion. If you tend to be more reserved, you must intensify your feelings about what you are doing in order for the emotions to be communicated. Make sure your topic pleases you; get involved with the developmental material; and constantly remind yourself that what you are planning to say will benefit the audience. Audiences do not listen without some motivation; they will expect some effort on your part.

Eye Contact

Although perception of speech communication seems to be primarily auditory, we concentrate better on the message when a visual bond is established between speaker and audience. In fact, in face-to-face communication we expect speakers to look at us while they are talking. If the speakers do not look at us, we will lose our need to look at them, and, thus, our desire to pay attention to them. The result is a break in the communication bond and a proportional loss of attention. As a speaker then, you have a certain amount of control over your listeners' attention simply by looking at them.

Not only does good eye contact help attention, it also increases audience confidence in the speaker. What do you think of individuals who will *not* look you in the eye when they speak with you? Your attitude toward them is probably negative. On the other hand, when speakers do look you in the eye, you are probably more willing to trust them. Eye contact is not material evidence of a speaker's sincerity. We do, however, regard it as psychological evidence.

But as you gain skill in speaking you will become aware of the most beneficial aspect of good eye contact; that is, your ability to study audience reaction to what you are saying. Communication is two-way. You are speaking with an audience, and it in turn is responding to what you are saying. In daily conversation, its response would be verbal; in public speaking, its response is shown by various cues given. An audience of people who are virtually on the edges of their seats with their eyes upon you is paying attention. An audience of people who are yawning, looking out the window, and slouching is not paying attention. You can determine what adjustments, what additions, changes, and deletions you need to make in your plans by being aware of audience reaction. As you gain greater skill, you will be able to make more and better use of the information learned through eye contact.

How do you maintain audience eye contact? It is, of course, physically impossible to look at your whole audience all at once. What you can do is to talk with individuals and small groups in all parts of the audience throughout your speech. Do not spend all of your time looking front and center. The people at the ends of aisles and those in the back of the room are every bit as important as those right in front of you.

Spontaneity

The third characteristic fundamental to effective speech delivery is spontaneity—the impression that the idea is being formed at the time it is spoken. At some time, you may have had to memorize some bit of prose or poetry. Remember when you were working on the assignment, you were not nearly as concerned with the meaning of the words as you were with the process of memorizing the flow of words. If you or other classmates had to recite, you will remember that the class was seldom inspired by the presentations. Why? Since the words sounded memorized, any semblance of meaning was lost. What was missing was spontaneity, the particular characteristic of voice that makes an idea sound new, fresh, and vital even if it has been practiced for days. Although good actors can make lines they have spoken literally thousands of times sound original, most of us do not have the ability or the know-how. Have you ever wondered why a public official often sounds so much better in off-the-cuff interviews than he does when reading a speech? Once the word is memorized or written down, it is no longer spontaneous communication, and the speaker is then required to become somewhat of an actor to make the idea sound spontaneous.

How can you make a planned speech seem spontaneous? The answer lies in how you use characteristics of your own conversational method. Since there is a tremendous difference between knowing ideas and memorizing them, you need to have a mastery of content, not words. If I asked you to tell me how to get downtown, you would be able to tell me spontaneously, because you have made the trip so many times the knowledge is literally a part of you. If I asked you to tell me about the tennis game you just finished, you could do it spontaneously, because key parts of the game would be vivid in your memory. If, on the other hand, I asked you to tell me a little about the material you studied for a history class, your ability to do it spontaneously would depend upon the quality of the effort you had made to master the material. If you had weighed and considered the material, if you had tried to understand the concepts rather than just memorize the details, you would have enough understanding to discuss the content spontaneously. Spontaneous presentation of prepared materials requires experience with the facts, vivid images of the facts, and true understanding of the facts.

Students will often say that they can speak so much better on the spur of the moment than when they try to give a prepared speech. What they mean, of course, is that given a topic about which they have had experiences, vivid images, and understanding they can communicate reasonably well on the spur of the moment. Since you have the opportunity to weigh and consider your subject matter, there is no reason why you should not be equally spontaneous with the prepared speech. How to show spontaneity will be considered further when we examine speech practice later in this chapter.

These three concepts—desire to communicate, eye contact, and spontaneity—when taken together, give a speaker what has come to be called a conversational quality. Speechmaking and conversation are not really quite the same. However, by using the best characteristics of conversation in the formal speech situation, the speaker will give listeners the feeling that he is conversing with them. These three characteristics of conversational quality provide the foundation for good delivery. Now let us look at the mechanics of delivery: voice, articulation, and bodily action.

Voice

Just as the words we use communicate, so does the sound of our voice. The meanings expressed by the way we sound (called *paralanguage*) may tell our audience what we intended and may contribute to the meanings of our words. However, *how* we sound may interfere with stimulating meaning and may at times even contradict our words.

Our voice has all the capabilities of a musical instrument. How we use it makes the difference between success or failure. To begin our discussion, let us take a brief look at the speech process.

Speech is a product of breathing, phonation, resonation, and articulation. During inhalation, air is taken in through the mouth or nose, down through the pharynx (throat), larynx, trachea, bronchial tubes, and into the lungs. We get the power for speech from exhaling the air we breathed. As air is forced from the lungs back up through the trachea and larynx by controlled relaxation of the diaphragm and contraction of abdominal and chest muscles, the vocal folds that help protect the opening into the trachea are brought closely enough together to vibrate the air as it passes through them. This vibration is called phonation, the production of sound. The weak sound that is emitted (like the sound made by vibrating string) travels through the pharynx, mouth, and in some cases the nasal cavity. Each of these three cavities helps to resonate the sound. This resonated sound is then shaped by the articulators (tongue, lips, palate, and so forth) to form the separate sounds of our language system. These individual sounds are then put together into words, or distinguishable oral symbols. We call the sound that we produce voice.[1] Now let us examine the major characteristics of voice pitch, volume, rate, and quality that work together to give us the variety, expressiveness, and intelligibility that assist communication.

Pitch   Pitch refers to the highness or lowness of the voice. As mentioned, voice is produced in the larynx by vibration of the vocal folds. In order to feel this vibration, put your hand on your throat at the top of the Adam's apple and say "ah." Just as the change in pitch of a violin string is brought about by making it tighter or looser, so the pitch of your voice is changed by the tightening and loosening of the vocal folds. Although you have no conscious control over the muscles that change the tension in the vocal folds, you can feel the change of position of the entire larynx by placing your hand on the Adam's apple again and saying "ah," first at a very high pitch and then at a low pitch. The pitch that one uses most frequently is called the "key" of the voice. Fortunately, most people talk in a pitch that is about right for them. Occasionally a person talks in a pitch that seems abnormally high or low. If you have questions about your pitch, ask your professor. If you are one of the very few persons with a pitch problem, your instructor will refer you to a speech therapist for corrective work. Since for most of us our normal pitch is satisfactory, the question is whether we are making the best use of the pitch range that we have at our disposal.

Volume   Volume is the loudness of the tone we make. When we exhale normally, the diaphragm relaxes, and air is expelled through the trachea. When we wish to speak, we need to supplement the force of the expelled air on the vibrating vocal folds by contracting our abdominal muscles. This greater force behind the air we expel increases the volume of our tone. To feel how these muscles work, place your hands on your sides with your fingers extended over the stomach. Say "ah" in a normal voice. Now say "ah" louder. Now say

---

[1] If you are interested in a more detailed analysis of the anatomy and physiology of the process, ask your instructor to recommend one of the many excellent voice and articulation books on the market. Two such books are Hilda Fisher, *Improving Voice and Articulation*, 2nd ed. (Boston: Houghton Mifflin, 1975), and Virgil A. Anderson, *Training the Speaking Voice*, 2nd ed. (New York: Oxford University Press, 1961).

"ah" as loud as you can. If you are making proper use of your muscles, you should have felt the stomach contraction increase as you increased volume. If you felt little or no muscle contraction you are probably trying to gain volume from the wrong source, resulting in tiredness, stridency, and lack of sufficient volume to fill a large room. Under ideal circumstances, you should be able to increase volume without raising pitch. Each of us, regardless of size, is capable of a great deal of vocal volume. The problem is that most of us do not use our potential. If you have trouble getting sufficient volume, work on exerting greater pressure from the abdominal area.

Rate   Rate is the speed at which we talk. As mentioned earlier, a normal rate is somewhere between 140 and 180 words per minute. Rate, like pitch, is an individual matter. There is no one rate that is best for everyone. Since some people talk more rapidly and some more slowly than others, the test is whether an audience can understand what a speaker is saying.

If your instructor believes you talk too rapidly or too slowly, he or she will tell you; and before improvement in normal conversation is possible, you must adjust your ear to a more appropriate rate. The most effective method is to read passages aloud, timing yourself to determine the exact number of words per minute you speak. Then you must make a conscious effort to decrease or increase the number of words per minute accordingly. At first, a different speech rate will sound strange to your own ear. But if you practice daily, within a few weeks you should be able to hear an improvement and you should be able to accustom your ear to the change.

Quality   Quality is the tone, timbre, or sound of your voice. Voices are characterized as being clear, nasal, breathy, harsh, hoarse, strident, and by other such adjectives. If your voice has too great a degree of some undesirable quality, consult your professor. Although you can make some improvement on your own, improvement requires a great deal of work and a rather extensive knowledge of vocal anatomy and physiology. Severe problems of quality should be referred to a speech therapist.

Vocal Variety and Expressiveness   In determining effectiveness of delivery, these qualities are not nearly so important individually as they are in combination. It is through the variety of pitch, volume, rate, and occasionally quality that you are able to give the most precise meaning to your words. An expressive voice is not flawed by the two most common faults of speech melody: *monotone* and *constant pattern.*

A monotonous voice is one in which the pitch, volume, and rate remain constant, with no word, idea, or sentence differing from any other. Although very few people speak in a true monotone, many limit themselves severely by using only two or three tones and relatively unchanging volume and rate. The effect of an actual or near monotone is that the audience is lulled to sleep. Without vocal clues to help them assess the comparative value of words, members of an audience will usually lose interest. To illustrate what proper vocal emphasis can do for meaning, say the sentence, "I want to buy ice cream," in such a way that the pitch, rate, and volume are held constant. Such a delivery would require the listener to decide what the sentence meant. Now say "buy" in a higher pitch, louder, or perhaps more slowly than the other words in the sentence. Through this vocal stress alone, you are communicating the idea that you want to *buy* ice cream rather than make it or procure it in some other way. With this sentence, meaning can be changed significantly by changing only the vocal emphasis of "I," "want," "buy," or "ice cream." During an actual speech, you should give such vocal clues in almost every sentence, to ensure audience interest and understanding.

The other prevalent fault detracting from expressiveness is the constant vocal pattern, in which vocal variation is the same for every sentence regardless of meaning. The resulting vocal pattern is nearly as monotonous as a true monotone. For instance, a person may end every sentence with an upward pitch or may go up in the middle and down at the end of every phrase. Vocal variety is of little value unless it is appropriate to the intended meaning. The best cure for a constant pattern is to correlate changes in voice with meaning. If you suffer from a relatively severe case of monotone or constant pattern, you should set up a work program that you can pursue every day. One method is to read short passages aloud to a friend. Ask your friend to tell you which words were higher in pitch, or louder, or faster. When you find that you can read or speak in such a way that your friend will recognize which words you were trying to emphasize, you will be showing improvement in using vocal variety to clarify meaning.

Articulation

Characteristics of voice are most noticeable on the vowel sounds. Whether or not our words are understandable is a question of how we form our consonant sounds. This process is called articulation, the shaping of speech sounds into recognizable oral symbols that go together to make up a word. Articulation is often confused with pronunciation, the form and accent of various syllables of a word. Thus, in the word "statistics," articulation refers to the shaping of the ten sounds (*s, t, a, t, i, s, t, i, k, s*); pronunciation refers to the grouping and accenting of the sounds (*sta-'tis-tiks*). If you are unsure of a pronunciation, look it up in a dictionary. Constant mispronunciation labels a person as ignorant or careless or both.

Although true articulatory problems (distortion, omission, substitution, or addition of sounds) need to be corrected by a speech therapist, the kinds of articulatory problems exhibited by most students can be improved individually during a single term. The two most common faults among college students are slurring sounds (running sounds and words together) and leaving off word endings. "Wutcha doin' " for "What are you doing" illustrates both of these errors. If you have a mild case of "sluritis," caused by not taking the time to form sounds clearly, you can make considerable headway by taking ten to fifteen minutes a day to read passages aloud, trying to overaccentuate each of the sounds. Some teachers advocate "chewing" your words; that is, making sure that you move your lips, jaw, and tongue very carefully for each sound you make. As with most other problems of delivery, you must work conscientiously every day for weeks or months to bring about significant improvement.

Bodily Action

Bodily action serves many key functions in our communication. It stands for words—a nod means "yes," arms extended palms down means "safe," thumbs down means disapproval. It supplements meaning—"The house is over there" (pointing), "It's about so big" (using hands to show the size), "You really make me mad" (stamping the foot). It shows our feelings—(wide-open eyes for surprise, a scowl for anger, palms pressed against temples to express a mistake). In normal conversation, bodily action often *defines* the meaning of ideas, and the same is true in public speaking. Consider the principal variables of bodily action, namely, *facial expression, gesture,* and *movement.*

Facial Expression   The eyes and mouth communicate far more than some people realize. You need only recall the icy stare, the warm smile, or the hostile scowl that you received from someone to validate the statement that the eyes (and mouth as well) are the mirror of the mind. Facial expression should be appropriate to what we are saying. We are impressed by neither deadpan expressions nor perpetual grins or scowls; we are impressed by honest and sincere expression reflecting the thought and feeling being communicated. Think actively about what you are saying and your face will probably respond accordingly.

Gesture By gesture we mean the movement of hands, arms, and fingers. Gestures are usually descriptive or emphatic. When the speaker says "about this high" or "nearly this round," we expect to see a gesture accompany the verbal description. Likewise, when the speaker says "We want you" or "Now is the time to act," we look for him to point a finger, pound his fist, or use some other gesture that reinforces his point. If you gesture in conversation, you will usually gesture in a speech. If you do not gesture in conversation, it is probably best not to force yourself to gesture in a speech. As aids in helping you "do what comes naturally," I would suggest that you try to leave your hands free at all times. If you clasp them behind you, grip the sides of the speaker's stand, or put your hands in your pockets, you will not be able to gesture even if you want to. If you wonder what to do with your hands at the start of the speech so that they will not seem conspicuous, you may either rest them on the speaker's stand partially clenched or hold them relaxed at your sides, or perhaps with one arm slightly bent at the elbow. Once you begin the speech, forget about your hands—they will be free for appropriate gestures. If, however, you discover that you have folded your arms in front of you or clasped them behind you, put them back in one of the two original positions. After you have spoken a few times, your professor will suggest whether you need to be encouraged to be more responsive or whether you need to be somewhat restrained.

Movement Some speakers stand perfectly still throughout an entire speech. Others are constantly on the move. In general, it is probably better to remain in one place unless you have some reason for moving. Nevertheless, because a little movement adds action to the speech, it may help you maintain attention. Ideally, movement should occur to help focus on transition, to emphasize an idea, or to call attention to a particular aspect of the speech. Avoid such unmotivated movement as bobbing and weaving, shifting from foot to foot, or pacing from one side of the room to the other. At the beginning of your speech, stand up straight and on both feet. If during the course of the speech, you find yourself in some peculiar posture, return to the upright position standing on both feet.

With all kinds of bodily action, be careful to avoid those little mannerisms that often are so distracting to the audience, like taking off or putting on glasses, smacking the tongue, licking the lips, or scratching the nose, hand, or arm. As a general rule, anything that calls attention to itself is bad, and anything that helps reinforce the idea is good.

**A PROGRAM OF
SPEECH PRACTICE**

The first thing we need to consider in terms of speech practice is the mode of delivery we will be using. Speeches may be delivered *impromptu,* by *manuscript,* by *memorization,* or *extemporaneously.*

Impromptu speaking is done on the spur of the moment, without previous specific preparation. Although nearly all of our conversation is impromptu, most people prefer to prepare their thoughts well ahead of time before they face an audience. Regardless of how good you are at daily communication, you would be foolhardy to leave your preparation and analysis for formal speeches to chance. Audiences expect to hear a speech that was well thought out beforehand.

A common and often misused mode is the manuscript speech. Because the speech is written out in full (and then read aloud), the wording can be planned very carefully. Although Presidents and other heads of state have good reason to resort to the manuscript (even the slightest mistake in sentence construction could cause national upheaval), most speakers have little need to prepare a manuscript. Often their only excuse is the false sense of security that the written speech provides. As you can attest from your listening experience, however, few manuscript speeches are very interesting. Because manuscript speeches are not likely to be very spontaneous, very stimulating, or very interesting and because of the natural tendency to write a speech in written style devoid of audience adaptation, you should avoid manuscript speaking except as a special assignment.

A memorized speech is merely a manuscript committed to memory. In addition to the opportunity to polish the wording, memorization allows the speaker to look at his audience while he speaks. Unfortunately for beginning speakers, memorization has the same disadvantages as the manuscript. Few individuals are able to memorize so well that their speech sounds spontaneous. Since a speech that sounds memorized affects an audience adversely, you should also avoid memorization for your first speech assignment.

The ideal mode is one that has the spontaneity of impromptu, yet allows for careful preparation and practice. The extemporaneous speech (the goal of most professional speakers) is prepared and practiced, but the exact wording is determined at the time of utterance. Most of the material in this text relates most directly to the extemporaneous method. Now let us consider how a speech can be carefully prepared without being memorized.

All that we have discussed so far is concerned with the standards of delivery, or what you should practice. Now we can apply the theory showing *when* and *how* you should practice your delivery.

Novice speakers often believe that preparation is complete once the outline has been finished. Nothing could be further from the truth. If you are scheduled to speak at 9:00 A.M. Monday and you have not finished the outline for the speech until 8:45 A.M. Monday, the speech is not likely to be nearly as good as it could have been had you allowed yourself sufficient practice time. Try to complete your outline a day in advance of a two- to five-minute speech and two or even three days in advance of longer speeches. The only way to test the speech itself is to make proper use of the practice period. Practice gives you a chance to revise, evaluate, mull over, and consider all aspects of the speech.

Like any other part of speech preparation, speech practice must be undertaken systematically. In order to make the practice period as similar to the speech situation as possible, you should stand up and practice aloud. The specific procedure may be outlined as follows:

1. Read through your outline once or twice before you begin.

2. Put the outline out of sight.

3. Look at your watch to see what time you begin.

4. Begin the speech. Keep going until you have finished the ideas. If you forget something, don't worry about it—complete what you can.

5. Note the time you finish.

6. Look at your outline again.

Now the analysis begins. Did you leave out any key ideas? Did you talk too long on any one point and not long enough on another? Did you really clarify each of your points? Did you try to adapt to your anticipated audience? Unless you are prepared to criticize yourself carefully, your practice will be of little value. As soon as you have completed the analysis of your first attempt, go through the six steps again. After you have completed two sessions of practice and criticism, put the speech away for a while. Although you may need to practice three, four, or even ten times, there is no value in going through all the sessions consecutively. You may well find that a practice session right before you go to bed will be extremely beneficial. While you are sleeping, your subconscious will continue to work on the speech. As a result, you will often note a tremendous improvement at the first practice the next day.

Should you use notes in practice or during the speech itself? The answer depends upon what you mean by notes and how you plan to use them. My advice would be to avoid using notes at all for the first short speech assignments. Then, when assignments get longer, you will be more likely to use notes properly and not as a crutch. Of course, there is no harm in experimenting with notes to see what effect they have on your delivery.

Appropriate notes are composed of key words or phrases that will help trigger your memory. Notes will be most useful to you when they consist of the fewest words possible written in lettering large enough to be seen instantly at a distance. Many speakers condense their written preparatory outline into a brief word or phrase outline. (See Figure 6.1.)

For a speech in the five- to ten-minute category, a single 3-by-5-inch note card should be enough. When your speech contains a particularly good quotation or a complicated set of statistics, you may want to write them out in detail on separate 3 by 5 cards.

During practice sessions you should use notes the way that you plan to use them in the speech. Either set them on the speaker's stand or hold them in one hand and refer to them only when you have to. Speakers often find that the act of making a note card is so effective in helping cement ideas in the mind that during practice

```
What compels selection of clothes?

   Physical comfort
      Temperature
      Weather

   Modesty
      Religion
      Culture

   Appeal to opposite sex
   Women
         Attraction
         Approval
   Men
         Distinction
         Status
```

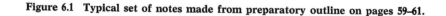

Figure 6.1 Typical set of notes made from preparatory outline on pages 59–61.

or later during the speech itself they do not need to use the notes at all.

How many times should you practice? This depends upon many things, including your experience, familiarity with subject, and the length of the speech. What you do not want to do is to practice the speech the same way each time until you have it memorized. An effective speaker needs to learn the difference between learning a speech and memorizing it. One has to do with gaining an understanding of ideas; the other has to do with learning a series of words.

When people memorize, they repeat the speech until they have mastered the wording. Since emphasis is then on word order, any mistake requires backtracking or some other means of getting back to the proper word order. Unfortunately, this kind of practice does not make for mastery of content, it does not give additional insight into the topic, and it does not allow for audience adaptation at the time of presentation. Another way that speakers memorize is to say the speech once extemporaneously and then repeat the same wording over and over again. The result is about the same in both instances.

When people stress the learning of ideas, they practice their speech differently each time. Utilizing the principles of proper speech practice, a description of the shaft of a pencil could take the following forms:

1.   The shaft is a cylindrical piece of wood about 6 inches in length. Its color is yellow. It houses a piece of graphite of about $\frac{1}{16}$ of an inch in diameter.

2.   It's the shaft that houses the graphite. The yellow shaft is about 6 inches long and is cylindrical in shape. The piece of graphite that does the actual writing is about $\frac{1}{16}$ of an inch in diameter.

3.   The main part of the pencil is made out of a soft piece of wood. Its shape is cylindrical. Its color is yellow. Its length is about 6 inches long. It houses a $\frac{1}{16}$-inch piece of graphite that runs the entire length of the shaft—and, of course, it is the graphite that leaves the imprint on paper.

4.   The main part of the pencil is a cylindrical shaft that houses the graphite writing compound. The shaft, painted a bright yellow, is about 6 inches long. The graphite runs the length of the shaft and is about $\frac{1}{16}$ of an inch in diameter.

Notice that in all four versions the same essential facts were included: the shaft is a cylindrical piece of wood; it is about 6 inches long; it is painted yellow; it houses a $\frac{1}{16}$-inch piece of graphite. These are the facts that would appear on the outline and that the speaker would attempt to include in every practice and in the speech itself. An interesting phenomenon is that each practice usually gets a little better. As a result, more often than not the actual speech will be similar to the best practice period rather than to the worst. Not being tied to a particular phrasing, the speaker could adapt to audience reaction at the time of delivery.

Exercise 9	Make a diary of your program of practice for your first formal speech. How many times did you practice? At what point did you feel you had a mastery of substance? How long was each of your practice periods?

Assignment	**Prepare a two- to five-minute speech. An outline is required. Criteria for evaluation will include (1)"content"—whether topic was well selected, whether the purpose was clear, and whether good material was used to develop or to prove the points; (2) "organization"—whether speech had a good opening, clear main points, and a good conclusion; (3) "style"—whether language was clear, vivid, emphatic, and appropriate; and (4) "delivery"—whether voice and body were used effectively to show a positive attitude, spontaneity, and to achieve directness.**

Outline: **First Speech**	*Since this outline is for the first speech given, notice the way it is written. Test each part against the recommendations for outlining on pages 57–59. Also note that this outline contains 267 words, a good length for a four- or five-minute speech.*

Specific Purpose: To share with you the experience of the high dive.

Introduction

   I. This summer I had a rather extraordinary job.

  II. I would like to share with you the experience of the high dive.

Body

   I. The high dive apparatus is composed of a set of interlocking ladders.
     A. They are fastened to the ground by guy wires.
     B. The platform is approximately one foot square.

  II. The high dive takes a great deal of preparation.
     A. It took me about a month to perfect my dive.
     B. I executed it first at lower heights and then moved up.

 III. The climb up the ladder is one of the more difficult parts.
     A. While climbing you are aware of the danger involved.
     B. During the climb I usually questioned why I was doing it.
     C. Try never to rush, because it is so easy to slip.
     D. Upon reaching the top you will be confronted with mixed feelings.
       1. On one hand is the feeling of power.
       2. On the other hand is the feeling of fear.

 IV. The dive itself produces one of the most exhilarating feelings you will ever experience.
     A. As you prepare to leave the platform, you will find it hard to swallow and your heart will beat wildly.

B. As you leave, nothing exists but you and the water.

C. Hitting the water rushes you immediately back to reality.

V. The entry into the water is a most critical part of the drive.

A. The diver must stretch and lock out every muscle.

B. Locking out and stretching helps you pierce the water.

C. I hated the entry because it concluded my journey and because the water always felt too hard.

Conclusion

I. Completion of the dive left me with a tremendous feeling of accomplishment.

II. I don't recommend this dive to everyone.

The High Dive

Read the sample speech through aloud in its entirety.[2] After you have judged its quality, read the speech again, noting the criticism included in the other column.

Analysis

This is a particularly good opening. It uses a question to get initial attention, identifies with audience interest, and reveals the novel topic in a vivid way. From these first words, the speaker was guaranteed a listening audience.

His first point gives an overall picture of the apparatus. He tries to describe both the physical and the psychological setting.

The second point explains the dive and the diver's preparation for it.

Throughout the development the speaker reminds us of the potential danger. This adds to the excitement of the speech.

Speech

How many of you would like to work at an amusement park? Think of it—free rides and a summer of fun and excitement. Maybe you'd like to try out for the job I had last summer. But you'd better hold on for a few minutes before you volunteer—you see, my job was daredevil high diver. From 100 feet in the air I dove into a tank of water only 14 feet deep. I'd like to share with you the experience of the high dive.

The high-dive apparatus consists of a set of interlocking ladders that are fastened down by guy wires to the ground. The perch or platform that the diver stands on to execute his dive is approximately 1 foot square. So, when I stood atop the 100-foot span, all I had was a small foot rest, a little ladder to hang on to, and a lot of air.

I can honestly say that the high dive is not an easy task, but with good coaching and complete concentration an experienced diver can learn to execute the dive without fear. It took me approximately one month to learn my dive. I perfected a double somersault with a half twist, from the lower heights. I then worked my way up the ladder about 6 to 10 feet at a time—always aware that I had to adjust to the increase in height each time, because one slight miscalculation and it would have been all over.

[2] Speech given in Fundamentals of Speech class, University of Cincinnati. Printed by permission of Tim McLaughlin.

Analysis

His next three points (climb, dive, and entry) are all developed in second person. He says "Come with me" and he then leads us through the dive. In these three points audience involvement is at its peak. We get a vicarious thrill as we listen.

In this fourth point, the dive, the speaker helps us feel the exhilaration.

As a result of his method, we actually feel the *smack* of the water.

This fifth point is well introduced. The development would even be better had the speaker defined "locking out" better. We get the idea, but he does not help us to be sure of our understanding.

The conclusion is satisfactory. Although the speaker doesn't summarize his points, his caution, "I don't recommend this line of work" reminds us of the danger and I believe brings back the picture of the 100-foot descent. The topic is excellent—it by itself is attention getting and gives great potential for informative and interesting development. In addition, the speech lives up to audience expectation. The speaker has good material and good organization—his wording is excellent. The speech is vivid and well adapted to the audience. I believe this is an excellent model for a first speech round.

Speech

Come with me as we go through the dive step by step. The 100-foot climb up the ladder is one of the more difficult parts of the act. While climbing the ladder, you're conscious of the danger. I was constantly asking myself just what I was doing here. You should, of course, never rush up the ladder, because one slip and you would fall helplessly to the ground below. Upon reaching the top of the long span, you're confronted with mixed feelings of power, looking out onto the audience of people watching every move you make— and the feelings of fear, wondering if you're going to survive this dive.

The dive itself is one of the most exhilarating experiences you will ever feel. As you make the decision to leave the platform, you'll find your heart beating wildly, and find it very hard to swallow; but when you have actually left the platform, all your problems will seem to disappear behind you. The world just seems to stop for a few seconds and nothing exists but you and the water below—and then, *smack*—hitting into the water you are instantly rushed back to reality.

The entry into the water is the last and perhaps most critical part of the dive. To enter properly, the diver must stretch and lock out every muscle in his body to prepare for impact of the water. By locking out and stretching, you are able to pierce the water and prevent injury. I always hated the entry, because it concluded the tremendous journey I just experienced and also because, uh, I never really hit the water too smoothly—I never completely locked out.

The successful conclusion of a high dive left me with a tremendous feeling of accomplishment. I knew that I had not only entertained my audience, but I had also conquered the 100-foot tower for another day. I don't recommend this line of work for everyone; I believe that an equal feeling of exhilaration and excitement can be achieved in other areas. But I do believe my experience this summer was extraordinary, and also one I'll never forget.

INFORMATIVE SPEAKING

PART THREE

PRINCIPLES OF INFORMATIVE SPEAKING

7

Up to now, we have considered the major principles and practices that underlie the preparation and presentation of any and all speeches. In this chapter, we want to examine principles of informative speaking. Although speech purposes overlap—in fact, as you read the speeches in the appendix, you may have difficulty deciding whether the speaker intended to inform or to persuade—studying informative speaking as a separate purpose gives us an opportunity to focus on creating understanding. Whether your intention is to explain how a zipper is made, to describe your new library, to discuss Thor Heyerdahl's findings on the Ra Expeditions, or to explain how scientists are working to predict earthquakes, your ultimate purpose is to *create understanding*. The next five chapters consider different forms of presenting information. Here we will examine some general principles of information exchange that will be useful to your development of any informative speech. Each of these principles will assist you in gaining your audience's reception and increasing your audience's retention of the information you present.

1. *Information is more readily received when it is relevant to audience experience.* Rather than acting like a sponge to absorb every bit of information that comes our way, most of us act more like a filter—we retain only that information we perceive as relevant.

Of course, the ultimate in relevance is for an audience to perceive information as *vital*. Topics like lifesaving, defensive driving, and understanding of household poisons, topics that are truly a matter of life and death, are automatically relevant. Since only a relatively few topics are vital to audiences, you will have to work to make your information relevant. You can ensure information relevance in two ways.

The first way is to frame your speech as an answer to stated or implied audience questions. For instance, when your instructor discusses the nature of the midterm test he is giving the next class meeting, you will notice the great interest of nearly everyone in class. Likewise, information on how to take a nice vacation on spring break with little money, how to get a summer job, or courses to take as electives is information that will answer many implied audience questions.

The second way to ensure relevance is to direct the information to a felt need. Consider the day's weather. If you need to stay in your room all day and study, you probably will not care about outside temperatures and weather conditions, because you have no felt need to know; however, if you are planning to go to a football game or take a hike, weather information will meet a felt need, and you will seek out and listen closely to weather forecasts. Information meets the tests of relevance, then, when it is presented so that the audience sees the need for it.

Almost any information can be made relevant to the audience. For every major statement of information you plan to present, ask, "What does it have to do with this audience?" Then *show* the audience what that relationship is. Can you make Bolivian politics and economics relevant to your audience? For starters point out the United States needs copper: from one-cent coins to the plumbing in our kitchen, copper is important to each of us. Since Bolivia is a major source of copper supply, the politics and economics of Bolivia has a lot to do with U.S. copper needs. The more remote the topic from our experience, the more difficulty in showing the relevance. But audience reception to that information may depend on how well you can show that relevance.

2. *Information is more readily received when it is new.* Any fact may be new to someone in the audience, of course. But we mainly think of facts as being new information when they add knowledge or give us new insights. Contrast the informative value of a speech naming the planets with a speech discussing the findings about Jupiter revealed by the Pioneer space probe. Whereas naming the planets may give new information to only a few members of our audience, information about Jupiter would be new information to most of them.

New information is received even more readily when it is novel. Novelty is newness with a twist, something that commands our involuntary attention. Novelty begins with the topic itself. In the speech about the summer job of the high diver you read at the end of the last part, the audience listened because it found the topic truly novel. But if the topic itself is not novel, the next best thing is to take a novel approach to the material by focusing on the features that make the information unusual. A Rolls Royce grill makes a standard Volkswagen novel; solar energy heating makes a three-bedroom ranch-style house novel. Novelty is often the product of the creative mind. We will consider creativity in speechmaking in far greater detail in the chapter on expository speaking.

3. *Information is more readily received when it is startling.* When something startles you, it means that it takes you aback or gives you an emotional jolt. Seeing your professor in a new sport coat may get your attention; seeing your professor come to class in a toga, a bear skin, or a loin cloth would be startling. Whereas novelty implies a long-lasting impression (a speech on the high dive is novel from beginning to end), startling means having momentary impact. As a result, the best use of the startling is as an attention getter—either to get attention initially or to rekindle attention at flagging moments.

The startling is often accomplished through action. Blowing up a balloon and letting it sail around the room to illustrate propulsion is startling. Taking off one's outer clothes in class to reveal a gym suit underneath would be startling. Sometimes, however, what you do may be so startling that the audience never recovers. So be careful. Although startling actions may get momentary attention, they can disrupt a speech if they are too overpowering.

Something akin to the startling action is a really good anecdote, illustration, example, or particularly provocative statement. For instance, consider this part of a speech to high school graduates:

> Our Bibles tell us that we are allotted three score and ten years on earth. Seventy years, more or less. Barring pestilence and wars, natural disasters and automobile accidents, today's average American can anticipate that life expectancy. So you members of the class of 1974 must realize that you have already consumed about one-quarter of your allotted years.
> Feeling old already?[1]

4. *Information is more readily received and retained when it is presented humorously.* You do not have to be riotously funny or sprinkle your speech with jokes—in fact, both are likely to be more detrimental to your information than useful. To be most effective, the humor should be related to the topic. If you discover an amusing way of developing some point in your speech, your audience will listen. For instance, here is how one speaker heightened audience interest in his speech on hotel management:

[1] Theodore Sendak, "Anchors and Rudders," *Vital Speeches*, August 1, 1974, p. 635.

Frankly, I think the hotel business has been one of the most backward in the world. There's been very little change in the attitude of room clerks in the 2000 years since Joseph arrived in Bethlehem and was told they'd lost his reservation.[2]

If trying to be funny makes you feel self-conscious, then do not force humor into your speech. But if you think humor is one of your strengths, then make the most of it.

5. *Information is more likely to be understood and retained if it is associated.* When you walk into a room of people, you seek out the familiar faces. Likewise, when you are confronted with information that you do not readily understand, your ear listens for certain familiar notes that will put the new information into perspective. A speaker can take advantage of this tendency on the part of the audience by associating new, difficult information with the familiar.

Association is defined as the tendency of a sensation, perception, or thought to recall others previously coexisting in consciousness with it or with states similar to it. That means when one word, idea, or event reminds you of another, you are associating. A speaker can associate through vivid comparisons and contrasts. For instance, if you were trying to show your audience how a television picture tube works, you could build an association between the unknown of the television tube and audience knowledge. The metaphor "a television picture tube is a gun shooting beams of light" would be an excellent association between the known and the unknown. The image of a gun shooting is a familiar one. A gun shooting beams of light is easy to visualize. If you made the association striking enough, every time your audience thought of a television picture tube, they would associate it with guns shooting beams of light. If you can establish one or more associations during your speech, you are helping to ensure audience retention of key ideas.

6. *Information is more likely to be understood and retained when it is related visually.* You are more likely to make your point if you can show it as well as talk about it. Visual aids are effective in simplifying and emphasizing information as well as in holding interest. Their impact is a result of appealing to two senses at the same time: we listen to the explanation and we see the substance of the explanation. This double sensory impact helps cement the ideas

[2] James Lavenson, "Think Strawberries," *Vital Speeches*, March 15, 1974, p. 346.

in our mind. Since visual aids are so important in information exchange, the entire next chapter is devoted to their use in speeches.

7. *Information is more likely to be understood and retained when it is repeated.* When you meet someone for the first time, you will be more likely to remember the name if you repeat it a few times immediately after being introduced; when you are trying to learn a new definition, a formula for a compound, or a few lines of poetry, you will master them only after you have repeated them often enough to remember. And as we all know, some of the most effective, as well as the most irritating, television commercials are based upon the simple device of repetition. As a student of public address, you should learn when and how to take advantage of this potent device. Unfortunately, for beginning speakers the words that are most often repeated are of the nature of "uh," "well," "now," and "you know." The artful speaker will determine the two, three, four, or five most important words, ideas, or concepts in the speech, and think of ways of repeating them for emphasis.

Exact duplication is called *repetition;* duplication of idea but not of words is called *restatement.* If you want the audience to remember the exact word, repetition is the proper device to use; if you want the audience to remember the idea, restatement is probably better. Thus, a speaker who wants you to remember a telephone number would say: "The number is 365–4217—that's 3, 6, 5, 4, 2, 1, 7." In contrast, a speaker who wants you to remember the approximate size of a city would say: "The population is 497,000—that's roughly half a million people." A speech with artful use of repetition and restatement will be remembered longer than a speech without them.

8. *Information is more likely to be understood and retained when it is well organized.* A clear, well-developed outline is the starting point of good speech organization. But in addition to your speech having a clear organization on paper, an audience must be consciously aware of the *presence* of that good organization. The old journalistic advice, "Tell them what you're going to tell them, tell them, and tell them what you've told them," recognizes the importance of emphasizing organization. The speaker who states, "In my speech I will cover three goals, the first is . . . the second is . . . and the third is . . ." will often have more success getting an audience to remember than one who does not. Likewise, such reminder statements as "Now we come to the second key point" or "Here's where we move from the third stage of development and go to the fourth" have proven effective in directing audience thinking. When

listeners perceive the clarity of idea development, they are likely to remember the material.

Now that we have examined principles of informative speaking, we can begin to put what we have learned into practice. In these next five chapters, we will pursue skills relating to using visual aids, explaining processes, describing, defining, and using resource material.

Assignment

> **Prepare a four- to six-minute informative speech. An outline is required. Criteria for evaluation will include means of ensuring reception and retention of information. The following questions can be used as a basis for evaluation of your speech:**
>
> **Did you develop relevance of information?**
>
> **Did you present information in a novel, startling, or humorous fashion?**
>
> **Did you use visual aids, association, and/or repetition to emphasize the information?**
>
> **Did you help the audience follow your organization?**

Outline

Specific Purpose: To explain four major classifications of nursery rhymes.

Introduction

I. "Hey diddle diddle, the cat and the fiddle, the cow jumped over the moon. The little dog laughed to see such sport, and the dish ran away with the spoon."

II. Did you know that there are four major classifications of nursery rhymes?—ditties, teaching rhymes, historically based, and modern use.

Body

I. Ditties are nursery rhymes with a prophetic purpose.
   A. A fortune-telling rhyme is told while counting the white spots on the fingernails.
   B. Just as in *Poor Richard's Almanack*, by Benjamin Franklin, Mother Goose had her merry wise sayings.
   C. Traditionally, a rhyme on the topic of love fidelity is said while plucking the petals of a daisy.

II. Some nursery rhymes were used as teaching aids.
   A. "Hickory Dickory Dock" is an example of onomatopoeia, which is an attempt to capture in words a specific sound.
   B. Song rhymes helped the children with their coordination.
      1. Historical background.
      2. Children's usage.
   C. Numbers in nursery rhymes obviously retain the traces of the stages by which prehistoric man first learned to count.

III. Many nursery rhymes have historical significance.
   A. Religious problems entered into the nursery rhymes with "Jack Sprat."

B. It became a tradition in England that some of these country rhymes may have been relics of formulas used by the druids in choosing a human sacrifice for their pagan gods.

C. Cannibalism is quite prevalent in nursery rhymes.

IV. A modern classification of the nursery rhyme is the parody.

A. The famous prayer "Now I lay me down . . ." was first published in 1737, but has now been parodied.

B. A joke has been created out of "Mary and Her Lamb."

Conclusion

I. Every song, ballad, hymn, carol, tale, singing game, dance tune, or dramatic dialogue that comes from an unwritten, unpublished word-by-the-mouth source contributes to the future culture of our nation.

II. Remember that with your next cute saying, teaching aid in the form of a rhyme, reference to our history, or modern use of the nursery rhymes, you may become the next Mother Goose.

Bibliography

Baring-Gould, William S., and Cecil Baring-Gould, *The Annotated Mother Goose.* New York: Clarkson A. Potter, 1962.

Bett, Henry, *Nursery Rhymes and Tales—Their Origins and History.* New York: Henry Holt and Co., 1924.

Ken, John Bellenden, *An Essay on the Archaeology of Popular Phrases and Nursery Rhymes.* London: Longman, Rees, Orme, Brown, Green, and Co., 1837.

Mother Goose, *Mother Goose and the Nursery Rhymes.* London: Frederick Warne and Co., 1895.

Classifications of Nursery Rhymes

Read the speech at least once aloud.[3] Examine it to see how the speaker made information relevant; whether she presented information in a novel, startling, or humorous way; whether she used association or repetition for emphasis; and how she helped the audience follow the information. After you have studied the speech, read the analysis in the other column.

Analysis

The speaker uses a common rhyme to capture our attention. From the beginning the novelty of the topic and the development get and hold our attention. Notice the clever wording "There's more to nursery rhymes than meets the ear."

Speech

"Hey diddle diddle, the cat and the fiddle, the cow jumped over the moon, the little dog laughed to see such sport and the dish ran away with the spoon." You recognize this as a nursery rhyme, and perhaps you always considered these nursery rhymes as types of nonsense poetry with little if any meaning. As we look at the four classifications of nursery rhymes, I think that you'll see as I did that there's more to nursery rhymes than meets the ear.

[3] Speech given in Fundamentals of Speech class, University of Cincinnati. Printed by permission of Susan Woistmann.

Analysis

**To increase our under-
standing, information
should be presented
clearly. Throughout the
speech, the speaker leads
us through the organiza-
tion. She begins the body
of the speech by identifying the first classification.
The next sentence gives us
the three subdivisions of
the major classification.
The commendable part of
this and all sections of the
speech is the use of the
specific examples to illustrate the various types
and subtypes. As far as
real information is con-
cerned, this main point
does not go much beyond
labeling and classifying
our own knowledge. The
last part is of some in-
terest in that it shows the
evolution of wording.**

**Again the main point is
clearly stated. She begins
this section with an in-
teresting look at a com-
mon rhyme. Once more,
an excellent use of specifics
to illustrate the point she
is making. Although speech
language should be infor-
mal it should not be im-
precise. Notice that the
antecedent for "he" in
"he's trying to show the
ticking" is unclear. You
should be careful to avoid
these common grammat-
ical errors. This section of
the speech illustrates how
information can sometimes
be communicated in such
an interesting way that we
are not even aware that we
have learned anything.**

**Again the speaker moves
smoothly into the state-
ment of the main point.
As far as the quality of
information is concerned,
this is probably the best**

Speech

One of the major classifications of nursery rhymes is ditties. Ditties are fortune-tellings, little wise sayings, or little poems on love fidelity, and they are the most popular form of nursery rhyme. There are various ways of telling your fortune through ditties. One is saying, "A gift, a ghost, a friend, a foe; letter to come and a journey to go." And while you say this little ditty, this fortune-telling, you count the little white spots on your fingernails. Or you can say, "Rich man, poor man, beggarman, thief, doctor, lawyer, merchant, chief," and count your buttons. Whichever button you end on is the type of guy you are going to marry. Another kind of ditty is the wise saying. Just as in *Poor Richard's Almanack* by Benjamin Franklin, Mother Goose had her own little sayings. She said, "A pullet in the pen is worth a hundred in the fen," which today we say as "A bird in the hand is worth two in the bush." Love fidelity, the third kind of ditty, can be proven while plucking the petals off a daisy. "Love her, hate her, this year, next year, some-time, never." But today's usage has brought it up to "Love me, love me not, love me, love me not."

Another classification of nursery rhymes is those used as teach-ing aids, such as the saying "Hickory dickory dock." This is the use of onomatopoeia, which is trying to develop a sound from the use of words. In this case, he's trying to show the ticking of a clock. London Bridge, although it has some historical background, is used for teaching children coordination, such as running around the circle raising their hands up and jumping back down. Similarly, in the ancient times, man made up rhymes in order to make things easier for him to remember, such as in the saying, "one, two, buckle my shoe; three, four, close the door." And as time went on, he eventually found out that he could use the fingers and toes to count. This is where "This little piggy went to market and this little piggy stayed home" originated.

Also, did you know that nursery rhymes have historical back-ground? The third classification of nursery rhymes are those of historical significance. In the Middle Ages, which is when most nursery rhymes were formed, the saying, "Jack Sprat could eat no fat, his wife could eat no lean; and so betwixt the two of them, they

Analysis

Speech

section of the speech. Notice that she continues to use her examples and illustrations very well.

Of all the single examples in the speech, this is probably the best.

Once more we are aware of the statement of a main point. The speaker returns to classifying and labeling information that as an audience we have in our possession.

From the foregoing criticism it can be seen that the speech is a very clear, extremely interesting informative speech. Two possibilities for strengthening the speech are worth considering. Since the third main point is so informative, it might have been better for the speaker to limit the entire speech to this particular subject. She could have mentioned the other three classifications in the introduction, then told us why she would focus on historical significance. The advantage of such a revision would, of course, be that the information level of the speech

licked the platter clean," refers to the Catholic Church and the government of the old Roman Empire. This is when the Catholic Church was blessing tithes, and wiping the country clean. The government came in and collected the taxes; and between the two of them, the country had no wealth and no money. The Druids, in their relics of old formulas for selecting human sacrifices, used the "eeny meeny, miny, moe." And cannibalism is quite prevalent in almost all the nursery rhymes. Such as in "Jack and the Beanstalk," the big giant eater, and "Fee, Fi, Foe, Fum, I smell the blood of an Englishman. Be he alive or be he dead, I'm going to use him to make my bread." This also came up again in Shakespeare with *King Lear* and *Midsummer Night's Dream*. "Little Jack Horner" is about a man named Jack Horner, who was steward of the abbot of Glastonberry. And in 1542, he was sent by this abbot to King Henry VIII of England with a pie. And in this pie were documents which were the documents of the ownership of land around the Abbey of Glastonberry, in Somersetshire. And on his way to the king, he stuck in his thumb and pulled out a document to the ownership of Meld, which he kept to himself. And until this day, over in Somersetshire, the Manor of Meld belongs to the Horner family.

The fourth classification of the nursery rhyme is the modern use, parodies and jokes, such as in "Mary had a little lamb, its fleece was white as snow," today the kids go around saying, "Mary had a little lamb and was the doctor ever surprised." Or else they tend to make parodies of these nursery rhymes. Such as the famous little prayer, "Now I lay me down to sleep. I pray the Lord my soul to keep. If I should die before I wake, I pray the Lord my soul to take." It was first published in 1737, so you can see the age of this prayer. But, nowadays, the children say in joke, "Now I lay me down to sleep with a bag of peanuts at my feet. If I should die before I wake, you'll know I died of a stomach ache."

would have been better. Secondly, since the bibliography accompanying the outline shows the amount of research, she should have taken better advantage of the research by including some of the scholarly methodology involved. She could have told us where the scholars uncovered their information. She could have told us which aspects of the analysis were fact and which were theory.

This conclusion ties the speech together pretty well. The wording of the summary gives the conclusion a necessary lift. The speech is light but still informative. Most importantly, information is presented in a novel way. Through the excellent examples, the speaker gets and holds attention throughout the speech. This is a good example of an informative speech.

So every song, ballad, hymn, carol, tale, dance rhythm, or any cute little saying that you might come up with may contribute to the future culture of our nation. So remember, the next time you start spouting wise sayings, using rhymes as a teaching aid, referring to our history, or when you start making jokes of the traditional nursery rhymes, who knows, you might be the next Mother Goose.

USING VISUAL AIDS

8

The visual aid is a unique form of speech amplification, for it gives the speech a new dimension. Speech, being primarily verbal, appeals to the ear; visual aids appeal to the eye. With the use of visual aids, the ideas of the speech gain a double sensory impact. Whether a picture is worth a thousand words or not, research has shown that people learn considerably more via the eye than via the ear.[1] Because visual aids are used most in informative speeches, let us consider the various kinds of visual aids and how they can be used effectively.

KINDS OF VISUAL AIDS

By definition, anything that is used to appeal to the visual sense of the audience is a visual aid. Going from the simple to the complex, the most common types are the speaker; objects; models; chalkboards; pictures, drawings, and sketches; charts; and slides, projections, and films.

The Speaker

Sometimes the best visual aid is the speaker himself. Through the use of gesture, movement, and attire, the speaker can supplement the words. For instance, descriptive gestures can show the size of a squash ball, the height of a volleyball net, and the shape of a lake. Posture and movement can show the correct stance for skiing, a butterfly swimming stroke, and methods of artificial respiration. Attire can illustrate the native dress of a foreign country; the proper outfit for a mountain climber, a spielunker, or a scuba diver; and the uniform of a fireman, a nurse, or a soldier.

Objects

Objects are usually excellent visual aids in that they eliminate most of the possible distortions of size, shape, and color. If you talk about a vase, a basketball, a braided rug, or an épée, the object itself is most suitable for display. Unfortunately, most objects are too small to be seen or too large to be carried to class, maneuvered, or shown. As a result, even though the actual object might be the best visual aid, its use may be impracticable.

[1] See *Speech Monographs*, Vol. 20 (November 1953), p. 7.

Models

A model is a representation used to show the construction or to serve as a copy. When the object itself is too large to bring to class, a model will usually prove a worthwhile substitute. If you were to talk about a turbine engine, a racing car, the Great Pyramid, or a dam, a model might well be the best visual aid. Especially if you are able to obtain or construct a working model, the speech will usually benefit from its use. Your most important test is whether the model is large enough to be seen by the entire audience. Some model cars, for instance, may be only 3 or 4 inches long—too small to be used for a speech; on the other hand, a model car made to the scale of 1 inch to 1 foot (perhaps 12 or 18 inches long) would be large enough. Although models distort size, their shape, color, and maneuverability make them excellent visual aids.

Chalkboard

Because every classroom has a chalkboard, our first reaction is to make use of it in our speeches. As a means of visually portraying simple information, the chalkboard is unbeatable. Unfortunately, the chalkboard is easy to misuse and to overuse. The principal misuse students and teachers make of it is to write a volume of material while they are talking. More often than not what we write while we talk is either illegible or at least partly obscured by our body while we are writing. Furthermore, the tendency is to spend too much time talking to the board instead of to the audience.

The chalkboard is overused because it is so readily available. Most people use it in an impromptu fashion, whereas good visual aids require considerable preplanning to achieve their greatest value. By and large, anything that can be done with a chalkboard can be done better with a pre-prepared chart, which can be introduced when needed.

If you believe you must use the chalkboard, think about putting the material on the board before you begin, or use the board for only a few seconds at a time. If you plan to draw your visual aid on the board before you begin, get to class a little early so that you can complete your drawing before the period. It is not fair to your classmates to use several minutes of class time completing your visual aid. Moreover, it is usually a good idea to cover what you have done in some way. If you do plan to draw or to write while you are talking, practice doing that as carefully as you practice the rest of the speech. If you are righthanded, stand to the right of what you are drawing. Try to face at least part of the audience while you work. Although it seems awkward at first, your effort will allow your audience to see what you are doing while you are doing it.

**Pictures,
Drawings,
and Sketches**

Pictures, drawings, and sketches probably account for a majority of all visual aids used in speeches in or out of the classroom. Because they may be obtained or made so much more easily and inexpensively, their use is undoubtedly justified. Obviously, any picture, drawing, or sketch gives up some aspect of realism in size, shape, color, or detail. Nevertheless, the opportunities for emphasis of key features usually outweigh any disadvantages.

Pictures, of course, are readily obtainable from a variety of sources. In your selection, make sure that the picture is not so detailed that it obscures the central features you wish to emphasize. Colored pictures are usually better than black and white; and, above all, of course, the picture must be large enough to be seen. The all-too-common disclaimer, "I know you can't see this picture, but . . ." is of little help to the audience.

Many times you will have to draw your own visual aid. Don't feel that you are at any disadvantage because you "can't draw." If you can use a compass, a straightedge, and a measure, you can draw or sketch well enough for speech purposes. If you were making the point that a water skier must hold his arms straight, his back

Figure 8.1

straight, and have his knees bent slightly, a stick figure (see Figure 8.1) would illustrate the point every bit as well as an elaborate, lifelike drawing. In fact, elaborate, detailed drawings are not worth the time and effort and may actually obscure the point you wish to make. Although actual representation is not a major problem, size, color, and neatness often are. For some reason, people tend to draw and letter far too small. Before you complete your visual aid, move as far away from it as the farthest student in class will be. If you can read the lettering and see the details, it is large enough; if not, you should begin again. Color selection may also cause some problem. Black or red on white are always good contrasts. Chartreuse on pink and other such combinations just cannot be seen very well.

Charts

A chart is another graphic representation of material that enables a speaker to compress a great deal of material and to show it in a usable, easily interpreted form. A frequently used type is the word chart. For instance, in a speech on causes of juvenile delinquency the speaker may print the items in Figure 8.2. To make the chart more eye-catching, the speaker may have a picture or a sketch to portray each word visually.

The chart is also used to show organization, chains of command, or steps of a process. The chart in Figure 8.3 illustrates the organization of a college department. Charts of this kind lend themselves well to what is called a strip-tease method of showing. The speaker prints the words on a large piece of cardboard, covers each with pieces of cardboard or paper mounted with small pieces of cellophane tape, then removes the cover as he or she comes to each point to expose that portion of the chart.

Maps are of great value to indicate key elements of a territory. For instance, through various maps you have the opportunity to focus on physical details such as mountains, rivers, valleys; or on the location of cities, states, nations, parks, and monuments; or on automobile, train, boat, and airplane routes. A professionally prepared map may have artistic advantages, but a map you make yourself can be drawn to include only the details you wish to show. Whether you use a professionally prepared map or your own drawing, the features you wish to point out should be easy to see. The weather map in Figure 8.4 is a good example of a focusing on selected detail.

If your speech contains figures, you may want to find or to draw some kind of graph. The three most common types are the line graph, the bar graph, and the pie graph. If you were giving a speech on auto fatalities in the United States, you could use the *line graph*

CAUSES

1. Poverty
2. Permissivness
3. Broken homes

Figure 8.2

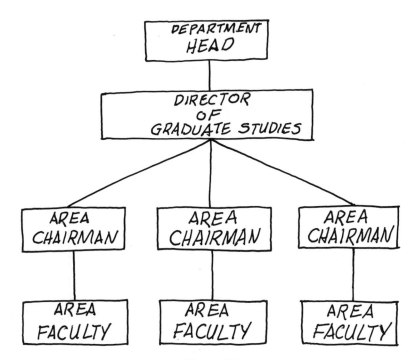

Figure 8.3

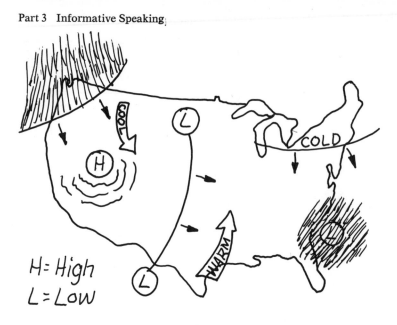

H = High
L = Low

Figure 8.4

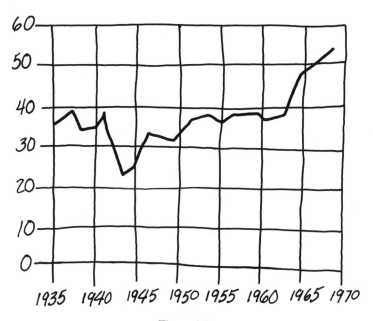

Figure 8.5

in Figure 8.5 to show the annual number of auto deaths, in thousands, for a thirty-five year period. If you were giving a speech on gold, you could use the *bar graph* in Figure 8.6 to show comparative holdings of the International Monetary Fund (IMF) and of world governments in billions of dollars (1972). In any speech where you want to show distribution of percentages of a whole, such as total government money spent on combatting crime in 1971, a *pie graph* like the one in Figure 8.7 could used.

To get the most out of your charts, however, you should be prepared to make extensive interpretations. Since charts do not speak for themselves, you should know how to read, test, and interpret them before you use them in speeches. The obvious tests of size and color are the same as for drawings.

Films, Slides, and Projections

Seldom will you have the opportunity to use films, slides, or projections. The scheduling of projectors, the need for darkened classrooms, and the tendency for these visual aids to dominate the speaker all combine to outweigh possible advantages of their use. Beginning speakers find it difficult enough to control the speaking situation without having to cope with the problems that films, slides, and projections involve.

Nevertheless, because they are used so much professionally and because they can make a classroom speech more exciting, we need to say at least a few words about three of the most easily used: slides, opaque projections, and overhead projections. Slides are mounted transparencies that can be projected individually. In a speech a few slides could be used much the same as pictures. For instance, for a speech on scenic attractions in London, a speaker might have one or more slides on the Tower of London, the British Museum, Buckingham Palace, and the Houses of Parliament. He could show the slides and talk about each of them as long as he needed to. Opaque and overhead projections can be used much the same way. An opaque projector is a machine that enables you to project right from a book, a newspaper, or a typed page. It is especially useful for materials that would be too small to show otherwise. An overhead projector is a machine that requires special transparencies. The advantage of an overhead is that the room need not be darkened and you can write, trace, or draw on the transparency while you are talking. Overheads are especially useful for showing how formulas work, for illustrating various computations, or for analyzing outlines, prose, or poetry. Many of the kinds of things teachers use a chalkboard for could be done better with an overhead projector.

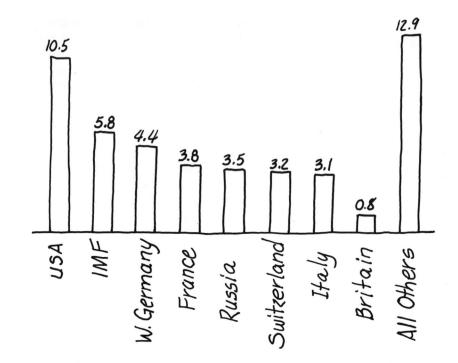

Figure 8.6

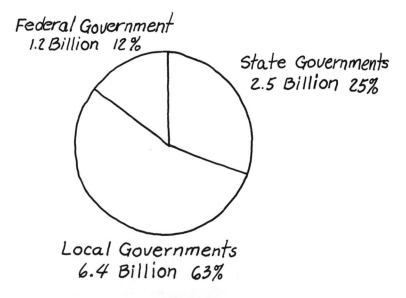

Figure 8.7

With each type of projection, you need to practice using the visual aid as often as you practice the speech itself. You will also notice that it takes longer to prepare mechanically projected visual aids than charts or sketches. It is often to your advantage to use a partner to run the machinery from the back of the room while you give your speech from a position next to the projection.

USING VISUAL AIDS   Since visual aids are very powerful types of speech amplification, you should take care to use them to your advantage. The following are some of the guidelines that will enable you to get the most out of your visual aids:

1.   Show visual aids only when you are talking about them. It takes a very strong-willed person to avoid looking at a visual aid while it is being shown. And while people are looking at a visual aid, they will find it difficult to pay attention to the speaker's words if they are not related to that visual aid. So, when you show a visual aid, talk about it; when you have finished talking about it, put it out of sight.

2.   Conversely, you should talk about the visual aid while you are showing it. Although a picture may be worth a thousand words, it still needs to be explained. You should tell your audience what to look for; you should explain the various parts; and you should interpret figures, symbols, and percentages.

3.   Show visual aids so that everyone in the audience can see them. If you hold the visual aid, hold it away from your body and let everyone see it. Even when the visual aid is large enough, you may find yourself obscuring someone's view inadvertently if you are not careful in your handling of your aid. If you place your visual aid on the chalkboard or mount it on some other device, stand to one side and point with the arm nearest the visual aid. If it is necessary to roll or fold your visual aid, you will probably need to bring transparent tape to hold the aid firmly against the chalkboard so that it does not roll or wrinkle.

4.   Talk to your audience and not to your visual aid. Even though most of the members of the audience will be looking at your visual aid while you are speaking, you should maintain eye contact with them. The eye contact will improve your delivery, and you will be able to see how your audience is reacting to your visual material.

5.   Don't overdo the use of visual aids; you can reach a point of diminishing returns with them. If one is good, two may be better; if two are good, three may be better. Somewhere along the line, there is a point at which one more visual aid is too many. Visual aids are a form of emphasis; but when everything is emphasized, nothing receives emphasis. If you have many places where visual aids would be appropriate, decide at which points the visual aids would be most valuable. Remember, a visual aid is not a substitute for good speechmaking.

6. Think of all the possible hazards before you decide to pass objects around the class. Since we are used to professors passing out materials, we sometimes became insensitive to the great hazards of such a practice. Audiences cannot resist looking at, reading, handling, and thinking about something they hold in their hands; and while they are so occupied, they are not listening to the speaker. More often than not, when you pass out materials you lose control of your audience—lessening your chances of achieving your purpose. Even when only two or three objects are passed around, the result may be disastrous. Most members of the class become absorbed in looking at the objects, looking for the objects, wondering why people are taking so long, and fearing that perhaps they will be forgotten. Anytime you pass something around, you are taking a gamble —a gamble that usually is not worth the risk.

Assignment

Prepare a three- to six-minute informative speech in which visual aids are the major kind of speech amplification. Criteria for evaluation will include selection and use of visual aids. For an example of a speech using visual aids, refer to the sample speech on explaining a process on pages 129–132 of the following chapter.

EXPLAINING PROCESSES

9

Much of our daily information exchange involves explaining processes: telling how to do something, how to make something, or how something works. We give instructions to our partner on how to get more power on a forehand table-tennis shot; we share ideas with our neighbor on how to make gourmet meals with ground meat; and we talk with an employee of the water works on how the new water-purification system works. In this chapter we want to consider the means of clear, accurate explanation.

SELECTING TOPICS

Chances are that the brainstorming lists you developed earlier contain several ideas that relate to explaining processes. Because topics of this kind are so abundant, you may be tempted to make your selection too hastily. For instance, "how to bowl" may sound like a good topic for a bowler. When we apply the tests outlined in Chapter 3, we see that it fails as a topic on at least two counts. First, because nearly all college students have bowled and because many bowl frequently, a topic this general is unlikely to provide much new information for most of the class. Second, the topic is so broad that it is unlikely that you would be able to get into much depth within the time limits. If bowling is your hobby, your brainstorming sheet should contain such ideas as "spare bowling," "scoring," "automatic pin setters," "selecting a grip," "altering the amount of curve," and "getting more pin action," any of which would be better than "how to bowl." For this speech, a principle for topic selection should be to reject such broad-based topics as "how to bake cookies," "how clocks work," and "how to play tennis," in favor of more informative and more specific topics such as "judging baked goods," "how a cuckoo clock works," or "developing power in your tennis strokes."

ESSENTIALS OF PROCESS EXPLANATION

Your explanation of a process is a success when an audience understands the process—or better yet, when an audience can apply what you have shown. The more complicated the process, the more care you will need to take with your explanation. Although explanations of processes are often considered the easiest types of informative speeches to give—they deal with specific, concrete procedures—you will still need to consider the essentials carefully.

Knowledge and Experience

Good, clear explanation requires knowledge and experience of the process. Have you ever used a recipe? A recipe is an example of clear explanation of a process. If you can read a recipe, you can make the dish. Right? —Wrong. As many of us have found out, in the hands of a novice the best recipe in the world for beef stroganoff may still lead to disaster. Why? Because cooking requires both knowledge and experience. Just because Julia Child can turn the recipe into a gourmet's delight does not mean we can. But, after Julia Child explains how to make a dish, we can often come up with something that tastes quite good. A recipe indicates ingredients, quantities needed, and a way to proceed. The success of the dish depends upon the execution of that recipe. Only our knowledge and experience tell us whether two eggs are better than one, whether an additional few minutes in letting dough rise is beneficial or disastrous, or whether the product will taste even better if one of the suggested ingredients is omitted or substituted. If you are experienced, you will have tried the many variations. During the speech, you can speak from that experience; and you will be able to guide your listeners by explaining whether alternate procedures will work equally well or whether such procedures might be ill-suited for this audience.

In addition to giving necessary know-how to barren instructions, knowledge and experience builds speaker credibility. In explaining a process, you are projecting yourself as an authority on that particular subject. How well an audience listens will depend upon your credibility as an authority. We listen to Julia Child tell us how to make chicken cacciatora, Catfish Hunter tell us how to pitch a curve, and Neil Armstrong tell us how a moon rover works. And your audience will listen to you if you make them confident in your knowledge and experience of the process you are explaining.

Grouping Steps

All but the simplest processes will have many steps involved in the explanation. Earlier, in our discussion of outlining, we talked about limiting main points to no more than five, yet your process may have nine, eleven, or even fifteen steps. And of course, you cannot leave any of them out. One of your problems will be to group the steps into units that can be comprehended and recalled. A principle of learning states that it is easier to remember and comprehend information in units than as a series of independent items.

Although you should not sacrifice accuracy for listening ease, you should employ this principle whenever possible. The following example of a very simple process illustrates this principle:

A	B
1. Gather the materials.	1. Plan the job.
2. Draw a pattern.	A. Gather materials.
3. Trace the pattern on the wood.	B. Draw a pattern.
4. Cut out the pattern so that tracing line can still be seen.	C. Trace the pattern on wood.
5. File to the pattern line.	2. Cut out the pattern.
6. Sandpaper edge and surfaces.	A. Saw so the tracing line can be seen.
7. Paint the object.	B. File to the pattern line.
8. Sand lightly.	C. Sandpaper edge and surface.
9. Apply a second coat of paint.	3. Finish the object.
10. Varnish.	A. Paint.
	B. Sand lightly.
	C. Apply a second coat of paint.
	D. Varnish.

Although both sets of directions are essentially the same, the inclusion of the arbitrary headings in B enables us to visualize the process as having three steps instead of ten. As a result, most people would tend to remember the second set of directions more easily than the first. Most processes will provide an opportunity for such an arbitrary grouping. The "plan-do-finish" organization cited above is a common type of grouping for explaining how to make something. A little thought on the best way of grouping similar steps will pay dividends in audience understanding and recall.

Our example also illustrates the major kind of organization for most process speeches. Both sets of directions represent a *time order* organization: each point is a step of the process that must be accomplished before the next step is in order. Because a process does require a step-by-step procedure, a time order is a preferable organization. Occasionally, however, you will find your material falling into a *topic order*. In such cases, the subdivisions of each topic will usually be discussed in a time order. For instance, you might want to show that there are three ways of making spares in bowling. Your main points would be the three ways: spot bowling, line bowling, and sight bowling; then each of the methods would be explained in terms of the steps involved.

Visualization

Although it is possible to enable your audience to visualize a process through vivid word pictures—in fact, in your impromptu explanations in ordinary conversation, it is the only way you can proceed—when you have time to prepare, you will probably want to make full use of visual aids.

When the task is relatively simple, you may want to complete an actual demonstration. If so, you will want to practice the demonstration many times until you can do it smoothly and easily. Remember that, under the pressure of speaking before an audience, even an apparently easy task can become quite difficult. Since demonstrations often take longer than planned and since motor control will be a little more difficult in front of an audience than at home (did you ever try to thread a needle with twenty-five people watching you?), you may want to select an alternate method even though the process could be demonstrated within the time limit.

One alternative is the modified demonstration. Suppose you had worked for a florist and you were impressed by how floral displays were made. Making some special floral display would be an excellent process for this speech. The following example illustrates how one speaker accomplished her goal with a modified demonstration. For her speech on flower arranging, she brought a bag containing all the necessary materials. Since her second step was to prepare the basic triangle to begin her floral arrangement, she began to put the parts together in their proper relationship. Rather than trying to get everything together perfectly in the few seconds she had available, she drew from a second bag a partly completed arrangement that illustrated the triangle. Her third point was to show how additional flowers and greenery could be added to bring about various effects. Again, she began to add flowers to give us the idea of how a florist proceeds, and then she drew from a third bag a completed arrangement illustrating one of the possible effects that could be made. Even though she did not complete either of the steps for us, we saw how a florist handles her materials. In effect, her use of visual aids was every bit as professional as the floral arrangement she showed us.

Technically, this would not be a demonstration, for she did not go through all the steps in their entirety. Since discretion is the better part of valor, however, with any complex subject it is probably better to have some of the steps completed beforehand.

Additional Considerations

Your speech will be even better if you keep the following pointers in mind as you prepare.

1. *Consider your materials.* The effectiveness of your explanation may depend upon the nature and the number of materials, parts, equipment, or ingredients you select to show. In your consideration, separate the essentials from the accessories. A bowler

needs a ball, bowling shoes, and access to an alley. Wrist bands, thumb straps, finger grip, and fancy shirts are all accessories that may not be worth mentioning. For some speeches, you will want to bring all the materials for display; for other speeches, a list of materials may suffice.

2. *Speak slowly and repeat key ideas often.* In most speeches the audience need retain only the ideas behind the words. When you explain a process, it is important for an audience to retain considerably more detail. Don't rush. Especially, during the visualization steps, you want the audience to have a chance to formulate and to retain mental pictures. Give sufficient time for your words and your visual aids to "sink in." It is a good idea to repeat key ideas to make sure that the audience has command of the material.

3. *Work for audience participation.* We learn by doing. If you can simulate the process so that others can go through the steps with you, it will help to reinforce these ideas. If the process is a simple one, you may want to give materials for the audience to work with. For instance, in a speech on origami—Japanese paper folding—you may want to give members of your audience paper so that they can go through a simple process with you. You could explain the principles; then you could pass out paper and have the audience participate in making a figure; finally, you could tell how these principles are used in more elaborate projects. Actual participation will increase interest and ensure recall.

Assignment

         Prepare a three- to six-minute speech in which you show how something is made, how something is done, or how something works. Outline required. Criteria for evaluation will include quality of topic, our belief in your knowledge and experience with the topic, your ability to group steps, and the visualization of the process.

**Outline:
Speech Utilizing
Visual Aids
(3–6 minutes)**

Specific Purpose: To explain the three steps involved in executing a successful grab start.

Introduction

     I. One distinction that I can draw between competitive swimming and recreational swimming is that competitive swimming involves three specialized techniques that recreational swimming does not: the grab start, racing stroke, and racing turn.

    II. Since competitive swimming goes on in a racing setting, where time is the most crucial element, I'm going to limit myself to the beginning—the grab start.

   III. I want to discuss with you the three steps of the grab start that are used in getting the swimmer into the water in an expedient, rapid way.

Body

     I. In the first step, a swimmer assumes a "get-ready" position.
       A. The swimmer places his arms on the racing block, grabbing the block with his hands.
       B. His arms are placed between his legs, and the legs must be spread a little wider than the spread of the shoulders.
       C. The swimmer's arms must be bent slightly.
       D. His toes must grab the edge of the block.

    II. In the second step, the swimmer coordinates his body in a way that provides thrust of entry.
       A. The swimmer must pull down hard with his arms to pull himself even more forward than he was in the "get ready" position.
       B. Then he projects his arms out and almost simultaneously uses his legs to supplement the thrust provided by the arms.

   III. In the final step, the swimmer enters the pool at a slight angle, but almost parallel with the surface.
       A. This allows the swimmer to surface rapidly.
       B. He can commence his stroke more quickly.

Conclusion

The three steps involved in the execution of a grab start are: assume a "get ready" position, provide the necessary thrust, and enter the water at a slight angle.

The Racing Start

Study this speech in terms of informative value of topic, apparent knowledge and experience of the speaker, clarity of the steps, and visualization of the process.[1] Read the speech through at least once aloud. After you have read and analyzed the speech, turn to the detailed analysis in the other column.

Analysis

This opening paragraph serves several purposes. First, it establishes the speaker's authority to talk on this topic—we see that he has done competitive swimming. Second, it gives us the three major contrasts. And, third, it focuses on the subject of this speech, the grab start. Had he not mentioned the other two, we might wonder whether this is the only difference. The introduction's only weakness lies in the very beginning. The speech would profit from a question or startling statement to secure attention to the opening.

Since there are three major contrasts, and since we will agree that the speaker can talk only about one in the time limit, we are likely to ask, "Why the grab start?" By talking about the importance of speed, the

Speech

Before I became a member of a competitive swim team, I never realized the difference between competitive swimming and recreational swimming. Now, I can draw one clear distinction between the two: competitive swimming involves three very specialized techniques that recreational swimming does not. These are the techniques of the swimmer's grab start, the swimmer's stroke, and the swimmer's racing turn. Today, I am going to deal with one of these techniques, the swimmer's grab start.

Before I do, I think it is important to note the purpose of this technique. Competitive swimming goes on in a racing setting—the most crucial element of this setting is time. Everything the swimmer does is directed toward the goal of maintaining maximum expediency. Therefore, the purpose of the grab start is to permit the swimmer to enter the water in a way that is most expedient, most rapid. The grab start involves the following steps:

[1] Delivered in Speech class, University of Cincinnati. Printed by permission of Craig Newburger.

Analysis   Speech

speaker shows us that the grab start is the first step and any second saved here will be important to any length race. Still, I would like for him to have pointed out that the grab start would be especially important in shorter races.

First, the swimmer assumes a "get-ready" position atop a racing platform. The racing platform [visual aid] is simply an object that provides additional elevation between the swimmer's body and the water. In assuming the "get-ready" position, the swimmer first places his arms on the racing block, grabbing the block with his hands. His arms are placed, or positioned, between his legs [visual aid]. The legs must be spread a little wider apart than the spread of the shoulders, and, thirdly, the swimmer's arms must be bent slightly. Finally, the swimmer's toes must grab the edge of the block. All of these things must be coordinated with precision to allow the swimmer to complete the next step with expediency and efficiency.

The speaker states the first step of the process clearly.

Notice that the speaker clearly describes each of the aspects of the position. The steps of this position are clearly stated, and easily followed. The stick-figure visual aids help to make the points simply and clearly, yet require little artistic ability.

The next step is called, uh, providing thrust. Thrust is exactly what the word says; the swimmer in this step uses his body in such a way and coordinates himself in such a way that he may provide himself with enough thrust to enter the water effectively. In this step, the swimmer, after hearing the bang of the starter's signal,

In this section the speaker does a little "uh-uhing." Although vocalized pauses should be avoided, a few will creep into almost anyone's speech, and probably will not even be noticed by the listener.

Analysis   Speech

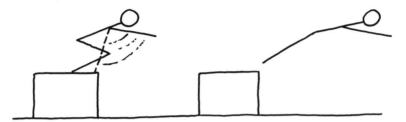

uh, must pull down hard—very hard with his arms to pull himself even more forward than he was in the get ready position [visual aid]. Secondly, he projects his arms out as we see here, and shortly after, almost but not quite simultaneously, he uses his legs to supplement the thrust provided by the arms. He does this by springing his legs forward [at this point the speaker leaps forward] to provide the final push that will allow him to enter the water properly.

Again, the main point is clearly stated. Each of the aspects of "providing thrust" is clearly stated and shown.

This is a good, clear transition taking us from the second to the third and final main point of the speech. And again the step is clearly stated.

I like the way the speaker emphasizes "slight angle." Apparently entering at too

This brings us now to the third and final step in the grab start, which is entering the water at a slight angle. It is important once the swimmer has departed from the racing platform to maintain his body posture at an angle whereby he can enter the water at a slight angle [visual aid]. Now, it is important for me here to emphasize the words "slight angle." By entering the water at a slight angle, the swimmer can surface rapidly and commence his stroke—whereas the swimmer who enters the water at more than a slight

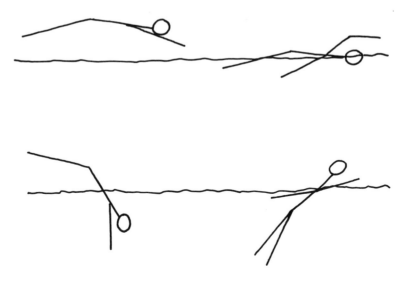

Analysis

Speech

much of an angle is one of the major problems in learning the grab start. By contrasting slight angle with the improper angle, the speaker is able to make his point especially clear.

angle, as we see here [visual aid], runs the risk of having to expend, as our swimmer is doing here, more time, precious time, and additional energy in reaching the surface to a point where he can commence his stroke.

To finish his speech, the speaker uses a simple but effective summary of the main points. In his summary, he makes a minor but common mistake. He begins to enumerate the steps, drops the enumeration with the second point, and picks it up again with the third. If you wish to enumerate, and it will help achieve clarity, carry the enumeration through.

Therefore, I think that we can all see that the grab start is a very specialized technique that involves the following steps [repeats all visual aids]: first, the swimmer assumes the "get ready" position; then he provides the necessary thrust for which his body needs to, uh, dive into the water—enter the water properly; and, third, the swimmer must enter the water at a slight angle.

By and large, this is a clearly explained, easily visualized process.

DESCRIPTIVE SPEECHES

10

Because description can help to create clarity and vividness in any speech, a descriptive speech assignment provides an excellent opportunity for developing language skill. Since the goal of the descriptive speaker is to give an accurate, informative description, we will first look at the essentials of description. Then we will consider topics, organization, and language of descriptive speeches.

ESSENTIALS OF DESCRIPTION

You achieve your goal in descriptive speaking by providing word pictures for your audience. In order for the listener to reconstruct a mental image that corresponds with your perception, an amount of essential data is required. If the object is simple and familiar (a light bulb, a rocking chair), the description need not be very detailed. If the object is complex and unfamiliar (a sextant, a nuclear reactor), the description must be more detailed. Even common objects must be described vividly if you want to differentiate them from the standard. Description is, of course, made considerably easier with visual aids. Since the purpose of this assignment is the development of verbal facility, your description should be clear enough and vivid enough to create a mental picture without visual aids. The essentials of description are size, shape, weight, color, composition, age and condition, and location of subordinate items.

Size

Size is described subjectively by "large" or "small" and objectively by dimensions. Ordinarily a meaningful description of size will contain a comparison. For instance, neither "The book is a large one," nor "The book is 9 inches by 6 inches," by itself creates an image. On the other hand, "The book, 9 inches by 6 inches by 3 inches, is a large one, the same length and width but twice the thickness of your textbook" would be descriptive.

Shape

Shape is described in terms of common geometric forms. "Round," "triangular," "oblong," "spherical," "conical," "cylindrical," and "rectangular" are all descriptive. A complex object is best described as a series of simple shapes. Since most objects do not conform to perfect shapes, you can usually get by with approximations and with comparisons to familiar objects. "The lake is round," "The lot is pie shaped," or "The car looks like a rectangular box" all give reasonably accurate impressions. Shape is further clarified by such adjectives as "jagged," "smooth," or "indented."

Weight

Weight is described subjectively as "heavy" or "light" and objectively by pounds and ounces. As with size, descriptions of weight are clarified by comparisons. Thus, "The suitcase weighed about 70 pounds; that's about twice the weight of a normally packed suitcase" would be descriptive.

Color

Color, an obvious necessity of description, is difficult to describe accurately. Although most people can visualize black and white, the primary colors (red, yellow, and blue), and their complements (green, purple, and orange), very few objects are these colors. Perhaps the best way to describe a color is to couple it with a common referent. For instance, "lime green," "lemon yellow," "brick red," "green as a grape," "banana yellow," or "blue as the sky" give rather accurate approximations. Just be careful with how far you carry the comparisons. Paint companies, fabric dealers, and cosmetics manufacturers stretch our imagination to the breaking point at times with such labels as "blimey blue" or "giddy green."

Composition

The composition of an object helps us to visualize it. A ball of aluminum does not look the same as a ball of yarn. A pile of rocks gives a different impression than does a pile of straw. A brick building looks different from a steel, wood, or glass building. Sometimes you will refer to what the object seems like rather than what it is. An object can appear metallic even if it is not made of metal. Spun glass can have a woolly texture. Nylon can be soft and smooth as in stockings or hard and sharp as in toothbrush bristles.

Age and Condition

Whether an object is new or old can make a difference in its appearance. Since age by itself may not be descriptive, it is often discussed in terms of condition. Although condition is difficult to describe objectively, it can be very important to an accurate description. The value of coins, for instance, varies tremendously depending on whether they are uncirculated or their condition is good or only fair. A 1915 Lincoln penny in fair condition may be worth two cents, whereas an uncirculated 1960 penny may be worth five cents. Books become ragged and tattered, buildings become run down and dilapidated, land is subject to erosion. Age and condition together often prove especially valuable in developing informative descriptions.

Location of Subordinate Items

If your object for description is complex, the parts must be fitted into their proper relationship before a mental picture emerges. Remember the story of the three blind men who described an elephant in terms of what each felt? The one who felt the trunk said the elephant was like a snake; the one who felt a leg said the elephant was like a tree; and the one who felt the body said the elephant was like a wall. Not only must we visualize size, shape, weight, color, composition, age, and condition, but also we must understand how the parts fit together.

Since the ultimate test of description is that it enables the audience to visualize, the speaker probably should include too much detail rather than not enough. Moreover, if some particular aspect is discussed in two or three different ways, everyone might get the mental image, whereas a single description might make the image vivid to only a few. Begin your practice sessions with more material than you could possibly get into the time limits for your speech. As you gain a mastery of the material in practice, you can begin to delete until you get the speech down to a workable length. Keep in mind, however, that with the descriptive speech perhaps more than any other you will have to resist the desire to memorize.

TOPICS FOR DESCRIPTIVE SPEECHES

The goal of the descriptive speaker is to give an accurate, informative description of something specific and concrete. It may be an object, a structure, a place, an animal, or a person. Although animals and people may seem like obvious subjects, the tendency to describe them in terms of subjective reaction rather than objective analysis makes them less suitable topics for informative description. I would also caution against selecting the first thing that comes to mind: your pencil sharpener on the wall, the statue on the shelf, or your favorite chair. Even though the goal is description, you should select your topic by using the methods and applying the tests outlined in Chapter 3. If you discover that your original lists do not include any subjects that would be appropriate for description, continue the brainstorming process until you have compiled several possibilities to choose from. For instance, if your hobby is camping, you might list "turtleback campers," "camp site," "kerosine lantern," "tent trailers," "tents," "sleeping bags," and other topics associated with camping. If your major is medieval history, you might list "moats," "castles," "jousting spear," "coat of mail," or "crossbows."

In evaluating your topic selection, remember that it must meet the principal test of informative speeches—the potential for new information. Description itself is, and must be, subordinate to informative intent. You want to describe what the object, place, or building looks like, but your intent must be informative rather than poetic. You want to create an accurate, vivid, verbal picture of what you are describing.

ORGANIZATION OF DESCRIPTION

Since at least one of the goals of a descriptive speech is to leave with the audience a visual image of your subject, arrangement of main points by space order will often prove the most workable. A description of a jet-powered racing car might go from back to front, front to back, outside to inside, or inside to outside. A description of a painting might go from foreground to background, background to foreground, left to right, or top to bottom.

Although space-order organization should be used most often, when you are describing a class of objects you might use a topic order with a space order of subdivisions. For instance, in a description of your campus, you might want to speak on the topics of buildings, the walk system, and the wooded park areas. Or, in a description of Yellowstone Park, you might talk about Old Faithful geyser and the Fountain Paint Pot as the two main topics. Each of the main topics would in turn be developed with a space order arrangement of subordinate detail.

A significant benefit of a space-order organization is that your decision about placement of main points is simplified. Once you determine that you will go from left to right, top to bottom, or inside to outside, every key feature that the eye encounters will become either a main point or an important subdivision of a main point.

LANGUAGE

Although a descriptive speech has several goals, it derives its major benefit as a language exercise. With this assignment you can concentrate on *clarity, vividness, emphasis,* and *appropriateness,* fundamental qualities of style we discussed in Chapter 5. You want to make your description so vivid that the audience will be able to visualize your subject accurately.

As you consider your wording of the speech, remember the function of description. You want your speech to be informative, not poetic. Be on the lookout for florid description, emotive words, and excessive adjectives and adverbs. A descriptive speech should not sound like a page from a literary magazine. By keeping the emphasis on the informative nature of the topic and not the beauty, by keeping the emphasis on the functional nature of the language and not the poetic, you should be able to make your speech clear, vivid, emphatic, and appropriate without being affected or artificial.

Earlier you were cautioned about not memorizing this speech. Since there are unlimited ways that you can describe in any part of your speech, in each practice keep the essentials in mind, and try to use slightly different wordings to express your descriptions. By adapting to your audience and by having a true spontaneity, you will be able to avoid memorization.

Assignment

Prepare a two- to four-minute speech describing an object, a building, or a place. Outline required. Criteria for evaluation will include clarity, vividness, emphasis, and appropriateness of the description.

**Outline:
Descriptive Speech
(2–4 minutes)**

Notice that three points of the outline follow a space order going from room to room inside the castle. The fourth point describes the overall castle.

Specific Purpose: To describe the Colleen Moore Fairy Castle.

Introduction

I. Have you ever dreamed of what it would be like to live in or even walk through a fairy castle?

II. Let me take you on tour through a fairy castle.

Body

I. The room we enter is the Great Central Hall.
   A. The floor is ivory, with rose vines leading to the ceiling.
   B. The domed ceiling two stories above depicts stories of Grimm and Anderson.
   C. On the walls hang paintings of famous characters.
   D. Tall etched-glass windows overlook the gardens.
   E. A spiral staircase in front of us leads up to the bed chambers.

II. Off to the right and through an archway is the Drawing Room.
   A. The floor is made of rose quartz.
   B. The ceiling is like a sea-blue sky with misty clouds.
   C. A diamond, emerald, and pearl chandelier hangs from the ceiling.
   D. On the walls are murals of the Cinderella story.
   E. A fireplace is in one corner.
   F. The furniture is made of silver.
   G. Special pieces are a rosewood piano, a silver secretary, and a grandfather clock.

III. Off to the right again is King Arthur's Dining Hall.
   A. The ceiling has rafters, the walls are marble, and the floor is inlaid wood.
   B. On the walls hang needlepoint tapestries depicting Arthurian epics.
   C. Dominating the room is the Round Table.
      1. Each knight's chair is in place with coat of arms emblazoned on the back.

2. Each place is set with solid gold service.

IV. This castle is for real and on display at the Science and Industry Museum in Chicago.

    A. The castle is 9 feet square and 12 feet high.

    B. It has its own electric and plumbing systems.

    C. It holds over 1,000 treasures.

    D. It's valued at half a million dollars.

Conclusion

The castle was a dream come true for actress Colleen Moore.

Colleen Moore's Fairy Castle

As you read this speech analyze the descriptions of size, shape, weight, color, composition, age, and condition, and location of subordinate items.[1] Which descriptions are vivid? Which need more detail? After you have read the speech at least once aloud, read the analysis in the other column.

Analysis

The speaker begins his speech with questions. He tries to get the listeners to think back to their childhood.

He ends his introduction with a clear statement of what he intends to do in the speech.

The speaker begins with a description of the entry way. Notice how each of the parts is clearly stated. We are able to visualize what he is describing very clearly and vividly.

This is a good transition taking us from the entry way to the drawing room. Again the description is very clear and vivid. The speaker itemizes each thing we see and gives us its size, shape, and color.

Speech

Have you ever dreamed what it would be like to live in a fairy castle? Or to just be able to walk through one—the kind that you read about when you were a little child? Well, today let me take you on a tour of one of my fairy castles.

We enter the castle through two large, huge oak doors from the beautifully appointed fountain gardens outside surrounding the castle with weeping willows that actually weep. We find ourselves standing first of all in a great central hall. The floor below us is made of fine ivory, covered with rose vines that climb up to the ceiling on golden pillars. And two stories above us is a domed ceiling illustrating the stories of Hans Christian Anderson and Brothers Grimm. And on the walls hang many famous paintings of Alice in Wonderland, Snow White, and Old King Cole. And the tall windows overlooking the gardens are etched in glass illustrating the stories of Prince Charming and Jack in the Beanstalk. Directly in front of us across from the two front doors we find a spiral staircase that leads us to the princess' bed chambers, and gives the appearance of a *floating* staircase.

Then, as we move up to the right through an archway, we find ourselves in the drawing room. This floor is made of shimmery rose quartz bordered by green jade made in China. And from the ceiling above us hangs a chandelier—a beautifully ornate chandelier made of green emeralds, diamonds, and pearls. In one corner of the room stands a fireplace with silver andirons. Above it is a bejeweled

[1] Delivered in Speech class, University of Cincinnati. Printed by permission of Frank Buschbacher.

Analysis   Speech

gold clock ticking away the fairy minutes. And the early fairy period furniture in this room is all made of silver, except for a grand piano, which is made of rosewood with ivory legs. And there's a silver secretary with a statue of William Tell carved in ivory, and across from the silver secretary we find a hickory-dickory grandfather clock.

Once more we have a clear transition statement taking us to the next room. What makes the description so good is the care with details. Each item is carefully placed and described briefly, yet in a way that we can visualize it.

As we move off to the right again, we find ourselves in King Arthur's dining hall, with a feudal raftered ceiling, warm walnut woodwork, marble walls that are highly polished, and a floor of inlaid wood. And on the walls hang many needlepoint tapestries depicting the epics of King Arthur and his knights. And, of course, dominating this room is King Arthur's Round Table, each knight's chair in its proper place, and emblazoned on the back of each chair is that particular knight's coat of arms. And at each place is set a solid gold dining service, with a goblet, plate, and wine glass.

I particularly like the way the speaker gets us back to reality. After doing an excellent job of taking us on the tour, he gives us the specific details of the castle. This climactic approach to the material makes the information a little more interesting and helps carry the fairylike motif throughout.

The care with detail, careful selection from among all he could have picked, and excellent wording make this a very clear as well as exceptionally vivid descriptive speech.

Now at this point in the tour you're probably wondering about me, thinking, "Has this guy got an imagination!" Well, this isn't my imagination. This castle is for real, and it's on display in the Science and Industry Museum in Chicago. But there is only one problem in taking such a tour as I have just described to you now. We have to shrink down to 5 inches in size, for this castle and all I have described to you is a miniature replica of a fairy castle. It is 9 feet square, and the highest tower stands 12 feet above the floor. It has its own electrical and plumbing systems. And in this castle there are over a thousand wee little treasures, giving the castle a value of half a million dollars. A long time ago, this castle was a dream come true for an actress named Colleen Moore. Today it is dedicated to those of us who still believe in fairy castles.

SPEECHES OF DEFINITION

11

Every time we use a dictionary, we are reminded that our working vocabularies are relatively small compared to the total number of words in the English language. Moreover, anyone who has attempted to answer small children's constant refrain, "What does that mean?" is well aware that even those words we use every day are often difficult to explain. As a result of our problems with vocabulary, our attempts at relating to others often fail—sometimes because we do not know the meaning of a word and sometimes because we accept one meaning when the communicator intended another. Yet, since we cannot solve problems, learn, or even think without meaningful definitions, the ability to define clearly and vividly is essential for the effective communicator. Since Plato first attacked the Sophists for their inability to define and to classify, rhetoricians have seen definition as a primary tool of effective speaking. In fact, Richard Weaver, representing the view of many modern scholars, has placed definition as the most valuable of all lines of development.[1] In this chapter, we are studying definition in an informative speaking context; you will find, however, that you will be applying the principles of sound definition to any and all kinds of speeches.

HOW WORDS ARE DEFINED

Although individuals have used numerous methods to define words for their audiences, you can improve your communication by mastering the following four.

Classification and Differentiation

When you define by classification and differentiation, you give the boundaries of the particular word and focus on the single feature that gives the word a different meaning from similar words. For instance, a dog may be defined as a carnivorous, domesticated mammal of the family Canidae. "Carnivorous," "mam-

---

[1] Richard Weaver, "Language Is Sermonic," in Richard L. Johannesen, ed., *Contemporary Theories of Rhetoric: Selected Readings* (New York: Harper & Row, 1971), pp. 170–171.

mal," and "family Canidae" limit the boundaries to dogs, jackals, foxes, and wolves. "Domesticated" differentiates dogs from the other three. Most dictionary definitions are of the classification-differentiation variety.

Synonym and Antonym

Synonyms are words that have the same or nearly the same meanings; antonyms are words that have opposite meanings. When you use synonym or antonym, you are defining by comparison or contrast. For instance, synonyms for "sure" are "certain," "confident," "positive." An antonym would be "doubtful." Some synonyms for "prolix" would be "long," "wordy," or "of tedious length." Antonyms would be "short" and "concise." Synonyms and antonyms are often the shortest, quickest, and easiest ways to clarify the meaning of a new word. Of course, the use of synonym and antonym presupposes that the audience is familiar with the synonyms and antonyms selected.

Etymology and Historical Example

Etymology is the derivation or an account of the history of a particular word. Depending upon the word being defined, etymology may or may not be a fruitful method of definition. Since words change over a period of time, origin may reveal very little about modern meaning. In many instances, however, the history of a word reveals additional insight that will help the audience remember the meaning a little better. Consider the following definition: "A sophist is an individual who is more concerned with ingenuity and specious effectiveness than he is with soundness of argument." In this case, the following explanation of the history of the word adds considerable insight to the rather barren classification definition:

In ancient Greece there were professional teachers who distinguished themselves for their teaching of practical politics, language, and speech. These men became some of the most renowned men in Greece. Although most of them were dedicated, intelligent, and valuable contributors to their cultures, some of them became so entranced with their powers of persuasion that they regarded belief as more important than truth. Plato was so incensed by the power of these men who could "make the worse case appear the better" that he devoted large segments of many of his dialogues to destroying the reputation of the sophists. He was so successful that today when we refer to someone as a sophist, we do not mean an excellent teacher of practical politics; instead we mean a rather slippery individual who is more interested in effectiveness than in truth.

Under certain circumstances, etymology and historical example can give an excellent assist in the definition of a word.

Uses and Functions

A fourth way to define is to explain the use or the function of a particular object. Thus, when you say, "A plane is a hand-powered tool that is used to smooth the edges of boards," you are defining the tool by indicating its use. Since the use or function of an object may be more important than its classification, this is often an excellent method of definition.

Regardless of the kind of definition you select, it should always differentiate, meet all circumstances, include all that is necessary, and, perhaps most important, be understandable.

TOPICS FOR SPEECH OF DEFINITION

The very best topics for definition are often general or abstract words, words that give you leeway in definition and possibility for creative development. On your brainstorming lists look for words like the following:

Expressionism	Rhetoric	Extrasensory
Existentialism	Epicurean	perception
Status	Fossil	Logic
		Acculturation

DEVELOPMENT OF SPEECHES OF DEFINITION

Definition can be used in your speeches in at least two basic ways—either as a form of support or as the framework for the speech itself. Since this chapter is concerned with an assignment of a speech of definition, we need to see how such a speech may be developed. One method is to develop the speech topically with coordinate headings each of which stands as a part of the definition. The other method is to develop the speech topically with subordinate headings in which the first point defines the word in general and subsequent points define the word in specific.

Coordinate Development

Webster's Eighth New Collegiate Dictionary defines "jazz" as "American music characterized by improvisation, syncopated rhythms, contrapuntal ensemble playing, and special melodic features peculiar to the individual interpretation of the player." Like most dictionary definitions, this is of the classification-differentiation variety that requires an understanding of the various terms used within the definition. Before its meaning would be clear, most people would have to look up "improvisation," "syncopation," "contrapuntal" (which refers to "counterpoint"), and "ensemble." Nevertheless, such a dictionary definition makes for a very good purpose sentence for a speech. By utilizing each aspect as a prospective topical development of the speech, a potentially sound organizational structure is provided with very little effort on your part. Assuming that you had the background to attest to the accuracy of the definition and to understand the various topics mentioned, your structural outline would look like this:

Specific Purpose: To explain the four major characteristics of jazz.

I. Jazz is characterized by improvisation.

II. Jazz is characterized by syncopated rhythms.

III. Jazz is characterized by contrapuntal ensemble playing.

IV. Jazz is characterized by special melodic features peculiar to the individual interpretation of the player.

With this method, then, the organization is suggested by the definition itself. The inventive process determines how you enlarge upon each aspect of the definition. Your selection and use of examples, illustrations, comparisons, personal experiences, and observations would give the speech original distinctive flavor. Furthermore, you would have the option of utilizing other methods of definition to reinforce various parts of the speech.

You can achieve the same coordinate development by starting from a definition you have evolved for yourself. In this case, your purpose sentence is evolved from various existing definitions and from individual analysis of the subject. Suppose you wished to define or clarify the concept "a responsible citizen." A dictionary would indicate that "responsible" means "accountable" and "citizen" means a "legal inhabitant who enjoys certain freedoms and privileges." But this definition does not really tell what a "responsible citizen" is. As you think about citizenship in relation to responsibilities, you might begin to list such categories as social, civic, financial, and political. From this analysis, you could evolve the following subjective definition: "A responsible citizen is one who meets his or her social, civic, and financial obligations." Once you are satisfied with the soundness of your definition, you may proceed in much the same way as the person who has adopted a dictionary definition. Your organization, developed topically, would look like this:

Specific Purpose: To show that a responsible citizen is one who meets his or her social, civic, and financial obligations.

I. A responsible citizen meets his or her social responsibilities.

II. A responsible citizen meets his or her civic responsibilities.

III. A responsible citizen meets his or her financial responsibilities.

This second method allows you to talk about concepts that have connotative or subjective meanings that are not usually found in dictionaries.

Subordinate Development

Sometimes you will discover that the word you wish to define is most clearly defined through various examples and illustrations that *limit* the boundaries of the definition. Under these circumstances, rather than developing the speech topically, with each main point standing as a part of the definition, you may elect to develop the speech subordinately. In subordinate development, your first major point presents the total definition *in general*. Then your remaining points present degrees, limits, or other specific aspects of the definition. In the speech offered as an example at the end of this chapter, the speaker defines the word *norm*. The definition itself is rather simple—norms are rules that define accepted behavior in society. Much of the real understanding of the word, then, must come through various examples that consider the degrees of norms. In brief, the skeleton of the outline looks like this:

Specific Purpose: To define the word *norm* in terms of two different degrees.

I. Norms are rules that define what is required in certain situations in society.

II. One degree of norms is illustrated by folkways.

III. Another degree of norms is illustrated by mores.

The strength of this kind of development is that in moving from general to specific, you give your audience a clear and vivid understanding of the word being defined.

In the following assignment you should not be restricted to either of these procedures. Your goal is to give the clearest, most meaningful definition possible, using any of the methods of definition suggested above.

Assignment	**Prepare a two- to four-minute speech of definition. Outline required. Select a word or concept that is not readily definable by most members of the class. Criteria for evaluation will include the clarity of the definition, organization of main points, and quality of the developmental material.**

**Outline:
Speech of Definition
(2–4 minutes)**

Specific Purpose: To define the word *norm* in terms of two different degrees.

Introduction

 I. We have all been on a bus at some point and have either given our seat to an elderly lady or seen someone else do it. This is normal behavior in that situation.

 II. Normal behavior is defined by norms.

Body

 I. Norms are rules that define what is required in certain situations in society.
   A. They imply that one should or must follow certain behavioral patterns.
   B. They are internalized rules and standards.
   C. Society regulates relationships through norms.
   D. People are punished for deviating from the norms.

 II. One degree of norms is illustrated by folkways.
   A. Folkways are ways of doing things that are natural.
     1. They are habitual or customary beliefs or styles of behavior.
     2. They are not strongly entrenched in the values of society.
     3. There is little or no punishment for deviation.
   B. Folkways are divided into customs and fashions.

 III. Another degree of norms is illustrated by mores.
   A. Mores are norms that are necessary for maintaining society in a given state.
     1. They are essential for the well-being of society.
     2. They are accompanied by strong moral feelings.
     3. Strong punishment follows deviation from mores.
   B. Mores are divided into conventions and laws.

Conclusion

 I. Now you can see that much of your behavior in society is regulated by norms.

II. The next time you give your seat to an elderly lady on a bus, you'll know that you are adhering to a norm and that norm is a folkway.

Norms

Study this speech in terms of quality of topic, clarity of definition, and development of the definition.[2] Before you attempt to evaluate, read the speech at least once aloud. After you have read and analyzed the speech, turn to the detailed analysis in the other column.

Analysis

The speech begins with a question that asks us to recall a common experience.

Once he has described the behavior, he gives it a name—a norm.

To develop the definition, the speaker moves from general to specific. During the first point of the speech, a classification definition of norm, he presents the various elements of the classification. Although we now know what norms are in general, we may still be unsure of their specific application. To complete our understanding of norms, the speaker moves to a discussion of specific degrees.

We see that the first degree he will discuss is folkways. Notice that the speaker continues the general-to-specific organization in his development. First he defines folkways; then he moves to specific types and gives us examples of each.

The effect of the specific examples is heightened by the humor of " 'groovy' was the groovy thing to say."

Speech

Haven't we all been on a crowded bus at one time or another in our lives when an elderly lady came on with many packages in her hands, and we decided to get up and give her our seat? I'm sure we've all been in this situation or seen this happen. Well, giving up a seat to an elderly lady is the "normal" behavior in that situation. How we behave in various situations in society is defined by *norms.*

Norms are rules of behavior; they define what is required and accepted under certain circumstances. Norms are internalized rules —they function within particular cultures, nations, or groups of people. A society regulates the relationships of the people through norms. Norms imply that individuals should or must follow behavioral, uh, certain behavioral patterns, and there is punishment for deviance from the norms. We can get a clearer understanding of the meaning of norms by considering two degrees of norms that operate in our society.

On one end of the spectrum there are folkways. The norms called folkways are habitual or customary beliefs or styles. They're ways of doing things that are "natural." They are not strongly entrenched in the values of society, so little or no punishment, uh, for deviation is followed. Two types of folkways are customs and fashions. The marriage ceremony, opening a door for a lady, or giving a seat to an elderly lady on a bus are all customs. Fads, styles of speech, and styles of dress are fashions. One time "groovy" was the groovy thing to say, or the Nehru jacket was the thing to wear. Whereas customs endure in a society, fashions are short-lived. They have a beginning and an end.

[2] Delivered in Speech class, University of Cincinnati. Printed by permission of Robert Sukys.

Analysis

Here the speaker moves clearly to the second degree of norms, mores. In his discussion of mores, the more important degree of norms, he spends more time with his explanation.

The speaker develops the importance of degree of punishment quite well.

Again, he offers good specific examples to clarify our understanding.

This standard summary is made considerably more effective with the restatement of the opening reference. All in all, this is a clear and interesting speech of definition.

Speech

On the other end of the spectrum are mores. Mores are norms that are necessary for maintaining society in a given state. They are essential for the well-being of a society. They are accompanied by strong moral feelings and are strongly entrenched in the values of society. And there is strong punishment for deviation. Two kinds of mores are conventions and laws. The specific difference between conventions and laws has to do with the punishment that follows deviation. The punishment for deviation from conventions is ostracism or negative responses, um, from fellow persons in society; the punishment for violation of laws is, of course, fine or imprisonment. An example of a convention would be behavior regarding privileged information. If a psychiatrist reveals the details of a case of a patient to another doctor or to another patient, the behavior is considered a violation of the conventions of medicine and the psychiatrist may be ostracized. Laws are the rules that are created by the political system in the society and punished also through the legal system in the society. So, when we travel 70 mph on the Interstate, we know we are breaking a law and we know our punishment could be a fine or even jail.

So we can see that norms are the rules of behavior of society. They may be folkways like fashions or customs, or they may be mores like conventions or laws. The next time you're on a bus and you give your seat to an elderly lady, you'll know that you are adhering to a norm and that particular norm is a folkway.

EXPOSITORY SPEECHES

12

Throughout history man has had an insatiable need to know. Unanswered questions stimulate research; research yields facts; and facts, when properly ordered and developed, yield understanding. Oral communication of the understanding of these questions is often made through expository speeches.

Most expository speeches are referred to as reports or lectures. Whether you call your speech a report, a lecture, or an exposition, it should be a carefully prepared informative speech that depends upon creative use of resource material for its effectiveness. In addition to considering research and creativity, in this chapter we will also consider the requirements of, and problems in developing, various types of expository speeches.

RESEARCH

You may have noticed that explaining processes and describing are methods of informing that depend more upon personal knowledge, experience, and observation than on research for speech development. Even definitions require a minimum of research in preparation. But expository speaking places such emphasis on the understanding of an idea that it requires outside source material to give the speech depth. We have already discussed sources of information in Chapter 3; now we want to consider means of testing information and methods of using source material in the speech.

Ensuring Comprehension

Quality research is a requirement of good exposition. Quality research will make your speech comprehensive. By comprehensive we mean covering the areas that need to be covered in order to satisfy your purposes. Or, put in another way, comprehensive means researching the best available material on the subject. Although comprehensive research on any expository subject could take a team of researchers weeks or more, for a class assignment, we would expect the speech to be comprehensive "within reason," which might be defined as using at least four or more sources of information. A review of sources of information (including the interview—perhaps one of the best sources for topics on contemporary issues) in Chapter 3 should help you get the best bibliography. My advice would be to look into eight or ten different sources.

As you gather the sources, which will be included in your bibliography, you may find that you have discovered more material than you can possibly read completely. In order to locate and record the best material, you should develop a system of evaluation that will enable you to review the greatest amount of information in the shortest period of time. Most students find that with a little practice they can increase their efficiency by skip reading. If you are appraising a magazine article, spend a minute or two finding out what it covers. Does it really present information on the phase of the topic you are exploring? Does it contain any documented statistics, examples, or quotable opinions? Is the author qualified to draw meaningful conclusions? If you are appraising a book, read the table of contents carefully, look at the index, and skip-read pertinent chapters asking the same questions you would for a magazine article. During this skip-reading period, you will decide which sources should be read in full, which should be read in part, and which should be abandoned. Every minute spent in evaluation will save you from unlimited amounts of useless reading.

Ensuring Accuracy and Objectivity

In addition to yielding comprehensiveness of analysis, a wide variety of sources are needed to ensure accuracy and objectivity. Because your goal is to find the facts regardless of what they may prove, you will need to get material on all sides of the topic being explored. Your material may reveal some contradictory aspects; your speech should reflect the nature of the conflict.

Any source that you read will be a representation of fact and opinion. A fact is anything that is verifiable; an opinion is an expressed view on any subject. That apples have seeds is a fact; that apples taste good is an opinion. Some opinions are related to, based upon, or extended from facts—some are not. Before you build your lines of development, you need to test the accuracy of the "facts" you have discovered and the objectivity of opinions. Determining accuracy of every item in a source can be a long and tedious and perhaps even an impossible job. In most cases accuracy can be reasonably assured by checking the fact against the original, or primary, source. If your source states that, according to the most recent Department of Labor statistics, unemployment went down 0.2 percent in December, you should look for those most recent Department of Labor statistics. If your history book footnotes the original source of an important quotation, you should go to that original source. Although checking sources in this way may appear to be an unnecessary task, you will be surprised at the number of errors that occur in using data from other sources.

If the original or primary source is not available, the best way of verifying a fact is to check it against the facts in a second source on the subject. Although two or more sources may on some occasion get their "facts" from the same faulty source, when two or more sources state the same fact or similar facts, the chances of verification are considerably better.

A second and equally important test is to determine the objectivity of an opinion. Facts by themselves are not nearly as important as the conclusions drawn from them. Since conclusions are more often than not opinions, they have to be weighed very carefully before they can be accepted. Researchers find that a good procedure is to study a variety of sources to see what they say about the same set of facts; then the researchers draw their own conclusions from the facts. Your conclusion may duplicate one source, or may draw from several sources, or occasionally may differ from the sources. But only after you have examined many sources, are you in a position to make the kind of value judgment that a thinking speaker needs to make. In your research you may be surprised how many times two sources will appear to contradict each other on the interpretation of a set of facts. Whether the issue is the cause of World War I, the effects of birth-control pills on women, or the importance of free trade to a nation's economic position, what the source says may depend on the biases of the author, the availability or selection of material, or care in evaluation of material. As a result, expository speakers must be sure that they are not communicating a distorted, biased, or hastily stated opinion as fact.

**Citing
Source Material**

A special problem of a research speech is how you can cite source material in your speech. In presenting any speech in which you are using ideas that are not your own personal knowledge, you should attempt to work the source of your material into the context of the speech. Such efforts to include sources not only will help the audience in their evaluation of the content but also will add to your credibility as a speaker. In a written report, ideas taken from other sources are designated by footnotes. In a speech, these notations must be included within the context of your statement of the material. In addition, since an expository speech is supposed to reflect a depth of research, citing the various sources of information will give concrete evidence of your research. Your citation need not be a complete representation of all the bibliographical information. In most instances, the following kinds of phrasing are appropriate:

According to an article about Senator Muskie in last week's *Time* magazine . . .

In the latest Gallup poll cited in last week's issue of *Newsweek* . . .

One conservative point of view was well summed up by Barry Goldwater in his book *Conscience of a Conservative.* In the opening chapter, Goldwater wrote . . .

But in order to get a complete picture we have to look at the statistics. According to the *Statistical Abstract,* the level of production for underdeveloped countries rose from . . .

In a speech before the National Association of Manufacturers given just last fall, Rockefeller said . . .

Although you do not want to clutter your speech with bibliographical citations, you do want to make sure that you have properly reflected the sources of your key information. If you will practice these and similar short prefatory comments, you will find that they will soon come naturally.

CREATIVITY AND ORIGINALITY

If you have selected a worthwhile topic and have gathered sufficient reliable material, your speech should have the necessary depth. Because you are engaging your audience in a learning process, you also want to do what you can to make your ideas interesting. By thinking creatively you can add originality to your speeches. An original speech is new; it is not copied, imitated, or reproduced. To you, the lecturer, this means that your speech must be a product of, but entirely different from, the sources you used. You find material, you put it in a usable form, then you inject your insights and your personality into the speech.

Originality is a product of the creative process. Some people have the mistaken idea that creativity is a natural by-product of a special "creative individual." Actually, we all have the potential for thinking creatively—some of us just have not given ourselves a chance to try.

To be creative, you must give yourself enough time to allow the creative process to work. Creative thinking is roughly analogous to cooking. You just can't rush it. Have you ever tried to make a good spaghetti sauce? It takes hours and hours of simmering the tomatoes, herbs, and spices. A good cook knows that success with the best ingredients and the best recipes is dependent upon allowing the proper length of time. So it is with speechmaking. Once you have prepared yourself fully (when you have completed your outline), you need two or three days for your mind to reflect upon what you have gathered. Let us take the practice period as an example of the result of giving the creative process time to work. You may find that the morning after a few uninspiring practices you suddenly have two or three fresh ideas for lines of development. While you were sleeping, your mind was still going over the material. When you awoke, the product of unconscious or subconscious thought reached the level of consciousness. Had there been no intervening time between practice sessions and delivery, your mind would not have had the time to work through the material.

But time alone is not enough. You must be receptive to new ideas, and you must develop the capacity to evaluate comparable ideas. Too often we are content with the first thought that comes to mind. Suppose, for your speech on plastics, you thought you would begin the speech with "Years ago when you learned that something was made out of plastic you often rejected it as an inferior product. Today you wouldn't give it a second thought. Let's examine some of the ways plastics have been developed to strengthen their quality." Now there is probably nothing wrong with such an opening, but is it the best you can do? There is no way for you to know until you have tried other ways. Here is where you can usefully employ the brainstorming method for a goal other than selecting topics. Try to start your speech in two, three, or even five different ways. Although several attempts will be similar, the effort to try new ways will stretch your mind, and chances are good that one or two of the ways will be far superior and much more imaginative than any of the others.

Being receptive also means taking note of ideas that come to you regardless of the circumstances. Did you ever notice how ideas will come to you at strange times? Perhaps while you are washing dishes, or shining your shoes, or watching a television program, or waiting for your date, or waiting for a stoplight to change. Also, have you often noticed that when you try to recall those ideas they have slipped away? Many speakers, writers, and composers carry a pencil and a piece of paper with them at all times; and when an idea comes, they take the time to write it down. They do not try to evaluate it, they only try to get the details on paper. Not all of these inspirations are the flashes of insight that are characteristic of creativity, of course, but some of them are. If you do not make note of yours, if you are not receptive to them, you will never know.

The greatest value of the creative process is to enable you to work out alternative methods of presenting factual material. In addition to methods already discussed, familiarity with possible lines of development will help guide your creative thinking. From a body of factual material, an infinite number of lines of development are possible. In any one speech, you may wish to use a single line of development or a combination of lines of development, depending upon the scope of the speech, the number of points you wish to make, and the time available to you. To illustrate the inventive process fully, let us suppose you are planning to give a speech on climate in the United States, and in your research you came across the data in Table 12.1.

Table 12.1

City	Temperature							Precipitation	
	Jan. Max.	Min.	Year High	Low	Extremes			July	Annual
Cincinnati	41	26	96	2	109	−17		3.3	39
Chicago	32	12	93	−6	103	−39		3.4	33
Denver	42	15	100	−5	105	−30		1.5	14
Los Angeles	65	47	88	39	110	28		T	14
Miami	76	58	96	44	100	28		6.8	59
Minneapolis	22	2	96	−21	108	−34		3.5	24
New Orleans	64	45	98	23	102	7		6.7	59
New York	40	27	97	11	106	−15		3.7	42
Phoenix	64	35	114	27	118	16		T	7
Portland, Me.	32	12	93	−6	103	−39		3.9	42
St. Louis	40	24	97	2	115	−23		3.3	35
San Francisco	55	42	86	33	106	20		T	18
Seattle	44	33	91	15	99	0		.6	38

Now what we want to show is how data can be used in a variety of ways to help yield an understanding of climatic conditions. The difference between this discussion and the one in Chapter 3 is that here we are going beyond finding materials; now we are talking about creating alternate lines of development using the *same set of facts*.

Development by Statistics

A statistical line of development is one in which a compilation of details, usually in numerical or percentage form, is used to illustrate the point. By examining the climatic data in Table 12.1, we could create a statistical way of showing the material. For instance:

Statement: Normal high temperatures in American cities vary far less than normal low temperatures.

Development: Whereas, of the thirteen cities selected, ten of them (77%) had normal highs between 90° and 100°, three cities (23%) had normal lows above freezing; six of them (46%) had normal lows between zero and 32°, and four of them (30%) had low temperatures below zero.

Development by Example

Development by example occurs when a single instance or a group of instances is used to illustrate the statement:

Statement: It hardly ever rains in California in the summer.

Development (single instance): The average rainfall during the whole month of July in San Francisco is less than one half of one inch.

Statement: It hardly ever rains on the West Coast in the summer.

Development (several instances): The average rainfall in July in Los Angeles and in San Francisco is less than one half of one inch. In Seattle, a city thought to be rather rainy, the average rainfall in July is only six tenths of an inch.

Development by Illustration

Development by illustration occurs when a single instance or example is presented in such a way that it becomes a story rather than an instance.

Statement: It hardly ever rains in California in the summer. (Same as the one above under *example*.)

Development: I had a chance to vacation in San Francisco for a couple of weeks last summer. And, like most people, I was concerned about whether I'd get good weather. During the first few days, the sky was crystal blue all day long. On about the fourth day some clouds swept in and a few drops of rain fell. For the rest of the stay some clouds blew in late in the afternoons, but we didn't have another drop of rain. Naturally, I thought I had really been lucky—two whole weeks and only a few drops of rain. For the fun of it I looked up the average rainfall in my almanac. Much to my surprise, I learned that my experience wasn't as unusual as I had thought. During the entire month of July, normal rainfall in San Francisco is less than one half of one inch.

Development by Comparison and/or Contrast

A comparative line of development places the emphasis on the similarities or on the differences involved. By and large, one of the best ways of giving meaning to figures and to abstract ideas is through comparison.

Statement: Whereas last year's high temperatures in major cities were much the same, low temperatures varied by more than 60°.

Development: Cincinnati, Miami, Minneapolis, and New York all had high temperatures of 96° or 97°; in contrast the lowest temperature for

Miami was 44°, whereas the lowest temperatures for Cincinnati, Minneapolis, and New York were 2°, −21°, and 11°, respectively.

Development by Analogy

An analogy is a special kind of comparative development in which a point is made about an unknown quantity by showing its similarities to a known quantity.

Statement: If you like the weather in St. Louis, you'll probably like the weather in Cincinnati.

Development: Normal high and normal low temperatures for St. Louis and Cincinnati are about the same; both cities have about the same amount of average rainfall per month; and both cities have rather hot and humid summers and rather mild winters.

TYPES OF EXPOSITORY TOPICS

In order to stimulate your thinking about topics and to help you anticipate and solve some of the problems associated with major types of expository speeches, let us consider four separate categories; first, the political, economic, and social issues; second, the historical events and forces; third, the theories, principles, or concepts; and, fourth, the critical appraisals.

Political, Economic, and Social Issues

Before you can hope to solve a problem, you must know something about it. Now, as perhaps never before, the ordinary citizen needs all kinds of information to help him cope with his environment. Take the battle with air pollution as an example. Although we may believe that something should be done about it, many of us do not know enough about the complexity of the causes and we have little knowledge about existing or proposed solutions. As an expository speaker, you have the opportunity and perhaps the obligation to make us aware of the various factors that should be considered before a decision can be made. You are not charged with the responsibility of proving the harm of an existing problem, nor do you attempt to move us to a particular action—these are all within the province of the persuasive speaker. You, as a lecturer, provide the facts about some phase of the problem. Your goal is to provide understanding.

One of the special problems met in dealing with contemporary issues is objectivity. You cannot hope to speak objectively (to discuss your topic in a detached manner) unless you are also objective in your analysis of the problem. For instance, you should not begin your research with the thought "I'm going to prove to them that

we've got to put more money into the solving of this problem now"
or "I'm going to show them why gas-fueled transportation should be
banned." What you can do is decide what aspect of the contemporary
issue needs to be discussed, then go ahead and find the material that
will yield understanding of that aspect. For instance, if after reading a few articles, you decide that the experts see the elimination of
the internal combustion engine for automobiles as an answer to air
pollution, you can speculate about alternative automotive power
plants. Further research might show that the present thrust in
automotive engineering is directed toward battery-driven and steam-
driven automobiles. As an expository speaker, then, you may talk
about why experts are considering the elimination of the internal
combustion engine, or you may talk about one or both of the
alternative systems. You would not attempt to prove that we should
abandon the gasoline engine, nor should you attempt to convince
us that either of the two alternatives is superior. So, objectivity is
ensured by reading widely on the topic, selecting an aspect of the
topic, then presenting the information as an addition to our knowledge and not as proof of a position.

Arousing audience interest may be even more difficult than
maintaining objectivity. Psychologically, you may face at least two
problems: antipathy toward matters of importance and audience
saturation. The first of these, antipathy, might be called the "spinach
syndrome." Just as some people rebel at eating spinach because it
is "good for them," they also rebel at listening to speeches that
will be "good for them." Since an understanding of contemporary
issues is obviously important, you must think of ways to make
these important topics interesting. The second related problem is
our tendency to "turn off" when we reach a saturation point; at
various times, all of us just get tired of hearing about energy,
pollution, inflation, recession, and other crises. The answer to the
saturation problem is to consider some aspects of a contemporary
issue that will be new to the audience. Although a speech on the
causes of the women's liberation movement may get a deaf ear, a
speech on the role of women in politics may arouse audience interest. Instead of giving the impression that you are going to give
another one of the innumerable talks about a "common" problem,
select some aspect that is fresh. In summary, new information presented in a fresh manner may counter both antipathy and saturation.

Although your topics should always grow from your brainstorming sheet, here and in each of the following sections several subject
areas will be listed to help stimulate your thinking.

Topics for Consideration

Methods of solving air pollution   Effects of marijuana
Modernization of police forces   Cable television
Progress on research on cancer   Women's rights
School financing   Effects of TV on children
Urban renewal   Nuclear power
Mass media   Inflation or recession

**Historical
Events and Forces**

It has been said that people who do not understand history are forced to repeat it. History can be fascinating for its own sake; moreover, through historical analysis we learn to appreciate the causal relationships that can help to explain or at least to illuminate contemporary society. Whether you talk about the strategy of war, mathematics, wrestling, or air pollution, you can find historical information to give an insight into the subject matter that is impossible to get in any other way.

Through thinking historically, you can uncover fascinating topics relatively quickly. For example, let us assume for a moment that you have an interest in machines, mechanics, building, construction, or related areas. As a result, you may be fascinated by the knowledge of all that is involved in creating a skyscraper or a bridge or a high-rise apartment. Let your mind wander a bit. Think of some of the famous constructions of the past—of the Great Wall of China, Stonehenge, or the Pyramids. In ancient times, man did not have such equipment as cranes, steamshovels, and bulldozers. How were these remarkable structures built? Why were they built? What materials were used? Why have they lasted? These are just examples. Every area of study is replete with topics of historical interest that are worth exploring.

Because history is a mirror of life, it may be dull or exciting. History can be made lively and interesting when you select examples, illustrations, and experiences that vivify your ideas. Recreation of actual events, actions, and description all will help add interest to historical analysis. If you have noticed, many people who say they do not like history enjoy historical fiction. Why? Because the history is made vivid and exciting.

Relevancy is a second major problem of historical analysis. Since your audience may not share your immediate or automatic interest, you must show a relevancy to contemporary times. Building pyramids may be related to modern construction problems, medieval jousts may be related to one or more modern sports, battle strategy may be related to modern warfare. As a lecturer you must seek out the tie between historical knowledge and our interests. Notice, I say seek out the tie. If the material has any intrinsic value or merit, it can be related to audience knowledge and needs.

Topics for Consideration

Pyramids	Oriental use of gunpowder
Greek drama	One-room schoolhouse
Roman chariots	Pirates
Circus Maximus	Establishing trade routes
Roman roads	Exploration
Genghis Khan	Napoleonic wars
Castles	Inventions
Chivalry	Battle strategy
Stonehenge	Witches

Theories, Principles, or Laws

The way we live is determined by natural laws, physical principles, and man-made theories. Yet as important as these are to us, many of us do not understand the laws, principles, and theories, either in themselves or in how they affect us. Take gravity, for example. We know that when we drop something it goes "down." We know that all of us stand upright on earth and that "up" to people on opposite sides of the earth happens to be opposite directions. Some of us may even remember that all heavier-than-air objects drop at the same rate of speed regardless of size or weight; or that, although speed remains the same, their momentum (weight times speed) differs. When astronauts reach a given height, they experience weightlessness. If you have an interest in physical laws, perhaps you could explain these and other phenomena having to do with gravity. Or you may be able to discuss applications of this law to other phases of our lives—applications that would be of tremendous informative and interest value to your audience. Because we are really so naïve about the forces around us, theories, principles, and laws make excellent expository topics.

The exposition of a theory, principle, or law brings about at least one problem that is peculiar to this kind of speech: the tendency to overuse or become dependent upon scientific terminology, formulas, and jargon. This dependence is one reason why some engineers, mathematicians, economists, and behavioral scientists find it very difficult to talk with people outside their professions. Your problem, then, is to explain scientific terms in a language that can be understood. Popularizers such as Vance Packard, Margaret Mead, and Isaac Asimov, have earned reputations for their ability to bridge the gap between the specialists and the common man. Good expository speakers must be such popularizers. They must understand the subject, and they must be able to discuss that understanding in an intelligible manner. An effective tool of the popularizer is the example. Any theory, principle, or law can be explained by using one or more examples. The more closely the example relates to the frame of reference of the listener, the more easily it can be understood. For instance, when you learned πr^2, the formula for the area of a circle, you probably needed one or more examples to give you a mastery of the formula. When your teacher wrote $22/7 \times 7 \times 7 = 154$ on the board, you saw how the formula worked. After she wrote $22/7 \times 10 \times 10 = 2200/7 = 314\frac{2}{7}$, you may have said, "I understand." The two examples then allowed you to put the formula into practice. You can help your audience gain a mastery by using examples to put the law, theory, or principle into practice. Furthermore, you can let the use of examples help you avoid a dependence upon jargon.

As with historical exposition, relevance is also a problem with theories, laws, and principles; however, one of their most exciting aspects is *how* they relate to us. The fact that plastic has the property of being molded into almost any form and the capacity for retaining that form under many stresses allows us to make many uses of plastic. The law that force is equal to mass times acceleration allows us to make jet engines. The "law" of supply and demand allows us to understand many modern business practices. And the formula $E = mc^2$ holds the key to our possible salvation or ultimate destruction. To assure your success you must show us what a particular law, theory, or principle means to us—with good topics, the challenge should not be difficult.

A third problem is to avoid misleading an audience. We hypothesize about many things in this world. From our hypotheses we formulate theories. Be sure that you know whether your topic is a theory or a fact. The formula πr^2 will give us the area of a circle, pure water boils at 212° Fahrenheit at sea level, and gravity can be measured. Relativity, evolution, and multiplier effect are theories that may or may not be valid. If you keep this differentiation in mind, you can avoid confusing yourself or your audience.

Topics for Consideration

Binomial theory	Colors—complement and contrast
Boyle's law	Condensation
Archimedes' law	Light refraction
Binary number system	X-rays
Einstein's theory of relativity	Multiplier effect
Harmonics	Magnetism

Critical Appraisals   Probably every university in the country offers courses in film, art, and music appreciation. The purpose of these and similar courses is to give insight into the standards of criticism. To appreciate means to understand *why* we respond the way we do. Because much of our pleasure and satisfaction is based upon our evaluation of paintings, musical composition, books, films, speeches, and other art forms, the critical appraisal is worth considering for your expository speech.

A major problem with this kind of assignment is recognizing the difference between objective evaluation and persuasive intent. We should, of course, be well aware that anything we say in a speech may have a kind of persuasive appeal for an audience. The difference, however, between a persuasive speech and an informative one is the intent of the speaker. A speech in which you tried to prove to the audience that Van Gogh's "Starry Night" is a great painting or is overrated, would be persuasive. In contrast, a speech on the characteristics of the painting that help to make it popular or a study of the painting in terms of Van Gogh's mental state would be informative.

In addition, as a critic you must have an accepted critical base from which to work. You should be familiar enough with the subject area to have some confidence in your knowledge and ability to explain and not just list. For instance, in appraisal of "Starry Night," you could comment on the use of heavy brush strokes. Although this fact in itself may be interesting, it would be better for you to explain what this kind of a stroke does to or for the painting and to show what kinds of effects are possible as a result. In other words, you must be prepared to go beyond superficial analysis and to give real insight into the work.

A third and a very real problem in a short speech is to give the audience enough orientation. With a speech on a Van Gogh painting, this can be done by showing a color reproduction of the painting itself; within a few seconds, an audience can get as much knowledge as it needs about the work being analyzed. If, however, you discuss a book, a film, or a speech, you may have to familiarize your audience with the work itself before you can go into a critical appraisal. The following guidelines will help you decide how much orientation will be necessary. If you select as a subject something that can be grasped by observation, you have no major problems. If you have a subject that is well known (for example, Lincoln's Gettysburg Address), you can assume an audience understanding. If the subject cannot be grasped on observance or is not familiar, you must make sure that you can explain it in no more than two minutes. If you cannot explain it in that time, it probably is not a good topic for this class and these time limits.

Subject Areas for Consideration

Painting:	*Literature:*	*Music:*
Picasso	Poetry	Jazz
Van Gogh	Novels	Folk rock
Rembrandt	Short stories	Symphony
Rockwell	Science fiction	Concerto

Speeches:	*Film:*
Inaugural addresses	Silent movies
Courtroom speaking	Foreign movies
Legislative speeches	

Assignment	**Prepare a four- to seven-minute expository speech. Outline and bibliography (at least four sources) required. Criteria for evaluation will include (1) how well you limit your topic, (2) how substantial is your resource material, (3) how well you have introduced bibliographical citations, and (4) how creative and informative you have made the development. A question period of one to three minutes will follow (optional).**
Alternate Assignment	**Prepare a four- to seven-minute report on some aspect of a topic that has been given to you. Criteria for evaluation are the same as above.**

Outline: Expository Speech (4–7 minutes)

Specific Purpose: To discuss three common errors in the use of the English language.

Introduction

    I. "Wishing to divest myself of all pomposity, I situate my presence before you in complete candor to speak in mellifluous tones, between you and I and, yes, even him whom is in that corner, in regards to a beguiling yet profound, substantive matter."

    II. If you don't get the meaning, it's because three common mistakes in English usage abound: abuse of grammar, misuse of words, and circumlocution.

Body

    I. Abuse of grammar is widespread.

        A. Commercials illustrate problems of English usage.

        B. Failure of students in English composition across the country points up the problem.

        C. Jean Stafford attributes much of the problem to television.

    II. A more subtle problem is misuse of words.

        A. It's a sneaky malfunction because it sounds quite good.

           1. Guestimate, thrust, and parameter are widely used.

           2. Viable is the new superword of planning.

        B. Many of these uses are quite funny when analyzed.

           1. "In depth" is really meaningless.

           2. "I teach college" is all-encompassing.

    III. Circumlocution, the art of using 50 words when 10 would do, may be the most distressing problem.

        A. Edwin Newman asks where simple, direct speech has gone.

        B. Random samples of statements illustrate current abuse.

C. The cap is former presidential press secretary Ronald Ziegler's meandering answer that means simply, "I need more time to think about it."

IV. Of course, the answer is not total purity.
    A. We need to have fun with language.
        1. Louis Armstrong's classic response to "What's jazz?"
        2. *Reader's Digest* column, "Toward More Picturesque Speech."
    B. Still, we must be conscious of problems that hinder communication.

Conclusion

I. In most cases, abuse of grammar, misuse of words, and circumlocution hurt rather than facilitate communication.

II. To what extent and with what results would seem to be the most important questions we can ask—"at this point in time," that is.

Bibliography

"Bonehead English," *Time*, November 11, 1974, p. 106.
Middleton, Thomas H., "Linguistic Inanities," *Saturday Review/World*, July 13, 1974, p. 56.
Newman, Edwin. *Strictly Speaking: Will America Be the Death of English?* Indianapolis, Ind.: Bobbs-Merrill, 1974.
Stafford, Jean, "At This Point in Time, TV Is Murdering the English Language," *New York Times*, September 15, 1974, p. 23.
"Toward More Picturesque Speech," *Reader's Digest*, October 1974, p. 74.

Problems of Communication

Read the transcription of this speech at least once aloud.[1] Examine the speech to see how well the topic has been limited, how substantial is the research, how well bibliographical citations have been introduced, and how creatively the information has been presented.

Analysis

The speaker begins with a very clever opening sentence illustrating the problems she will discuss. The attention comes from the bewildering complexity and obscurity of the language. Incidentally, if you reread the sentence carefully you will see that it does tell you what she

Speech

"Wishing to divest myself of all pomposity, I situate my presence before you in complete candor to speak in mellifluous tones between you and I, and, yes, even him whom is in that corner, in regards to a beguiling yet profound substantive matter." Get the meaning? Well, neither do I. But as strange as it may sound to your ear, the sentence I just spoke may be more typical than we'd like to admit. It contained three common problems of everyday communication that some experts say are ruining the English language: abuse of grammar, misuse of words, and circumlocution.

[1] Delivered in Speech class, University of Cincinnati. Printed by permission of Betty Zager.

Analysis

Speech

plans to do. At the end of the introduction the speaker states her goal quite smoothly.

She moves into her first point, abuse of grammar.

As the speech continues, we begin to see the strength of her development: clear, vivid examples.

Since such a point as abuse of grammar is difficult to illustrate with examples alone, the speaker makes good use of statistics to show the scope of the problem she is considering.

Notice the way the speaker cites her sources. Her references are short and unobtrusive, but they serve the purpose. They let us know the scope and depth of her research.

The speaker moves smoothly into her second main point, misuse of words.

Another of the strengths of the speaker's lecture is her humor. Although her topic and her information are serious, the light touch adds to both interest and retention of her points. These two examples are excellent in making her points in a creative way.

The third point, circumlocution, continues the

Abuse of grammar is a criticism we've heard for years. And after all, we've come a long way since the controversy over "Winston tastes good, like a cigarette should." Now our commercials give us such sentences as "You get a lot of dirt with kids, you get a lot of clean with Tide."

Is the misuse of grammar really a problem? Well, a recent article in *Time* magazine stated, "almost half the freshmen at the University of California at Berkeley failed the English composition test in the fall. Bonehead English was instituted to help them out." At the University of Houston, 60 percent of the current freshmen failed their first composition essay. At Harvard University, similar results are reported. Some people argue that schools have deemphasized grammar too much. Jean Stafford, a noted novelist, takes another view. In an article in the September 15, 1974, issue of the *New York Times* she pointed an accusing finger at television with the title, "At This Point in Time TV Is Murdering the English Language." When asked during the recent Watergate hearings, "Who is 'We'?" a lawyer defendant replied, "We is us."

Something more subtle than the outright abuse of grammar is the misuse of words. It's a rather sneaky malfunction because, when used expertly, the language sounds quite good. For instance, "Guestimate" now replaces an educated guess. "Thrust" is a new "in" word, as in "What is the thrust of the situation?" "Parameter" is used to make you sound educated. The term was once confined to mathematics, but now it pops up everywhere. Rather than talking about the limits or boundaries, we have to know the "parameters of a problem." And the new superword of planning, "viable"—it has to be a viable alternative or a viable solution. Sometimes these misuses are pretty funny if we think about them. How about the common phrase, "This study will be conducted in depth"? Well, unless the researchers are conducting the experiments on the bottom of the ocean, the phrase is really very meaningless. Or think about the lovely lady on TV pushing headache tablets. She testifies, "I teach college"—with such an all encompassing subject, no wonder she has a headache.

But perhaps the most distressing malfunction of language is circumlocution—the art of using 50 words when 10 would do. Edwin

Analysis

Speech

topic order of the speech development.

In a speech that abounds with good examples, I consider the ones in this section the very best.

I believe the speaker is wise in making this the third point. Whereas abuse of grammar and misuse of words may still communicate, circumlocution short-circuits the communication process completely.

This is an excellent example to use to conclude this point.

This short point helps put the speaker's lecture in proper perspective—and it continues the humorous thread that runs throughout the speech.

These last sentences ably summarize the speaker's points. And, of course, this final sentence from the Watergate era is a kind of topper that ends the speech on a high note. The speaker uses excellent material, develops it creatively, and organizes it clearly. All in all this is an excellent expository speech on abuses of language.

Newman, NBC-TV correspondent, took pen in hand for the first time to write his book *Strictly Speaking: Will America Be the Death of English?*, which appeared on the market in 1974. Mr. Newman asked, "Where has simple direct speech gone?" I have jotted down a few examples for your review. If you listen closely to what people are saying, I'm sure you'll hear statements like these. Teachers are "busy constructing behavioral objectives that individualize instruction to the point where the learner's self-concept is enhanced." Business executives must "set up study groups to evaluate committees that have been created to delve into the cortex of complexities swirling in the power hierarchy in order to get at the parameters of the problem." Politicians are "concerned with the meaningful rethink of the issues, including specificity." Children when leaving the home nest "opt for life-styles or living situations allowing them the greatest feedback from their input in education, which in turn focuses the thrust of the future contributions to mankind." Mr. Newman's concern is that the stilted and pompous phrase, the slogan, and cliché are going to come to dominate the entire language. As a cap to this point, let's look at presidential press secretary Ron Ziegler's explanation when defending a request for a four-day extension on subpoenas for special files. He replied that James St. Clair, the President's attorney, "needed to evaluate to make a judgment in terms of a response." Why didn't Ziegler just say he needed more time to think about it?

Now, I'm not saying that these critics are calling for total purity in language. We have to be able to have some fun with language. For instance, no one should be concerned with Louis Armstrong's double negative in his answer to the question, "What's jazz?" Armstrong replied, "If you got to ask what it is, you ain't never gonna know." Moreover, our language is enriched with many usages that stretch meanings to the breaking point. The *Reader's Digest* column "Toward More Picturesque Speech" has been collecting quaint usages for years. Who would question the value of the observation about the orchestra conductor "who kept throwing tempo tantrums"?

Still, our language suffers abuses that we should be aware of and do our best to correct. In most cases, abuse of language, misuse of words, and circumlocution hurt rather than facilitate communication. To what extent and with what results would seem to be the most important question we can ask—"at this point in time," that is.

PERSUASIVE SPEAKING

PART FOUR

13

Have you ever had a fantasy involving your persuasive powers? You imagine that as a result of a stirring speech given by you war is averted, poverty abolished, or you get a date with that person you've had an eye on for six weeks. Although everything works superbly in our fantasies, our real-life attempts at changing attitudes or modifying behavior are not always so successful. Let's face it: speaking persuasively is perhaps the most demanding of speech challenges. Moreover, there is no formula for success—no set of rules to guarantee effectiveness. Still, in the centuries that man has been studying the process, he has learned to identify many of the variables of persuasion. In this chapter we want to explore the principles of persuasive speaking that you will want to consider.

BEGIN WITH A CLEAR BEHAVIORAL OBJECTIVE

Although any statement may have some behavioral effect on another person (merely saying "The team's having a great year, isn't it?" may "persuade" another person to go to a game), the successful persuader does not leave the effect of his message to chance. He starts his planning with a clearly stated purpose statement firmly in mind.

The persuasive purpose statement, often called a *proposition*, indicates specifically what you want your audience to do or to believe. Ordinarily, the proposition will be phrased in one of three ways: to *reinforce a belief* held by an audience, to *change a belief* held by an audience, or to *move the audience to act*. "Every eligible citizen should vote" and "Everyone should love his country" are examples of propositions for speeches to reinforce beliefs. In both instances, the speaker would be trying to strengthen a prevailing attitude. "Capital punishment should be reinstated" and "The Ohio State Lottery should be abolished" would indicate the purpose of changing the beliefs of the audience. Even though some classmates would be in favor of the propositions, each calls for a change from current policy. Speeches of this kind are often called *speeches to convince*. "Buy Easter Seals" and "Eat at the Manor Restaurant" are both phrased to gain action. In these instances, the speaker wants more than intellectual agreement—he wants us to act. Before deciding on a wording for your proposition, you will want to weigh the following three principles.

① *Persuasion is more likely to occur when the proposition meets an audience need or grows out of an audience attitude.* If a person has a need for food, he will be more likely to be receptive to a message about where to eat, where to shop, or what to buy than if he does not have that need. Likewise, if a person is strongly in favor of the school basketball team, he is more likely to be receptive to a proposition asking him to buy tickets for an upcoming game. Thus, if you are able to identify audience needs and attitudes, you are in an excellent position to know how to begin your persuasive strategy.

Psychologist Abraham Maslow conceived a hierarchy of human needs based upon five categories: physiological needs, safety needs, belongingness and love needs, esteem needs, and self-actualization needs.[1] He said that safety needs will be considered relevant by an audience only if their physiological needs are met, and belongingness needs will be considered relevant by an audience only after safety needs are met, and so forth, up the ladder. In Chapter 15 we will make a more detailed analysis of these needs, but for now let me point out the importance of locating the level of unmet needs in your audience. It is folly to frame a proposition requiring fulfillment of a need that is not important or that does not exist for the particular audience. So, if you determine that one of the paramount needs in operation within your audience is a safety need (such as the need for reducing instances of murder, rape, and assaults) a proposition indicating a plan of action for achieving that goal will be listened to by that audience.

Framing a proposition related to a prevailing audience attitude also helps to ensure the persuasiveness of that proposition. An attitude is an individual's predisposition to behave in a particular way. People's attitudes have three essential characteristics: direction (from favorable to unfavorable), intensity (from strong to weak), and saliency (from very important to not very important). A person's behavior is an outgrowth of his attitude. Although a behavior may not always be consistent with an attitude (a person may not approve of gambling, yet he may on occasion play poker

[1] Abraham H. Maslow, *Motivation and Personality* (New York: Harper & Row, 1954), pp. 80–92.

with his friends), you are very likely to produce a behavior if it is an outgrowth of the person's attitude. If you know that your audience's attitude is favorable toward a group of people, you may be able to enlist their support for the group, you may be able to get them to give money to support the group, or you may be able to get them to attend a function sponsored by or involving the group.

②) If the speech calls for a change in attitude or behavior, persuasion is more likely to be achieved when the proposition is not too far from the focus of audience belief. Attitudes can be changed and behavior can be modified, but to expect 180-degree shifts in attitude or behavior as a result of a single speech is unrealistic and probably fruitless. William Brigance, one of the great speech teachers of this century, used to speak of "planting the seeds of persuasion." If we present a modest proposal seeking a slight change in attitude, we may be able to get an audience to think about what we are saying. Then later when the idea begins to grow, we can ask for greater change. For instance, if your audience believes that taxes are too high, you are unlikely to make them believe that they are not. However, you may be able to influence them to see that taxes are not really as high as they originally thought or not as high as other goods and services.

The further your goal is from the focus of audience belief, the more time it will take you to achieve that goal. Major attitude change is more likely to be achieved over a period of time rather than in a one-shot effort. One author encourages "seeing persuasion as a campaign—a structured sequence of efforts to achieve adoption, continuance, deterrence, or discontinuance."[2] Attitude change is most effective over a long-range, carefully considered program in which each part in the campaign is instrumental in bringing about later effects. Still, much of your speaking allows for only one effort—and you want to make the most of it. So, we have to look for principles to guide us when we have just one opportunity.

③) Persuasion is more likely to occur when the proposition is phrased so that it does not call for more than the audience can do or wishes to do at that time. When we call for members of an audience to act, we are usually asking them to modify their behavior in some way. This action or behavior modification is always done at some cost (in time, money, or energy) to the audience. When the cost is negligible or token, an audience may well go along with

[2] Wallace Fotheringham, *Perspectives on Persuasion* (Boston: Allyn and Bacon, 1966), p. 34.

you. For instance, if you ask your listeners to write a note to their congressman, the time and expense involved in the writing and mailing may be more than they care to handle at that time. However, if you *give* them pre-addressed post cards, they are likely to take a minute right then to dash off a few lines. Or if you ask them to give five dollars to a particular charity, they may see that as more than they can spare or they will not have the cash on them or they say they will do it "sometime." The result is, no money gets contributed. If, on the other hand, you ask them to reach into their pocket and pull out the change they are carrying and drop it in the hat as it is being passed, they are more likely to follow through.

The greater the demand you place on the audience, the more prepared you must be to meet resistance and the more prepared you must be to get less than maximum involvement. Even when you are asking for minimal expense of time, energy, or money, you must continue to show the audience how easy it is to follow up on your proposition.

CONSIDER AVAILABLE MEANS OF PERSUASION

The available means of persuasion are the factors that cause an audience to respond to a proposition. These means include the persuasive effect of information, credibility, reasoning, and motivation. Any given speech may be a product of one or more of these means.

1 *Persuasion may occur as the product of sound information.* The basic philosophy behind demonstrating a product is that once people see what that product can do, they will persuade themselves that they need it. For instance, in the housewares section of large department stores, you often see someone *demonstrating* a new product or some household gadget. When the family chef sees that neat little gadget that slices, chops, dices, and cuts everything from tomatoes to potatoes and all for $3.95, the urge to own one is often irresistible. The demonstrator seldom makes a sales pitch—he or she doesn't have to. People are likely to buy the product solely because they received information that they perceived as useful.

Don't forget all you have learned about effective information exchange—a vivid description of your apartment may be an important step in persuading a person to move to the same building; a clear and complete explanation of care and time put into making a product may be an important step in persuading a person to buy that product; and a clear and vivid description of the decor and bill of fare of a restaurant may be the most important step in persuading a person to eat at that restaurant.

② *Persuasion is more likely to be achieved when the audience likes, trusts, and has confidence in the speaker.* The Greeks had a word for this concept—they called it *ethos.* But whether we call it ethos, image, charismatic effect, or the word I prefer—credibility —the effect is the same: almost all studies confirm that speaker credibility has a major effect on audience belief and attitude.[3]

Why are people willing to take the word of someone else on various issues? Since it is impossible for us to know all there is to know about everything (and even if it were *possible*, few of us would be willing to spend the time and effort), we seek shortcuts in our decision making—we rely on the judgment of others. Our thinking often goes something like this: Why take the time to learn about the new highway when someone we trust tells us it is in our best interest? Why take the time to try every restaurant in town when someone we are willing to rely on tells us that Barney's is the best? Why take time to study the candidates when our best friend tells us to vote for Smith for Councilman? Each of us places such trust in some people in order to take shortcuts in our decision making.

How do we determine who we will rely on? Is it blind faith? No, the presence (or our *perception* of the presence) of certain qualities will make the possessor a *high credibility* source. Although the specific number of aspects of credibility differs somewhat in every analysis of that quality, most analyses include the importance of competence, consideration, character, and personality.

Competence is a quality that commands our respect. It may well be that your attraction toward your favorite professor is based upon competence. Although all professors are supposed to know what they are talking about, some are better able to project this quality in their speaking. As a rule of thumb, we believe that people are competent when we believe they know far more than what they are telling us now. For instance, when a student interrupts with a question, the competent professor has no difficulty in discussing the particular point in more detail—perhaps by giving another example, perhaps by telling a story, perhaps by referring the student to additional reading on the subject. Often our judgment of competence is based upon a past record. If we discover that what a

[3] Kenneth E. Andersen and Theodore Clevenger, Jr., "A Summary of Experimental Research in Ethos," *Speech Monographs,* Vol. 30 (1963), pp. 59–78.

person has told us in the past has proven to be true, we will tend to believe what that person tells us now.

A second important aspect of credibility is _consideration_—particularly consideration for other people. When a student interrupts our favorite professor with a question, we will expect that professor to provide an answer, even though it interrupts the flow of thought or prevents him or her from covering quite as much material. To put this another way, we like and respect people who put others' needs before their own. For instance, when a sales person tells you that of the two coats you like, the less expensive one looks better on you, you perceive that person as putting your best interest above his or her commission—as a result, your estimation of the person's credibility goes up. With some people, however, perhaps because of their negative record, you are led to respond to an apparent act of generosity with the cynical question "What's in it for them?" A past record of consideration for others builds confidence in a speaker; a past record of selfishness makes us question the speaker's motives.

A third important aspect of credibility is _character_. Character is sometimes defined as what a person is made of. We believe in people who have a past record of honesty, industry, and trustworthiness. Notice, however, that now we are not asking whether our professor knows the subject matter; instead, we are judging the professor as a person. Would he or she give good advice on a personal problem? Prepare an exam that is a good test of our knowledge? Grade us on what we do and not on extraneous factors? Judging another's character comes down to our basic respect for the individual.

The fourth important aspect of credibility is _personality_. Sometimes we have a strong "gut reaction" about a person based solely on a first impression. Some people strike us as being friendly, warm, nice to be around. Some would argue that personality or likeability is the most important of all aspects of credibility. The old sports saying that "nice guys finish last" is just not true in interpersonal relationships. Whether we are talking about public speakers or people we meet at a party, we make a judgment about whether we like them. If we do, we are more likely to buy their ideas or products. If we don't, we are likely to shun them.

Credibility is not something that you can gain overnight or turn off or on at your whim. Nevertheless, you can avoid damaging your credibility and perhaps even strengthen it somewhat during a speech or series of speeches. You will probably see the cumulative effect of credibility during this term. As your class proceeds from speech to speech, some individuals will grow in stature in your mind and others will diminish. Being ready to speak on time, approaching the assignment with a positive attitude, showing complete preparation for each speech, giving thoughtful evaluation of others' speeches and demonstrating sound thinking—all of these contribute to classroom credibility. Some people earn the right to speak and to be heard. Having once earned that right, they command the confidence of their listeners. Others never earn the right and nothing they do will have a very real, lasting effect on their audience. Think about how you are representing yourself to your audience. What kind of a person are you projecting to the class? Credibility is an important means of persuasion.

Although credibility takes time to build, there are some things that can be done during your speech. Personality and character are projections of what you are, but competence and consideration can be affected by what you say. How do you illustrate your competence and your consideration? You should try to establish your credentials during the speech. A few sentences of explanation of your point of view, your concern, or your understanding may make a big difference. For instance, if you were speaking on prison reform, you might say, "I had read articles about conditions in prisons, but before I came before you with any suggestions, I wanted to see for myself, so I spent two days observing at . . ." Assuming you had visited the prison, this short statement would help to increase your credibility with the audience. Or to show the amount of work you have done you might say, "I had intended to read a few articles to prepare for this speech, but once I began, I became fascinated with the subject. I hope word doesn't get around to my other teachers, but quite frankly this past week I've put everything else aside to try to find the most accurate information I could." Or a speaker might show fairness by saying "It would be easy for me to say we could get by without new taxes—such a move might get me elected, but I just don't see any way out of new taxes."

The key to the effectiveness of these and similar statements is the honesty of your representation. Whereas an arrogant, know-it-all approach will often backfire, a short, honest statement of qualifications, experience, or ability may build your speaker credibility.

3. *Persuasion is more likely to be achieved when you can show the audience logical reasons for supporting the proposition.* Most listeners want some justification for changing their attitude or modifying their behavior. They want to know *why* they should respond as you ask. You need not necessarily give complete proof of the proposition, often only enough substantiation or justification to satisfy the audience's need. Statements that provide substantiation or justification are called *reasons*. Why should off-track betting be legalized? The statement "It would channel gambling revenues to the state" is a reason. Usually the more compelling the reason, (or reasons), the better its chance of changing attitude or behavior.

But presenting reasons alone will not necessarily make a speech "logical"; the reasons may be poor or insupportable. It is up to the speaker to select the best possible reasons for his proposition. The next chapter describes the nature of reasoning, how to select and support reasons, and how to test the logic of the reasons.

A speech may succeed in persuading without logical reasons, but reasoning is the greatest protection against unethical, manipulative rhetoric.

4. *Persuasion is more likely to be achieved when the language of the speaker motivates the audience.* Through reasoning we may be convinced of the soundness of an idea. Yet intellectual agreement may not be enough to affect behavior. I may believe that giving to the United Appeal is a good idea, but I may not have given. I may believe that the handicapped should be helped by the government, but I may not have voted for legislation directed toward helping the handicapped. What makes the difference between believing in something and acting in its behalf? Often it is the degree of motivation inherent in the case for the action. Motivation is the driving force behind our actions. It is the prod that pokes or nudges us from passive to active. Unless properly motivated we may sit idly by and *do* nothing.

The speaker's major means of motivating is through language that is adapted to the needs of the specific audience and language that touches the emotions and drives us to respond. In any speech, but especially in a speech where your goal is audience action, you must ask, "How can I make my points so that they will have the greatest emotional effect on this audience?" In Chapter 17, we will consider the various facets of identifying audience needs and phrasing ideas with emotional impact in detail.

5. *Persuasion is more likely to have a lasting effect if it is ethical.* So far we have looked at information development, credibility, reasoning, and motivation, but overriding all of these is the principle of ethics. Especially when we believe strongly in the righteousness of our cause, we are faced with the temptation of bowing to the belief that the end justifies the means—or, to put

it into blunt English, that we can do *anything* to achieve our goals. And as we observe the world around us, we are all too well aware of the many people who have ridden roughshod over any moral or ethical principles operating within the society. Yet, just when we appear to be ready to give up on mankind something happens that proves that a society does have its ethical limits.

What are *ethics?* Ethics are the standards of moral conduct that determine our behavior. Ethics include both how we ourselves act and how we expect others to act. Whether or how we punish those who fail to meet our standards says a great deal about the importance we ascribe to our ethics. Although ethical codes are personal, society has a code of ethics that operates on at least the verbal level within that society.

What is your code of ethics? The following four points reflect the standards of hundreds of students that I have seen in my classes during the last few years. I believe that these four make an excellent starting point for the consideration determining your standards. These are not rules someone made up. They are statements of attitudes held by large numbers of individuals within the society.

1.   Lying is unethical. Of all the attitudes about ethics, this is the one most universally held. When pepole *know* they are being lied to, they will usually reject the ideas of the speaker; if they find out later, they often look for ways to punish the speaker who lied to them.

2.   Name calling is unethical. Again, there seems to be an almost universal agreement on this attitude. Even though many people name-call in their interpersonal communication, they say they regard the practice by public speakers as unethical.

3.   Grossly exaggerating or distorting facts is unethical. Although some people seem willing to accept "a little exaggeration" as human nature, when the exaggeration is defined as "gross" or "distortion," most people regard the exaggeration the same as lying. Because the line between "some" exaggeration and "gross" exaggeration or "distortion" is often so difficult to distinguish, many people see *any* exaggeration as unethical.

4.   Damning people or ideas without divulging the source of the damning material is unethical. Where ideas originate is often as important as the ideas themselves. And although a statement may be true regardless of whether a source is given, people want more than the speaker's word when a statement is damning. If you are going to discuss the wrong-doing of a person or the stupidity of an idea by relying on the words or ideas of others, you must be prepared to share the sources of those words or ideas.

Remember, these are but starting points in your consideration of ethical standards. Effective speaking should be ethical speaking.

ORGANIZE ACCORDING TO EXPECTED AUDIENCE REACTION

Although the nature of your material and your own inclination may affect your organization, the most important consideration is expected audience reaction. Let us first look at means of classifying audience reaction and then at various organizational patterns.

Classifying Audience Reaction

Earlier, in discussing the proposition, we defined attitude in terms of direction, strength, and saliency (importance). Since much of your success will depend on the kind of audience you face for the particular speech, you must have an appraisal of whether the members favor your proposition, to what degree they favor it, and how important their attitude is to them. Audience attitude may be distributed along a continuum from hostile to highly in favor (see Figure 13.1). Even though any given audience may contain one or a few members on nearly every point of the distribution, audience attitude will tend to cluster at some point on the continuum.

Except for polling the audience, there is no way of being sure about your assessment. But by examining the data in the way described in Chapter 3, you will be able to make reasonably accurate estimates. For instance, skilled workers are likely to look at minimum wage proposals differently from business executives; men will look at women's rights proposals differently from women; Protestants are likely to look at property tax levy for schools differently from Catholics. The more data you have about your audience and the more experience you have in analyzing audiences, the better your chances of judging their attitudes somewhat accurately. By and large, a very precise differentiation of opinion is not necessary.

Through a sample of attitude, an insight into audience behavior, or a good guess, you can place your audience in one of the following classifications: *no opinion*—either no information or no interest; *in favor*—already holding a particular belief; *opposed*—holding an opposite point of view. Although these classifications may overlap, since you will have neither the time nor the opportunity to present a line of development that would adapt to all

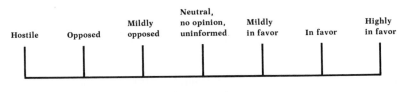

Figure 13.1

possible attitudes within the audience, you should assess the prevailing attitude and knowledge and work from there.

No Opinion   With some topics, your audience will have no opinion. Often this lack of opinion results from a lack of knowledge on the subject. Suppose you wanted to persuade the class "that elementary schools should explore the feasibility of ungraded primary schools." Unless your class is composed of prospective elementary teachers, only a few will know what an ungraded primary school is. Even those who know the term may not have enough knowledge to formulate an opinion. In this instance, yours will be a problem of instruction before you can hope to create a favorable attitude. Since they lack preconceived biases, you can usually approach the uninformed audience directly. If you can show enough advantages to meet their requirements, you have a good chance of persuading them. Despite this advantage, you may have a burden of explanation that must precede argumentation. If you have only five minutes to speak and it takes that long to explain the program, you will have a very difficult time creating any attitudes.

A lack of audience opinion may also result from apathy. When apathy is the problem but knowledge does exist, you can spend your entire time in motivation. Although an apathetic audience is difficult to motivate, you will have nearly the entire speech time to create interest and commitment. An apathetic audience presents a challenge and an opportunity for the persuasive speaker.

In Favor   In your analysis, you may find that the audience is already favorably disposed toward the proposition. Although this sounds like an ideal situation, it carries with it many hazards. When an audience is already in favor, they are seldom interested in a rehash of familiar material and reasons. Because of an ill-considered approach, a favorable audience can become hostile or apathetic to you as a speaker—a result as undesirable as negative commitment. If your campus is typical, a common complaint is the lack of on-campus parking. As a result, the subject matter of a speech in favor of increased parking space would already be accepted. In situations of this kind, the best line of argument is to develop a specific course of action satisfying the felt need. A speech on the need for an underground garage or a highrise parking garage on a present site or a new system of determining priority would build upon the existing audience attitude. The presentation of a well-thought-out specific solution increases the potential for action. In summary, when you believe your listeners are on your side, do not just echo their beliefs. Try to crystallize their attitudes, recommit them to their direction of thought, and bring the group to some meaningful action that will help to solve or alleviate the problem.

Opposed   With many of the kinds of propositions that call for a change in existing attitudes and procedures, your audience attitude may range from slightly negative to thoroughly hostile. These two degrees of negative attitude require a slightly different handling. For instance, with the proposition "The United States is spending too much for space exploration," most people will have an opinion. Since this is a debatable proposition, about half the audience will probably be at least slightly negative. Yet, the other half may even be slightly favorable to strongly favorable. Usually, the best way to proceed is with the generalization that your listeners can be persuaded if you can give good reasons and if you can motivate them. A straightforward, logically sound speech may convince those who are only slightly negative and will not alienate those in favor.

However, suppose the topic were "The federal government should guarantee a minimum annual income to all its citizens." With this proposition, there is an excellent chance that the majority of the audience would be negative to hostile. Hostile audiences can seldom be persuaded with one speech. In fact, a hostile audience may well turn itself off when it hears the topic. To get this kind of an audience even to listen calls for a great deal of motivation. If you have done a good job, you will be able to plant the seeds of persuasion. The next week, the next month, or even the next year, one or more of that audience might well come to your way of thinking—but do not expect too much to happen during the speech.

Methods of Organization

The following organizational methods may prove useful to adopt as stated or they may suggest an organization that you believe will work for your audience given the material you have to work with.

Statement of Reasons Method   When you believe your audience has no opinion on the subject, is apathetic, or is perhaps only mildly in favor or opposed, the straightforward topical statement of reasons may be your best organization. The following chapter provides a more complete explanation of this method. In brief, in the statement of reasons method, each reason presented is a complete sentence statement of justification for the proposition. Thus, in outline form, the statement of reasons method will look like this:

Proposition: Support the United Appeal.

I. It is a worthy cause.

II. One gift supports a wide variety of agencies.

III. Administrative costs are very low.

The Problem-Solution Method   We indicated earlier that persuasion is usually a problem-solving activity. If you are attempting to prove to the audience that a new kind of procedure is needed to remedy some major problem, the problem-solution method will provide you with the framework for clarifying the nature of the problem that needs to be solved and for illustrating why the new proposal is the best measure for accomplishing the purpose. Like the statement of reasons method, the problem-solution method works best when an audience has no opinion, is apathetic, or perhaps only mildly in favor or against. When you follow the problem-solution method, your speech will always have three main points: (1) that there is a problem that requires a change in attitude or action, (2) that the proposal you have to offer will solve the problem, and (3) that your proposal is the best solution to the problem. For the proposition, "To persuade the audience that the federal government should guarantee a minimum annual cash income to all its citizens," you could state three reasons:

I. A high percentage of our citizens are living in a state of abject poverty.

II. A guaranteed cash income would eliminate poverty.

III. A guaranteed cash income would be the best way to solve the problem.

Comparative Advantages Method   In your proposed speech, you may not be trying to solve a grave problem as much as you are suggesting a superior alternative course of action. Under such circumstances, your concern is with superiority of your proposal over any others. Let us say that you want to persuade your listeners to take their dry cleaning to a particular establishment. Since people are already taking their clothes to some dry cleaner, the problem of how the class should take care of their cleaning is already being solved. You are trying to persuade them that a particular cleaner has advantages over any of the places where they may already take their clothes. Your speech then is built with the advantages of your proposal over any other proposal. The advantages then become the main points of your outline.

Purpose: To persuade the audience to take their clothes to Ace Dry Cleaners.

I. Ace always does that little bit extra for no additional charge.

II. Ace gives students a 10 percent discount.

Criteria-Satisfaction Method   In some situations, particularly with hostile audiences, you may find it to your advantage to establish audience agreement—a yes-response—before you attempt to present the proposition and reasons. Although reasons are still the basis for the persuasion, the preliminary statement of criteria is essential to the method. If your proposition were "To persuade the audience to vote for Jones," you might organize your speech to show the criteria and how Jones meets them.

I. You want a man who meets certain criteria.
   A. He must be wise.
   B. He must have a plan of action.
   C. He must be fearless.

II. Jones meets these criteria.
   A. Jones is wise.
   B. Jones has a plan of action.
   C. Jones is fearless.

The Negative Method   The other method that is particularly effective for hostile audiences is the negative method. In this, you show that something must be done but that the alternative suggestions just will not work. Of course, this method will work only when the audience must select one of the alternatives. To persuade a hostile audience to vote for taxes, you might use this development:

I. Saving money by reducing services will not help us.

II. The federal government will not help us.

III. The state government will not help us.

IV. All we have left is to raise taxes.

SHOW CONVICTION

Effective delivery for persuasion is no different from effective speaking for any speech. Still, because delivery is so important it is worth a moment to focus on one key aspect of delivery that is especially relevant to persuasion: the effective persuader shows conviction in his subject. With some people conviction is shown through considerable animation. With others it is shown through a quiet intensity. However it is shown, it must be perceived by the audience. If the audience does not perceive some visual or auditory sign of conviction, what you say is likely to be suspect. And if you really do have a strong conviction, there is a good chance that your voice and your bodily action will reflect it.

At the beginning of this chapter we said that no formula for success could be given. But we did promise a set of principles that can serve as guidelines for your procedure. Let us summarize these basic principles in terms of steps of preparation:

1.   Determine a specific statement of belief or action you seek.

2.   Gather the materials that you will use ethically to develop your credibility, prove your points, and arouse the emotions of your audience.

3.   Organize your speech following some pattern that adapts to the prevailing audience attitude.

4.   Deliver your speech with conviction.

The assignment that follows would be appropriate for several situations: (1) as an assignment for a persuasive speech when time permits only a single persuasive speech assignment for the term; (2) as a diagnostic persuasive speech assignment that precedes one or more of the skills assignments that follow; or (3) as a final assignment for the persuasive speech unit to be given after students have practiced with one or more of the following chapter assignments.

The speech on pp. 216–218 is not only an excellent speech of motivation, but also exemplifies many of the principles we have considered in this chapter.

Assignment   **Prepare a four- to seven-minute persuasive speech. Outline required. Criteria for evaluation will include appropriateness of proposition to this audience's needs, interests, or attitudes; quality of information provided to give explanation of the proposal, to demonstrate speaker credibility, to prove soundness of argument, and to motivate; clarity and appropriateness of organization; and convincing delivery.**

14

Some portion of any persuasive speech you give may involve reasoning with your audience. Perhaps reasoning will be your primary method of persuasion, or perhaps it will be but a part of your total development. But before you can decide how reasoning will be used in your speech, you need to understand the principles of reasoning. In this chapter we will define reasoning, look at the basic principles, discuss means of testing the soundness of our reasoning, and then for practical application of the principles we will discuss a speech of conviction assignment that requires presentation of sound reasons.

PRINCIPLES OF REASONING

Reasoning is the process of drawing inferences from facts. Thus, if we are given the facts that today's temperature is 38 degrees, the wind is blowing, and rain is falling, we may infer (reason or conclude) that "It's a miserable day." To explain the reasoning process we need to examine the three basic requirements of the process. These requirements are called the *data*, the *conclusion*, and the *warrant*.[1] Your understanding of these words will enable you to construct and analyze the simplest or the most complex forms of reasoning.

Data means the evidence, assumption, or assertion that provides the basis for a conclusion—in our example, the data are the 38° temperature, the wind blowing, and the falling rain. The conclusion means the product of the reasoning, the inference—in our example, the conclusion is "It's a miserable day." The warrant is a statement denoting the substantive relationship between data and conclusion —it is the key that provides the essential test of the reasoning, and the only one of the essentials that is usually not included in the statement of the reasoning. Since in our example no warrant is pro-

[1] This analysis is based upon the ideas set forth by Stephen Toulmin, *The Uses of Argument* (Cambridge, England: Cambridge University Press, 1958).

vided, we have to frame one. One way of stating a warrant for the example is "low temperature, wind, and rain are three major criteria or characteristics of a 'miserable day.'" Using (*D*) for data, stated or observed; (*C*) for conclusion; (*W*) for warrant; and an arrow to show the direction of the reasoning, our example could be laid out schematically as follows:

(*D*)   Temperature 38°.
Wind blowing.   ⟶   (*C*)   It's a miserable day.
Rain falling.

      (*W*)   (Low temperature, wind, and rain are three
              major characteristics of a miserable day.)

The warrant is written in parentheses because it is implied rather than actually stated. The warrant, then, indicates how we drew the conclusion, the inference, from the data supplied.

So far we have seen how we can lay out a unit of reasoning. Now we need to see how we can test the essentials in order to judge the validity of the reasoning.

The tests we apply to reasoning are twofold. First we test the data. For a logical conclusion to follow, the data must be sufficient in quantity and quality. If either no data or insufficient data are presented, you must supply more; if the data are inaccurate, biased, or from a questionable source, the conclusion will be suspect. If you are satisfied that "temperature 38°," "wind blowing," and "rain falling" are accurate, you can examine the logic of the warrant. The warrant is tested by casting it as a yes or no question: "Is it true that low temperature, wind, and rain are the major characteristics of a miserable day?" If the answer is yes, the reasoning is sound; if the answer is no, the reasoning process is fallacious.

Analyzing reasoning schematically in the data, conclusion, warrant framework does not ensure the infallibility of the logic. But if you take the time to write the process out in this manner and ask whether the warrant is supported by research, the chances of discovering illogical reasoning is increased considerably.

Although warrants could be phrased in many ways for any given unit of reasoning and literally hundreds of variations are possible in the kinds of reasoning, most methods of reasoning will fall into one of five categories: *generalization, causation, analogy, sign,* and *definition.* Since these categories do supply so many warrants, you should familiarize yourself with them. The tests following the warrants indicate under what circumstances the warrants are reasonable.

Generalization

A generalization warrant says that what is true in some instances is true in all instances (or at least enough instances to validate the generalization). Although exceptions to generalizations can and do occur, they do not necessarily invalidate the generalization. However, if exceptions prove to be more than rare or isolated instances, the validity of the generalization is open to serious question. The following illustrates the kind of generalization you might make about your professors.

(D) Larsen is an excellent
      teacher.
      Greenberg is an
      excellent teacher.   (C) The professors at
      Jackson is an   Paradise U. are excellent
      excellent teacher.   teachers.

      (W) (What is true in representative instances
           will be true in all instances.)

The following example about collegiate athletic expenses further illustrates the method.

(D) Miami U. lost $605,000 in
      its athletic program.
      Ohio U. lost $740,000   (C) Athletic programs at
      in its athletic program.   Ohio universities are
      Cincinnati U. lost $908,000   losing propositions.
      in its athletic program.

      (W) (What is true in representative universities
           is true in all universities.)

A generalization warrant may be tested by these questions:

Are enough instances cited? Are Larsen, Greenberg, and Jackson enough teachers? Are Miami, Ohio, and Cincinnati enough universities? Since instances cited should represent most to all possible, enough must be cited to satisfy the listeners that the instances are not isolated or hand picked.

Are the instances typical? Are the three professors typical of all professors at Paradise U.? Are the three Ohio universities typical of all universities in Ohio? "Typical" means that the instances cited must be similar to or representative of most or all within the category. If instances are not typical, they do not support the generalization.

Are negative instances accounted for? Are there professors at Paradise U. who are *not* excellent teachers? Are there athletic programs in Ohio that did *not* lose money? Although negative instances by themselves may not invalidate a generalization, if negative instances are numerous and typical, no valid generalization can be drawn from those cited.

Causation

In causation, a special kind of generalization, we assume that one or more circumstances listed always produce a predictable effect or set of effects. The following illustrates causal reasoning that you might make concerning a fellow student.

(*D*)   You've got a good head.
     You've been studying.   ——→ (*C*)   You'll pass the course.
     Your attitude is good.

      (*W*)   (Intelligence, study, and good attitude are causes of or result in passing grades.)

The following example illustrates causal reasoning from a single fact.

(*D*)   We've had a bumper crop. ——→ (*C*)   Food prices will come down soon.

      (*W*)   (An abundance of good crops causes or results in lower food prices.)

A causation warrant may be tested by these questions:

Are the data alone important enough to bring about the particular conclusion? Are intelligence, study, and attitude by themselves important enough to result in passing a course? Is the presence of a bumper crop alone important enough to result in lower food prices? If the data are truly important, it means that if we eliminate the data, we would eliminate the effect. If the effect can occur without the data, then we can question the causal relationship.

Do some other data that accompany the data cited really cause the effect? Are there some other factors (like luck, whim of a professor, attendance) that are more important in determining whether a student passes? Are there some other factors (like amount of profits, consumption, supplier willingness) that are more important in determining food prices? If accompanying data appear equally or more important in bringing about the effect, then we can question the causal relationship between cited data and conclusion.

Is the relationship between cause and effect consistent? Do intelligence, study, and attitude always (or usually) yield passing grades? Does a bumper crop always (or usually) result in lower prices? If there are times when the effect has not followed the cause, then we can question whether a causal relationship really exists.

Analogy

Analogy is another special kind of generalization. In reasoning by analogy, you are attempting to show that similar circumstances produce similar conclusions. A warrant in the form of an analogy would be stated, "What is true or will work in one set of circumstances is true or will work in another comparable set of circumstances." Perhaps you have used this form of reasoning in situations like this:

(D)   Joe was inducted into the $\longrightarrow$ (C)   You should be
      organization last year.   inducted this year.

      (W)   (Since Joe had certain qualifications and
            was inducted last year and you have the
            same or similar qualifications, you will be
            inducted this year.)

Let us examine an analogy warrant in a different context:

(D)   New York is making money $\longrightarrow$ (C)   Ohio should adopt
      from off-track betting.   off-track betting.

      (W)   (Since off-track betting is working well in
            New York and since New York and Ohio are
            similar in many key respects, off-track bet-
            ting will work in Ohio.)

An analogy warrant may be tested by these questions:

Are the subjects being compared really similar in all important ways? Are Joe and you eligible? hard workers? supportive of goals? Are New York and Ohio similar in form of government? capability of handling betting? attitudes of residents? If subjects do not have significant similarities, then they are not really comparable.

Are any of the ways that the subjects are dissimilar important to the outcome? Do you have less prestige? Are you less well known? Is Ohio's dissimilarity in size a factor? Is the dissimilarity in concentrations of population a factor? If dissimilarities exist that outweigh the subjects' similarities, then conclusions drawn from the comparisons are not necessarily valid.

Sign

When the presence of certain events, characteristics, or situations always or usually accompany other unobserved events, characteristics, or situations, we say that the observed events are a *sign*. A sign warrant would be stated "When one variable that is usually or always associated with another variable is observed, we can predict the existence of the other unobserved variable." Signs are often confused with causes, but signs are indicators, not causes. A fever is a sign of sickness. It occurs when a person is sick, but it does not cause the sickness. You may have used sign reasoning in a situation similar to the following:

(D)   Professor Smith has a   ⟶   (C)   Professor Smith
       runny nose, watery eyes,   has a cold.
       and is sneezing.

    (W)   (A runny nose, watery eyes, and sneezing
        are signs of a cold.)

A sign warrant in a different context could be illustrated as follows:

(D)   New car sales are   ⟶   (C)   The recession is over.
       skyrocketing.

    (W)   (Dramatic increases in car sales are a sign of
        a healthy economy.)

A sign warrant may be tested by these questions:

Do the data cited always or usually indicate the conclusion drawn? Do a runny nose, watery eyes, and sneezing always (or usually) indicate a cold? Do skyrocketing car sales always (or usually) indicate a healthy economy? If the data can occur independent of the conclusion, then they are not necessarily indicators.

Are sufficient signs present? Are a runny nose, watery eyes, and sneezing enough to indicate a cold? Are skyrocketing new-car sales in themselves enough to indicate a healthy economy? Events or situations are often indicated by several signs. If enough of them are not present, then the conclusion may not follow.

Are contradictory signs in evidence? Is Professor Smith bouncy and enthusiastic? Are housing starts down? If signs that usually indicate different conclusions are present, then the stated conclusion may not be valid.

Definition

    The above four are usually considered the major forms of reasoning. You will, however, often observe the use of reasoning from definition, a minor form of reasoning. A definition is a verbal classification that follows the application of specific criteria for that classification. A definition warrant is usually stated, "When a situation has all the characteristics that are usually associated with a term, then we can use that term to describe the product of those characteristics."

The following is an example of a typical definition warrant.

(D)   He takes charge.
       He uses good judgment. ⎫
       His goals are in the best ⎬ ⟶   (C)   Bill is an excellent
       interest of the group.   ⎭   leader.

> (W) (Taking charge, showing good judgment, and
> considering the best interests of the group
> are the characteristics most often associated
> with excellent leadership.)

The following is another definition warrant:

(D) It's centrally located.
It's in the heart of an
area that has the greatest $\longrightarrow$ (C) Chicago is the best
number of members.   location for the Speech
It has excellent facilities.   Communication Associa-
                                                            tion convention.

> (W) (Location, proximity to schools with high
> membership, and facilities are characteris-
> tics most associated with location for con-
> ventions.)

A definition warrant may be tested by these questions:

Are the characteristics mentioned the most important ones in determining the definition? Are taking charge, good judgment, and sensitivity to group goals the most important criteria of excellent leadership?
Are location, proximity to members, and facilities the most important
criteria for "best location"? If the data presented are not usually considered criteria for the classification, then the definition does not follow.

Is an important aspect of the definition omitted in the statement of
the definition? Do we need to consider Bill's influence or power? His
desire to lead? Do we need to consider desirability of location of a convention city? The need to meet in different parts of the country? If items
that are ordinarily a part of the definition are missing, then the conclusion does not necessarily follow from the criteria listed.

Are those criteria best labeled by some other term? Are taking
charge and judgment better labeled by "autocrat" rather than "leader"?
Are location, proximity, and facilities better labeled by "expedient"
rather than "best"? If another label fits the criteria better, then the conclusion is not valid.

We have defined reasoning and shown how to analyze and test
various forms. Now we need to consider how a speaker uses reasoning in a speech. A speaker uses reasoning to form arguments. An
argument is a method of putting the product of reasoning into ad-
vocacy form. Or, to look at it in another way, an argument is the
process of reasoning moving in opposite directions—instead of a
person *drawing* inferences *from* data, the person *sets forth* a proposition (the conclusion of the reasoning process) and *cites* the data
for support. To illustrate the argument form, let us look at one ex-

ample of each of the types of reasoning we discussed previously pictured in argument form:

Argument from generalization (based upon the example of reasoning from generalization on p. 187):

Proposition: Professors at Paradise U. are excellent teachers.

Support: I. Larsen is an excellent teacher.

        II. Greenberg is an excellent teacher.

      III. Jackson is an excellent teacher.

Argument from analogy (based upon the example of reasoning from analogy on p. 189):

Proposition: You should be inducted into the organization this year.

Support: Joe was inducted last year.

Argument from causation (based upon the example of reasoning from causation on p. 188):

Proposition: You'll pass the course.

Support: I. You've got a good head.

        II. You've been studying.

      III. Your attitude is good.

Argument from sign (based upon the example of reasoning from sign on p. 190):

Proposition: Professor Smith has a cold.

Support: I. He has a runny nose.

        II. He has watery eyes.

      III. He is sneezing.

Argument from definition (based upon the example of reasoning from definition on pp. 190–191):

Proposition: Bill will make an excellent leader.

Support: I. Bill takes charge.

        II. Bill uses good judgment.

      III. Bill's goals are in the best interest of the group.

In all cases, whether we show the example in reasoning form or in argument form, the same warrants indicating the relationship between data (support) and conclusion (proposition) apply.

So, as you study your resources you try to draw conclusions from the data. Then, when it comes time to prepare the speech, you use the product of your reasoning to form arguments. Now we will consider the process of preparing a speech in which the emphasis is on reasoning with the audience.

PREPARING A SPEECH OF CONVICTION

We can put what we have learned about reasoning into practice by preparing and presenting a speech of conviction. A speech of conviction, or a speech of reasons as it is sometimes called, is an attempt to develop the proposition with clear reasons and sound support for the reasons. Your goal in accomplishing this assignment is to gain conviction through sound reasoning, by presenting a sound argument.

This assignment is not without real-life application. When you consider your persuasive strategy, you may decide that as a result of the audience position on a proposition or as a result of the nature of the audience itself, presenting the merits of the proposition is your best procedure. Under these circumstances the speech of conviction model will be the one you will follow. This does not mean your speech will be devoid of motivation nor that you as a speaker can ignore the value of your credibility. It does mean that the final evaluation of your effort will be on the soundness of your case.

Determining the Specific Purpose

The specific purpose of a speech of conviction is usually a proposition phrased to change a belief held by an audience—for example, "All states should adopt a no-fault automobile insurance program" or "Jones is the best man for president." In both cases, the assumption would be that the propositions are in opposition to the attitude or belief of the audience to which the speeches will be given.

Determining the Main Points

In order to determine what should be the main points of a speech of conviction, we go through the reasoning process discussed earlier in the chapter. As a result of examining data, we draw conclusions. We then put the product of our thinking in argument form. Sometimes the sources we read suggest our arguments for us by presenting clearly stated reasons in support of the proposition. How can we recognize reasons? We look for statements that answer *why* a proposition is justified. These statements are reasons. As you are doing reading on the subjects of medical safety, the most valuable player in the NBA, and guaranteed incomes, you might well find the sources suggesting the following reasons:

Proposition: You should read labels on products carefully before you use them. (Why?)

  I. Taking time to read labels saves time in the long run.

 II. Taking time to read labels may save money.

III. Taking time to read labels prevents errors.

Proposition: Kareem Abdul-Jabbar is the best player in the National Basketball Association. (Why?)

  I. He is one of the leading scorers in the league.

 II. He is an outstanding playmaker.

III. He is an excellent defender.

Proposition: The federal government should guarantee a minimum annual cash income to all its citizens. (Why?)

  I. A minimum cash income would eliminate the present poverty conditions that breed social unrest.

 II. A minimum cash income would eliminate the need for all the overlapping state and federal welfare agencies.

III. A minimum cash income would go directly to the people in need.

If the reasons given to justify the proposition are sound, then the attempted persuasion is logical; if the reasons satisfy the audience, then the reasons are persuasive. Thus, in developing a speech of conviction, you have two goals in mind: (1) to select reasons that prove the proposition and (2) to limit the speech to the reasons that are likely to be most persuasive—the reasons that are likely to have the greatest impact on your audience.

After you have a list of five or more reasons, you can select the best ones on the basis of which are most adaptable to your audience. You may discard some reasons on your list because you do not have and cannot get material. From those that are left, you can determine which will probably have the greatest effect on your specific audience. For most speeches, you need at least two and probably not more than four of the best, most applicable reasons.

But your job is not done with the discovery and selection of reasons. They in turn must be supported with further data—with evidence.

Basically, all supporting material may be reduced to two kinds of statements: *fact* and *opinion*. For instance, in one of our examples, it was stated that Kareem Abdul-Jabbar is the best player in the

National Basketball Association because he is one of the leading scorers in the league. If this statement were supported by quotations from other players, sports journalists, and fans, the support would be opinion. On the other hand, if we checked the records and found him second in scoring this year, first last year, and third the year before, our support would be fact.

The best support for any reason is fact. Facts are statements that are verifiable. That metal is heavier than air, that World War II ended in 1945, and that marijuana is a mild hallucinatory drug are all facts. If you say, "It's warm outside; it's 60°," and if the thermometer registers 60°, than your support is factual.

Although factual support is the best, there are times when the facts are not available or when the facts are inconclusive. In these situations, you will have to support your conclusions with opinion. The quality of opinion is dependent upon whether the source is expert or inexpert. If your gasoline attendant says it is likely that there is life on other planets, the opinion is not expert—his expertise lies in other areas. If, on the other hand, an esteemed space biologist says there is a likelihood of life on other planets, his opinion is expert. Both statements are only opinions, not facts, but some opinions are more authoritative than others. Opinions are also more trustworthy when they are accompanied by factual data. If it is an automotive engineer's opinion that a low-cost electric car is feasible, his opinion is valuable, since automotive engineering is his area of expertise. If accompanying his opinion, he shows us the advances in technology that are leading to a low-cost battery of medium size that can run for more than 200 hours without being recharged, his opinion is worth even more.

TESTING THE LOGIC OF YOUR DEVELOPMENT

Since the speech of conviction is an exercise in logical development, you must assure yourself that the speech development is sound. First you make sure your speech representation meets the tests of the speech outline; then you subject the outline and its parts to a data, conclusion, warrant analysis.

Testing the Logic of Structure

The logic of structure of a speech is tested by use of the speech outline. If the outline meets the key tests discussed on pp. 57–59 you will know the proposition is clear, the main points are support for the proposition and that data are present. In slightly abbreviated form, an outline on the subject of direct election of the President might look like this:

Proposition: To prove that the United States should determine the President by direct election.

Introduction

    I. In 1968, we barely avoided the electoral catastrophe of selecting the President in the House of Representatives.

   II. The time to reform the electoral system is now.

  III. Direct election of the President offers the best alternative to the electoral college.

Body

    I. Direct election of the President is fair.

       A. It follows the one-man, one-vote policy laid down by the Supreme Court.

       B. It allows every vote to count equally, regardless of where it is cast.

       C. It eliminates the possibility of the election of a candidate who receives a lesser number of popular votes.

   II. Direct election of the President is certain.

       A. The identity of the new President would be public knowledge once the votes were counted.

       B. The election of the President would not be subject to political maneuvers.

  III. Direct election of the President is a popular plan.

       A. A recent Gallup Poll showed that the majority of people favor direct election.

       B. Many political leaders have voiced their approval of this plan.

Conclusion

    I. The time to anticipate possible catastrophe is now.

   II. Support direct election of the President.

This outline meets the key tests. Although this outline illustrates sound idea relationships, it does not describe the reasoning process nor does it test the logic. These goals are accomplished by subjecting the outline to a data, conclusion, warrant analysis.

Testing the Logic of Argument

In subjecting the outline to a data, conclusion, warrant analysis, the first step is to examine the logic of the entire speech. In schematic form, the speech in its entirety would look like this:

(D)   Direct election is fair.   (C)   The United States should
       Direct election is certain. ⟶   determine the President
       Direct election is popular.   by direct election.

(W) (Fairness, certainty, and popularity are the
three major criteria for determining how a
President should be elected.)

To test this warrant, we ask, "Is it true that fairness, certainty, and
popularity are the criteria for selecting a method of election?" If experience, observation, and source material indicate that these three
are of fundamental importance, the speech is logical. If, on the other
hand, source material indicates that some other criterion is more important, or that two or three others are of equal importance, then
the warrant does not meet the test of logic and the argument should
be reconsidered.

Assuming that this warrant does meet the test of logic, we can
be assured that the overall structure of the speech is logical. But
what of the individual units that make up the speech? Each of the
three items of data listed above is in itself a conclusion of an argument that must be tested. Let us make a schematic examination of
the first of those statements, "Direct election is fair":

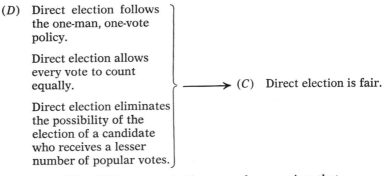

(D) Direct election follows
the one-man, one-vote
policy.

Direct election allows
every vote to count
equally.   (C) Direct election is fair.

Direct election eliminates
the possibility of the
election of a candidate
who receives a lesser
number of popular votes.

(W) (Fairness of election procedure requires that
all votes must count equally and that the
majority rules.)

First, we should test the data. Since we are working with an abbreviated outline (probably only half as detailed as an outline you
would be working with), for purposes of this analysis, we will assume our data are representative and accurate. Next, we would test
the warrant by asking, "Is it true that election method fairness requires that all votes must count equally and that majority rules?"
If we find from experience, observation, and source material that
election system fairness does require these, then the argument is
logical. But if election fairness is determined by criteria apart from
those included as data, the warrant is faulty and the argument would
need to be revised.

| Assignment | **Prepare a three- to six-minute speech of conviction. Outline required. Criteria for evaluation will include the clarity of the proposition, the clarity and quality of the reasons, the quality of the data used to support the reasons, and the logic of the units of argument presented.** |

Outline:
Speech of Conviction
(3–6 minutes)

Because this is the first complete persuasive speech outline and will as a result stand as a model for persuasive speech outlining, it will be analyzed in detail via the data, conclusion, warrant method.

Analysis

Outline

A proposition is the purpose sentence for a persuasive speech that indicates specifically what you want your audience to believe or to do.

Proposition (Specific Purpose): To prove that the listeners should purchase insurance while they are young.

As with the informative speech outline, the material included in the introduction should allow you to gain attention and lead into the body of the speech.

Introduction

I. Insurance in my mind was always a form of savings for older people.

II. There are four reasons for young people to buy life insurance.

Main point I is a clear reason. If you ask, "Why should people buy insurance while they're young?" the reason "because it provides financial savings and gain" answers the question.

Body

I. Buying insurance while you are young provides a financial savings and gain.

The logic of main point I is described as follows:

Data: Between 21 and 25, rates per thousand are lower than they would be at older ages.

A. Between the ages of 21 and 25, the rates per thousand are low.
    1. Age 25—about $16 per thousand.
    2. Age 35—about $23 per thousand.
    3. Age 45—about $33 per thousand.

Between 21 and 25, dividends per thousand are higher than at older ages.

B. In addition to lower rates the dividends are higher.
    1. Dividends left to accumulate between ages 25 and 65 amount to $727 per thousand.

Conclusion: Buying insurance while you are young provides a financial savings and gain.

    2. Dividends left to accumulate between ages 35 and 65 amount to $432 per thousand.
    3. Dividends left to accumulate between ages 45 and 65 amount to $250 per thousand.

Analysis

Outline

Warrant: (By definition, paying lower rates means making a financial saving and accumulating higher dividends means making a financial gain.)

Main point II is a clear reason. If you ask, "Why should people buy insurance while they are young?" the reason, "because it provides a systematic, compulsory savings" answers the question. Technically, this point includes two separate but related reasons, systematic and compulsory. Ordinarily it is better to limit each main point to one idea. Since they do overlap, handling them together in this case is acceptable.

The logic of main point II is described as follows:

Data: Periodic reminders of premiums due are sent to you.

Money invested in insurance cannot be withdrawn.

Conclusion: Buying insurance provides a systematic, compulsory savings.

Warrant: (By definition, if payments are made at fixed intervals, they are systematic; and if payments must be made and cannot be withdrawn, they are compulsory.)

Main point III is a clear reason. If you ask, "Why should people buy insurance while they are young?" the reason "because it enables you to have an insurability clause put into the contract" answers the question.

The logic of main point III is described as follows:

II. Buying insurance while you are young provides a systematic, compulsory savings.

   A. Each month, quarter, or year a reminder is sent to you of your premium's being due. This service is not provided by a bank, building and loan, or the stock market.

   B. Once money is invested it is saved. There is no put and take with insurance.

III. Buying insurance while you are young enables you to have an insurability clause put into the contract.

   A. This means that from the age of 21 to 40 you can reinvest the same amount up to $15,000 every three years at the standard rate for your age.

   B. By this I mean that your premium doesn't go up due to medical reasons or a job considered dangerous provided you are in good health and in a safe job at age 25.

Analysis

Outline

Data: From age 21 to 40 you can reinvest the same amount every three years at the standard rate for your age.

Premiums do not go up due to medical reasons if you are in good health.

Conclusion: Buying insurance while young enables you to have an insurability clause put into the contract.

Warrant: ?
In this case, there does not seem to be a clear relationship between the data and the conclusion. The data explain what an insurability clause is. The explanation is important to the speech. But in order for the conclusion stated to follow, the data must include proof that an insurability rider can be put in "while you are young." This part of the outline needs some repair.

Main point IV is a clear reason. If you ask, "Why should people buy insurance while they are young?" the reason "because it protects your personal financial value" answers the question.

The logic of main point IV is described as follows:

Data: You have a lifetime of earning power.

Your family is dependent upon your potential life's earnings.

Conclusion: Buying insurance enables you to protect your potential earnings.

Warrant: (If an insurance plan provides the same

IV. Buying insurance while you are young enables you to protect your personal financial value.
   A. Your background and future are monetarily valuable.
   B. Your family is dependent on this value for their support.
      1. At age 25 your value may be $400,000.
      2. If you die uninsured at the age of 27, your family is unprotected with a loss of $380,000.
      3. Insurance provides the money if you die.

Analysis

Outline

money that you would
have made if you had
worked, then by definition
the insurance plan protects
your financial value.)

This conclusion, a sum-
mary, is satisfactory for a
speech of reasons.

Now let us describe and
test the logic of the entire
outline:

Data: Insurance while
young provides financial
savings.

Insurance provides sys-
tematic, compulsory sav-
ing.

Insurance while young
enables you to attach an
insurability rider.

Insurance while young
enables you to protect
your financial value.

Conclusion: You should
buy insurance while you
are young.

Warrant: (Financial saving,
compulsory saving, having
an insurability rider, and
financial protection are
major criteria for deter-
mining whether and when
you should buy insurance.)

Because these criteria are
for the most part the key
criteria, the outline is
logical.

Conclusion

You should buy insurance while you are young because it provides a financial savings; it provides a systematic, compulsory savings; it enables you to attach an insurability rider; and it protects
your financial value.

| Buying Insurance While You Are Young | *As you analyze this speech of conviction, judge whether each of the reasons is clearly stated in the speech and whether the developmental material supports the reasons clearly, completely, and interestingly.[2] After you have made your own analysis, study the analysis given here.* |

[2] Speech given in Fundamentals of Speech class, University of Cincinnati. Printed by permission of Elaine Horan.

Analysis

Speech

The speaker begins with a sentence that establishes a point of audience agreement from which she can begin her argument. The next sentence shows that the speaker approached the topic with an open mind and suggests that the audience should do likewise. Since the speech of conviction calls for direct presentation, her preview of major reasons is appropriate.

I'm sure you're all familiar with the value of insurance for older people. However, the more I learned about it the more I realized it's wise to buy it while you're young. And what I'd like to do this morning is give you four reasons why we should invest in life insurance while we're young. It's a financial saving; it's a method of compulsory saving; you can have an insurability rider put into your contract; and it is wise to secure your own personal financial value.

Since it is usually not a good idea to state main points as labels, her first sentence would be better stated, "First, buying insurance now, while you're young, means a financial saving to you." The data showing costs per thousand provide the necessary specifics. Incidentally, the statement of those statistics would be improved by using the verb "costs" rather than "is." Active verbs are preferable to "is," "are," "was," and "were." Her developmental material indicates that the financial saving will come in the areas of "costs of insurance" and "increased dividends." The reason is a good one; the support is clear and logical.

First, the financial saving. When you are young, the rates are lowest. For instance, at age twenty-one, insurance is about 16 dollars per thousand. Purchased at age thirty-five, it's 23 per thousand, and at the age of forty-five, it's 33 per thousand. This is an indication that while you're young your rates are lowest. In addition to saving money while buying while you're young, you also gain a higher dividend. For instance, if your money is invested in insurance, and it remains from the age of twenty-five to sixty-five, your dividend is 727 dollars per thousand. At the ages of between thirty-five to sixty-five, the dividend is 432 dollars per thousand and if it's left to remain between forty-five and sixty-five, your dividend is about 250 dollars per thousand. So you see there is an increase of about 500 dollars if your money is left to remain from between the ages of twenty-five to sixty-five rather than forty-five to sixty-five. This is all done by the process called compound interest.

The speaker uses a good transition to lead her to her well-stated second reason. Her whole idea grows

Compound interest leads me into the second reason why it's wise to buy life insurance at a young age, that is, it is a method of compulsory savings. After each month, or quarter, or each year, your life insurance company will send to you a reminder that your pre-

Analysis

Speech

from the assumption that we want to save money, but that most plans do not provide the necessary motivation. Notice that she does not say that insurance savings would be greater than bank savings. By staying with the subject of motivation she adds strength to her argument. The subpoints which show that we are obligated to pay premiums at regular intervals and that we can't withdraw the money are clear and logical.

mium is due. This is a service not rendered by a bank, a building and loan or mutual fund. In addition, when you invest in life insurance, your money remains there; it cannot be withdrawn such as in a bank account, where you might be tempted to withdraw it for various reasons. Instead, it remains until your policy is redeemed and compounds interest for you. Of course it's not wise to invest all your money in life insurance because you do want some money available to purchase a house or car. Nevertheless, it is good to put your money in a safe place where you cannot touch it. There's no put and take in life insurance.

Although we know when the speaker begins her third reason, her statement of the reason is unclear. What is a "rigid" reason? Could she have simplified the entire point by saying, "By purchasing insurance now, we can guarantee our opportunity to buy more insurance later at standard rates"? Although her approach is somewhat clarified by the developmental material, she may have lost a few less interested listeners. Moreover, better audience adaptation in her examples of jobs or conditions would have increased audience interest.

The third reason why you should invest in life insurance at a young age is rather complicated but a very rigid reason. That is, you can have an insurability rider put into your policy contract. Now, an insurability rider allows you to purchase the same amount of insurance every three years until the age of forty, based on standard rates for your age. And, you ask, what does this mean? Well, it means that if you are in good health, between the ages of twenty-one and twenty-five and you have a safe secure job, your rates are at the standard rates. However, if you should contract an ulcer, or accept a dangerous job such as piloting an aircraft or even a spacecraft, the premiums are going to go up, unless you have this insurability rider. So with an insurability rider it means you pay only the standard rate for a person of your age every three years between the ages of twenty-five and forty and you may purchase the same amount of life insurance up to |$15,000 during this period.

The fourth reason is clearly stated and logically developed. Even though the speaker improves her direct audience adaptation in this section, she misses an excellent opportunity for direct adaptation. Instead of saying "Now, take, for example, a man twenty-five," she could have said, "Now, take, for example, one of the fellows in this room. Let's say that after he graduates he gets a job paying . . ." You

The fourth reason why it is wise to invest in life insurance at a young age is to secure your own personal financial value. Now, this means that your parents, or yourself, have invested a lot of money in your education and in the attainment of a certain social status. With your background you are capable and have the potential of securing a high paying job which increases your own personal value. Now, take, for example, a man twenty-five. Upon graduation from college, he receives a job paying $10,000 a year. Assuming that he maintains this at the same salary, his own personal financial value is worth 400,000 dollars, which will be used to support his family. Now, in case this man should die at the age of twenty-seven, the family not only loses him, but his potential earnings of 380,000. For this reason, a man must protect his own personal financial value in order to se-

Analysis

Speech

should relate to your audience wherever and whenever possible.

Her final examples about women aren't as vivid as her examples about men.

The conclusion, a summary, meets the requirements of a speech of reasons. Although summaries are always acceptable, they are usually better when they are coupled with an appeal, an example, or an anecdote that will leave the audience with a little more vivid impression of the specific purpose.

This is a good example of a speech of conviction. The proposition is clearly stated, three of the four reasons are clearly presented, and each reason is clearly supported. The speech would have been improved with the addition of sources for some of the statistics, better examples to illustrate some points, and more direct audience adaptation.

cure the support for his family. A woman too has a personal financial value. As the housekeeper and mother she has certain duties. However, upon her death a maid or housekeeper must be brought in to assist and assume these duties for her. For this reason, a woman, too, has her own personal financial value, which must be protected.

So what I have tried to do this morning is to give to you four reasons to buy life insurance while you're young. First, there is a financial savings, second, it is a method of compulsory saving, third, you can have an insurability rider put into your contract, and, fourth, it is wise to secure your own personal financial value.

MOTIVATING AUDIENCES: SPEECHES TO ACTUATE

15

Reasoning provides a solid logical base for your persuasion and a sound rationale for change of audience attitude. But what if sound reasoning is not enough to bring action? What can you do to complement or supplement reasoning? What can you do when your listeners recognize the relative merits of your proposition—but they are not acting? The catalyst for firing the imagination, causing commitment, and bringing to action is the psychological aspect of persuasion called *motivation*. In this chapter we will consider how to motivate by relating to audience needs and by appealing to audience emotions; and for practice in focusing attention on the development of motivation in speeches, we will consider a specific speech assignment, the speech to actuate.

RELATE MATERIAL TO BASIC AUDIENCE NEEDS

To be an effective speaker, you will have to recognize that an audience is composed of individuals whose responses to your words will be dictated by different motives for action operating within them. These motives that help each individual make the choices he faces are related to or grow from basic needs within all men. Abraham Maslow[1] classifies basic human needs in five categories:

1. Physiological needs

2. Safety needs

3. Belongingness and love needs

4. Esteem needs

5. Self-actualization needs

Notice that he places these needs in a hierarchy: one set of needs must be met or satisfied before the next set of needs emerge. Our physiological needs for food, drink, temperature are the most basic; they must be satisfied before the body is able to consider any of its

[1] Abraham H. Maslow, *Motivation and Personality* (New York: Harper & Row, 1954), pp. 80–92.

other needs. The next level consists of safety needs—security, simple self-preservation, and the like; they emerge after basic needs have been met, and they hold a paramount place until they, too, have been met. The third level includes our belongingness or love needs; these involve the groups that we identify with, our friends, our loved ones, our family. In a world of increasing mobility and breakdown of the traditional family, however, it's becoming more and more difficult for individuals to satisfy this need. Nonetheless, once our belongingness needs are met, our esteem needs predominate; these involve our quest for material goods, recognition, and power or influence. The final level is called, by Maslow, the self-actualizing need; this involves developing one's self to meet its potential. When all other needs are met, this need is the one that drives people to their creative heights, that urges them to do "what they need to do."

What is the value of this analysis to you as a speaker? First, it provides a framework for and suggests the kinds of needs you may appeal to in your speeches. Second, it allows you to understand why a line of development will work on one audience and fall flat with another. For instance, if our audience has great physiological needs—if they are hungry—an appeal to the satisfaction of good workmanship, no matter how well done, is unlikely to impress them. Third, and perhaps most crucial, when our proposition is going to come in conflict with an operating need, we will have to be prepared with a strong alternative in the same category or in a higher-level category. For instance, if our proposition is going to cost money—if it is going to take money in the form of taxes—we will have to show how the proposal satisfies some other comparable need.

Let us try to make this discussion even more specific by looking at some of the traditional motives for action. The few we will discuss are not meant to be exhaustive—they are meant to be suggestive of the kind of analysis you should be doing. You have a proposition; you have determined reasons for its acceptance. Now try to relate those reasons to basic needs and discover where you may be getting into difficulty by coming into conflict with other motives or other needs.

Wealth

Wealth, the acquisition of money and material goods, is a motive that grows out of an esteem need. People are concerned about making money, saving it, losing it, or finding it. People who do not have money may be motivated by a plan that will help them gain money, save money, or do more with what they have. People who already have money may be motivated by a plan that will enable them to enlarge it or to use it in a way that will indicate their wealth. For example, those who have little money could perhaps be motivated to buy a Toyota or a Volkswagen primarily because they are economical; on the other hand, those who have a great deal of money could perhaps be motivated to buy a Rolls-Royce or a Ferrari because they are prestigious. Does your proposition affect wealth or material goods in any way? If it does in a positive way, you may want to stress it. If your plan calls for giving up money, you will need to be prepared to cope with an audience's natural desire to resist giving up money—you will have to involve another motive from the same category (esteem) or from a higher category to override the loss of any money it will have to give up.

Power

For many people, personal worth is dependent upon their power over their own destiny, the exercising of power over others, and the recognition and prestige that comes from such recognition or power. Recognition, power, and prestige are all related to people's identity, to their need for esteem. If people control things, if they are well known, these feelings of control and recognition will raise their self-esteem and make them feel important. Consider whether your speech allows the person, group, or community to exercise power; if it does, it may offer a strong motivation. On the other hand, if your speech proposition takes away power from part or all of your listeners, you will need to provide strong compensation to be able to motivate them.

Conformity

Conformity is a major source of motivation for nearly everyone. It grows out of people's need for belongingness. People often respond in a given way because a friend, a neighbor, an acquaintance, or a person in the same age bracket has so responded. Although some will be more likely to do something if they can be the first one to do it or if it makes them appear distinctive, most people feel more secure, more comfortable when they are members of a group. The old saying that there is strength in numbers certainly applies. If you can show that many favor your plan, that people in similar circumstances have responded favorably, that may well provide motivation.

Pleasure

When you give people a choice of actions, they will pick the one that gives them the greatest pleasure, enjoyment, or happiness. On at least one level, pleasure is a self-actualizing need—more often it is an esteem need. Pleasure sometimes results from doing things you are good at. If you are able to shoot a basketball through the basket a higher percentage of times than most others, you probably enjoy the experience. At other times, pleasure is a result of accomplishing something that is difficult. Getting an A in a class you regard as difficult may give you more pleasure than getting an A in a class that you regard as easy—challenges will often give people pleasure. Just as you respond to things that are pleasurable, so will your classmates respond favorably when they see that your proposition will give them pleasure. If your speech relates to something that is novel, promises excitement, is fun to do, or offers a challenge, you can probably motivate your audience.

As we have already said, these are only a few of the possible motives for action. Freedom, recognition, security, workmanship, sex, responsibility, justice, and many others operate within each of us. We can and should have an understanding of such motives and some idea of which of these are likely to be most easily aroused in our audience on the specific proposition. Then we need to determine the hierarchy of the motives operating to make sure that the audience will be free to be receptive to the need we appeal to.

But knowing which motives are in operation and appealing to them are two different things. To maximize our effectiveness we need to understand how to trigger these motives.

PHRASE IDEAS TO APPEAL TO EMOTIONS

As we think back over causes for our actions we may hear ourselves saying that something impelled us to act. It is as if something inside of us took control of us and directed our actions. That something is often our emotional response to various stimuli. What is an emotion? *Webster's* says it is a "strong feeling" or a "psychological excitement." We recognize the presence of such emotions as love, sadness, happiness, joy, anxiety, anger, fear, hate, pity, and guilt. We hear ourselves and others say "I'm feeling anxious about the test," "I feel anger toward him for slighting me," "I feel sad that he's no longer able to work." Many of these emotions we feel are triggered by physical happenings: a dog jumps from behind a tree and frightens us, a friend falls and sprains his ankle and we feel sad; that person puts his or her arm around us and we feel joy. But emotions are also triggered by words. A person says, "You idiot, what did you do a dumb thing like that for?" and we feel angry. A person says, "I'd love to go with you," and we feel happiness. A friend says, "Go ahead with the gang—I'll be all right alone," and we feel guilty. We are interested in the conscious effort of a speaker to phrase his ideas in a way that appeals to the emotions of the audience.

Let us see how this can work in practice. Suppose you want your audience to give money to United Appeal. You believe your audience has nothing against United Appeal—in fact, you are reasonably certain they agree that United Appeal is a worthy charity. You see your goal, then, not of convincing them that United Appeal is worthy but in getting each member of the audience to give some money *now* and getting those who are willing to give *more* than what they had planned. Your problem is how to make them feel so strongly about the topic that they will *act*. What feelings are most likely to result in your listeners' opening their pocketbooks to give to United Appeal?

For this topic, you might work on three emotions: If you can make your listeners feel sad about people who are suffering, they may contribute money. If you can make them feel guilty that they have so much when the sufferers have so little, that may do it. If you can make them feel the responsibility of being their brother's keeper—if you can make them care enough to see that no person goes without food to eat—that may do it.

Now this procedure does not call for you to use emotional appeals the way you use statistics or examples. To think "I'll put in one angry statement here" will not work. Emotional appeal grows out of an emotional climate. You are the catalyst to developing that climate. The best use of emotional appeals comes out of your sincere feelings about the topic. If you can really imagine children suffering from lack of food, money, or shelter; if you can visualize their pleading eyes and constant sad looks; if you can picture living in a world where bare existence is all you dare hope for each day, perhaps you can find the words to describe that feeling to your audience. If you can, you can bring out that feeling in the audience.

Now, emotional appeals can go too far. If we as listeners are too aware of obvious or clumsy attempts to appeal to our emotions, we may put up our defenses so strongly that the appeals have no effect; sometimes, in fact, we may even react the opposite of what was intended. A poor try at making us sad may make us laugh.

In Chapter 5, we discussed the means of making language clear, appropriate, and vivid. These language skills are the beginning of emotional appeal. You must select the right words, you must speak vividly, and you must involve the audience directly to bring the emotional reactions you seek. In developing a speech of emotional appeal, then, try the following procedure:

1. Get in touch with your own feelings about the topic. When you think of United Appeal, do you feel joy? sadness? guilt? pleasure? love?

2. Picture what you see when you are thinking vividly about the topic. When you think vividly about Barney's restaurant, do you picture a cozy atmosphere? a juicy steak? an elegant decor?

3. Practice describing your feelings and your mental pictures so that the audience can get the same feeling or picture. Your first attempts may be clumsy. But as you work with your descriptions, you will find yourself becoming more and more vivid.

As a guideline for helping you test your emotional development, read through the speech at the end of this chapter. Notice how the speaker put words together to try to get the audience to see and to feel the same feelings.

In addition to heightening the sensual or emotional reaction to the ideas, language can be used to create an emotional atmosphere for your message. Let us consider three special language strategies —*yes-response*, *common ground*, and *suggestion*—that are used by persuasive speakers to condition an audience response. Like most means of persuasion, they apply equally well to ethical and unethical persuasion. You should learn to use them ethically and to recognize their unethical use by other persuaders.

Yes-Response A favorable climate for persuasion is built upon audience agreement. Psychologists have found that when listeners get in the habit of saying yes, they are likely to continue to say yes. If you can phrase questions that establish areas of agreement early in your speech, the audience will be more likely to listen to you and perhaps to agree with you later. In contrast, if you create areas of disagreement earlier, you may not be able to get agreement later. For instance, an insurance salesman might phrase the following questions: "You want your family to be able to meet their needs, don't you? You want to be able to provide for them under all circumstances, don't you? You want your family to have the basic needs, don't you? Then of course you want to have an insurance program that meets all these criteria, don't you?" With this set of yes-responses, the potential client is led to a yes-response he might not have made earlier; that is, he may well say yes to the suggestion that he buy an insurance policy.

The criteria-satisfaction organization we considered in Chapter 13 illustrates a yes-response organization. Thus, in a speech trying to get the audience to support a bill giving more funds for hiring more police you might follow this pattern:

You want a safe community? (Yes)

You want your sons and daughters to be able to walk the streets at night? (Yes)

You want to be able to leave your house without the constant fear of loss from burglary? (Yes)

Then you want a police force that can help make these a reality. (Yes!)

Common Ground Common ground relates to credibility and commonality of experience. Why is it that a good friend can tease us about a mistake we make, but a stranger or an enemy cannot? Why are we leery of "outsiders" trying to solve "our" problems? Because we respect, believe in, and trust those with *common experience.* Why when we meet someone from home when we are out of state or out of the country do we treat him like a long-lost friend, when perhaps back at home we hardly ever see each other? Because under a certain special set of circumstances (strangers in a strange land) we share a common experience; when those special circumstances no longer exist (when we are back home), that bond is no longer a strong common experience.

When you can show your audience that you have common experiences, you can build an affinity between you and your audience that lays a groundwork for bridging differences of opinion. Let us see how two different speakers build and use common ground.

This speaker, in her commencement address to the women of Hartford College, attempted to build common ground early in her speech this way:

I do commend you for what you have accomplished thus far. Working with you during the past year, I identified with many of you and recalled my own struggles, lacking financial and emotional support, to get a college education. I learned in my time, as you have learned in your day, that the president of Hartford College had her own affirmative action program for women long before it was fashionable. I am only one of many products of that program.

I know what some of you have sacrificed for your achievement.[2]

Notice that the emphasis is on common experience. What is the implication of her words? If we have had the same experiences, then we can talk together as equals.

Vernon Jordan, a black, uses common ground to make an appeal to his audience of Jews. Throughout his speech he shows what blacks and Jews have in common. Then he says:

Because I feel at home with you, because I am among friends, I wish to speak with the bluntness of a true friend; with the honesty that must characterize relations between friends who respect each other and who have each other's interests at heart. To the degree that tensions or misunderstandings exist between Jews and blacks today, some of the responsibility must be laid upon the indifference to issues touching the very core of black interests on the part of some Jews.[3]

[2] Mary Lou Thibeault, "The Hazards of Equality," *Vital Speeches*, July 15, 1974, p. 588.
[3] Vernon E. Jordan, Jr., "The Black and Jewish Communities," *Vital Speeches*, August 1, 1974, p. 630.

In effect, Jordan is criticizing some members of his audience—he could not have made his criticism and been heard without first building the common ground. Did the Jews in the audience accept the criticism as coming from a friend? No doubt much better than if he had made the criticism without building common ground.

Suggestion   Suggestion involves planting an idea in the mind of the listener without development. It is an idea stated in such a way that its acceptance is sought without analysis or consideration.

Suggestion may be direct, as in bumper stickers that say SEE MAMMOTH CAVE or VOTE FOR SMEDLEY. Suggestion may also be indirect. The speaker who says "Let's see, we could act now—a stitch in time often saves nine" has found an indirect way of saying, "If I were you I'd act now before the problem gets any worse, causing us to take even more drastic action later." Suggestion may be positive ("Play soccer") or negative ("Don't walk on the grass"). Positive suggestion is usually more effective. Negative suggestion often leads to the very behavior it decries. Who can avoid putting his finger on the wall when the sign says DO NOT TOUCH—WET PAINT? Suggestion may be in the form of countersuggestion. *Countersuggestion* is a manipulative form that can and often does backfire. You use countersuggestion when you want to go swimming, and you say to a bullheaded friend, "Let's go fishing"—and he replies, as you hoped, with "Naw, let's go swimming." Of course, if he said yes to fishing, your countersuggestion backfired.

One writer, Robert Oliver, says that suggestion works best when "(1) the audience is inclined to be favorable to the proposition; (2) the audience is in a generally agreeable state; and (3) the audience is polarized to such a degree that judgment is inhibited."[4]

As an example of a program of suggestion, see what the following speaker says about his hotel's efforts to boost sales of dessert in the restaurants. His point is that the waiter can try for other goodies, but no matter what, he can sell strawberries:

"So sell 'em strawberries!" we said. "But sell 'em." And then we wheeled out our answer to gasoline shortages, the dessert cart. We widened the aisles between the tables and had the waiters wheel the cart up to each and every table at dessert time. Not daunted by the diet protestations of the customer, the waiter then went into raptures about the bowl of fresh strawberries. There was even a bowl of whipped cream for the slightly wicked. By the time our waiters finish extolling the virtues of our fresh strawberries flown in that morning from Cali-

[4] Robert T. Oliver, *The Psychology of Persuasive Speech* (New York: David McKay, 1957), pp. 151–152.

fornia, or wherever he thinks strawberries come from, you not only had an abdominal orgasm, but one out of two of you order them.[5]

As an ethical speaker, however, you will find your use of suggestion limited. One prevalent use of suggestion in speechmaking is the use of directive. Such expressions as "I think we will all agree," "As we all know," and "Now we come to a most important consideration" are forms of suggestion that will help you to direct audience thinking. Another use of suggestion is to associate the name of a prominent individual to add prestige to a proposal. Of course, ethical use of this method is limited to those individuals who have given their backing to that particular proposal. In contrast to saying that a proposal is favored by notable men, you can say that Senator X, who received an award for his work on air-pollution control, favors the proposal to curb air pollution. This kind of use helps the audience to make the association between the proposal and responsible public officials. A third way to use suggestion is by phrasing ideas in specific, vivid language. Audiences are drawn to favor proposals that are phrased in memorable language. In 1946, Winston Churchill, regarded by many as the most effective speaker of the twentieth century, introduced the use of the term "Iron Curtain" in a speech at Fulton, Missouri. This term suggested an attitude about Russian ideology that has permeated Western thinking for more than twenty years. Because the subtle, less obvious statement of an idea may be more easily accepted by an audience, suggestion is an aid to persuasive speaking.

PREPARING
A SPEECH
TO ACTUATE

Practice with motivation may be best accomplished with a speech of actuation assignment, a speech calling for the speaker to bring his audience to action.

Propositions

Propositions for speeches to actuate are often phrased as directives, such as "Eat at Barney's," "Give to the United Appeal," "Go to the Antique Automobile show." Although you may call for any action, you may be wiser to select propositions about which your audience is in favor of in principle, is apathetic, is ignorant, or is only mildly opposed. For example, you can try to get a group of hardcore Republicans to vote for a Democrat or get a group of conservatives to support a social welfare program, but you are probably doomed to failure before you begin. It takes a highly skilled

[5] James Lavenson, "Think Strawberries," *Vital Speeches*, March 15, 1974, p. 348.

speaker and particularly favorable circumstances to bring an audience from hostile or strongly opposed to willingness to take direct action in one speech.

Development

Any persuasive speech is built upon sound reasons. Regardless of how you decide to proceed in the speech, you must have a logical framework to support your proposition. Although your speech may not be a "one, two, three" statement and development of reasons, it should be logically conceived and logically based.

As we said in Chapter 13, there are many organizations of reasons to choose from. Under some circumstances the statement of reasons method may prove best; under others a more indirect approach such as criteria-satisfaction method may be better.

The success of your speech will depend on how you appeal to audience needs and emotions. Here are a few suggestions:

1.   Keep the language audience-oriented. In this speech it is especially important to use personal pronouns, to build common ground, and to involve the audience emotionally.

2.   Either avoid pedantic and dry statement of points or supplement such statements with emotional language. For instance, you may decide to use the statement "one out of every eight children suffers some birth defect." As impressive as that statement appears to be, you will develop far more emotion involvement by supplementing the statement with a short case history or one specific example. People do not see or feel statistics.

3.   In writing the outline, make sure that every main point and major subdivision is stated with emotional appeal in mind. "The atmosphere is good" is not nearly as impressive as "The quiet, soft lit room is conducive to luxuriant dining."

4.   Put special emphasis on your introductions and your conclusions. You cannot persuade an audience that is not listening. If only ten of a class of twenty-five are listening to you, your potential is severely limited. Likewise, you must leave your audience excited about the action you call for. Think creatively to determine the very best way of closing your speech.

Delivery

If there is any speech where delivery effectiveness is crucial, this is it. You must practice this speech until you are in total command. The more careful you are in practice of wording and delivery, the better you will be in the actual speech.

Assignment

Prepare a four- to seven-minute persuasive speech on a topic designed to bring your audience to action. Outline required. In addition to clarity of purpose and soundness of rationale, criteria for evaluation will include your credibility on the topic, your ability to satisfy audience needs, and your ability to phrase your ideas in a way that will motivate.

Outline:
Speech to Actuate
(4–7 minutes)

Specific Purpose: To persuade listeners to donate their eyes to an eye bank.

Introduction

   I. Close your eyes and imagine living in a world of darkness.

   II. Millions live in this world.

Body

   I. The windows through which we see the world are the cornea.
      A. They are tough, dime-sized, transparent tissues.
      B. Normally they are clear.
      C. When they are distorted, they blot out the light.

   II. Those with injured cornea have the hope of normal sight through a cornea transplant.
      A. The operation works miracles, but it cannot work without donors.
      B. If eyes are transplanted within 72 hours after death of the donor, the operation can be 100 percent successful.
      C. The operation has turned tragedy into joy.

   III. There are many reasons for donating.
      A. The donor knows a part of him goes on living.
      B. The donor knows he can be as useful to mankind in death as in life.

   IV. I hope you will consider becoming a donor.
      A. Leaving your desire in your will is not enough—the operation must come within 72 hours of death.
      B. Get forms and details from Cincinnati eye bank.
      C. Then, when you die, someone who needs the chance can see.

Conclusion

   I. Close your eyes again—now open them.

   II. Won't you give someone else the chance to open theirs?

Open Your Eyes

Read this speech at least once aloud and analyze the use of motivation.[6] What motives is the speaker appealing to? What are her methods of heightening motivation? After you have analyzed the speech, read the analysis given here.

Analysis

Much of the strength of this speech is a result of the speaker's ability to involve members of the audience personally and get them to feel what she is saying. This opening is a striking example of audience involvement. She does not just tell the audience what it would be like—she has them experience the feeling. The speaker very successfully lays the emotional groundwork for total audience reception of her words.

Here the speaker begins the body of her speech by telling us about the role of the cornea. Notice throughout the speech the excellent word choice, such as "The bright world we awake to each morning is brought to us by. . . ."

Here again she does not just tell us what it is like but asks us to imagine for ourselves what it would be like if. The "rain-slashed window pane" is an especially vivid image.

The speaker continues in a very informative way. After asserting that corneal transplants work, she focuses on the two key points that she wants the audience to work with—the operation works, but it must be done within seventy-two hours.

Speech

Would all of you close your eyes for just a minute. Close them very tightly so that all the light is blocked out. Imagine what it would be like to always live in a world of total darkness such as you are experiencing right now, though only for a moment. Never to see the flaming colors of the sunset, or the crisp green of the world after the rain—never to see the faces of those you love. Now open your eyes, look all around you, look at all of the things that you couldn't have seen if you couldn't have opened your eyes.

The bright world we awake to each morning is brought to us by two dime-sized pieces of tough, transparent, semielastic tissue; these are the cornea, and it is their function to allow light to enter the lens and the retina. Normally, they are so clear that we don't even know they are there; however, when they are scratched or scarred either by accident or by disease, they tend to blur or blot out the light. Imagine peering through a rain-slashed window pane or trying to see while swimming under water. This is the way the victims of corneal damage often describe their vision.

"To see the world through another man's eyes." These words are Shakespeare's, yet today it can literally be true. Thanks to the research by medical workers throughout the world, the operation known as a corneal transplant or a corneal graft has become a reality, giving thousands of people the opportunity to see. No other generation has held such a profound legacy in its possession. Yet, the universal ignorance of this subject of cornea donation is appalling. The operation itself is really quite simple; it involves the

[6] Speech given in Speech class, University of Concinnati. Printed by permission of Kathleen Sheldon.

Analysis

Speech

Notice that there is still no apparent direct persuasion. Her method is one of making information available in a way that will lead the audience itself to thinking about what effects the information might have on them personally.

corneas of the donor being transplanted into the eyes of a recipient. And if this operation takes place within seventy-two hours after the death of the donor, it can be 100 percent effective.

In this segment of the speech, she launches into emotional high gear. Still. her approach remains somewhat indirect. Although we stress the importance of directness in language in this speech, the use of "no one" repeatedly throughout the examples is done by design. Although a more direct method might be effective, in this case the indirectness works quite well.

The real effectiveness of the section is a result of the parallel structure and repetition of key phrases: "no one who has seen . . . human tragedy . . . great joy . . . can doubt the need or the urgency." As this portion of the speech was delivered, the listeners were deeply touched by both the examples themselves and their own thoughts about the examples.

No one who has seen the human tragedy caused solely by corneal disease can doubt the need or the urgency. Take the case of a young woman living in New Jersey who lost her sight to corneal disease. She gave birth to a baby and two years ago, thanks to a corneal transplant, she saw her three-year-old baby girl for the first time. And no one who had seen this woman's human tragedy caused solely by corneal disease nor her great joy at the restoration of her sight can doubt the need or the urgency. Or take the case of the five-year-old boy in California who was playing by a bonfire when a bottle in the fire exploded, flinging bits of glass, which lacerated his corneas. His damaged corneas were replaced with healthy ones in an emergency operation, and no one who had seen this little boy's human tragedy caused solely by corneal laceration nor the great joy to his young life of receiving his sight back again can doubt the need or the urgency. Or take the case of Dr. Beldon H. Scribbner of the University of Washington School of Medicine. Dr. Scribbner's eyesight was damaged by a corneal disease that twisted the normally spear-shaped cornea into cones. A corneal transplant gave Dr. Scribbner a twenty-twenty corrective vision and allowed him to continue work on his invention—the artificial kidney machine. And no one who has seen this man's human tragedy caused solely by corneal disease, nor the great joy brought not only to Dr. Scribbner but to the thousands of people his machine has helped save, can doubt the need or the urgency.

Also note how the examples themselves are ordered. The first two represent a personal effect; the final one a universal effect.

At this point in the speech the audience should be sympathetic with the problem and encouraged by the hope of corneal transplants. Now the

There are many philosophies behind such a gift. One of them was summed up by a minister and his wife who lost their daughter in infancy. They said, "We feel that a part of her goes on living." Or take the case of the young woman who was dying of cancer. She donated her eyes and did so with this explanation: "I want to be

Analysis

Speech

speaker must deal with the listener's reactions of "That may be a good idea for someone else, but why me?" It is in this section that she offers reasons for our acting. If the speech has a weakness, it may be here. I'd like to have heard a little further development of the reasons or perhaps the statement of an additional reason.

Here she brings the audience from "Good idea —I'll do something someday" to "I'd better act now."

She reminds them of the critical time period. And tells them how they can proceed to make the donation. In this section it might be worth a sentence to stress that the donation costs nothing but a little time.

Here the speaker brings the audience full circle. Although she could have used different images, the repetition of those that began the speech takes the emphasis off the images themselves and places it in what the audience can do about those who are in these circumstances.

The last line of the speech is simple, but in the context of the entire speech it is direct and quite moving. This is a superior example of a speech to actuate.

useful; being useful brings purpose and meaning into my life." Surely if being useful is important there are few better ways than to donate your eyes to someone who lives after you. But no matter which philosophy you do adopt, I hope each of you will consider donating your eyes to another who will live after you and who otherwise would have to survive in the abyss of darkness. It will do you no good to leave your eyes in your regular will if you have one; for as I mentioned earlier, there is a seventy-two-hour critical period. If you wish to donate your eyes, I would suggest you contact Cincinnati Eye Bank for Sight Restoration at 861–3716. They will send you the appropriate donor forms to fill out, which should be witnessed by two of your closest friends or by your next of kin so that they will know your wishes. Then, when you die and no longer have need for your sight someone who desperately wants the chance to see will be able to.

Will all of you close your eyes again for just a moment? Close them very tightly, so that all the light is blocked out. And once more imagine what it would be like to live always in a world of total darkness such as you are experiencing right now, never seeing the flaming colors of a sunset, or the crisp green of the world after a rain—never seeing the faces of those you love. Now open your eyes . . . Won't you give someone else the chance to open theirs?

COUNTERATTACK: SPEECHES OF REFUTATION

16

For every assignment suggested in this book so far, you have been concerned with preparing a speech, delivering it to the audience, and then retiring to your seat to listen to either another speech or an evaluation of your speech. Although your professor may provide question or discussion periods for some speeches, he or she probably has not asked you to defend or attack any position taken. A useful assignment in a persuasive speaking unit is one that provides an opportunity for direct confrontation of ideas, a speech of refutation. In order to make the best use of your potential in social, legislative, vocational, and other decision-making bodies, you must develop some confidence in your abilities to reply.

Specifically, refutation means disproving, denying, or invalidating an idea that was presented. A speech of refutation assignment gives an experience with confrontation without all the trappings of formal debate. We will focus on what can be refuted and how refutation is prepared and presented. Then we will consider three assignments that allow for differing amounts of direct refutation, and present a debate illustrating the use of refutation.

**WHAT CAN
BE REFUTED**

Refutation, like all other aspects of speechmaking, can and should be handled systematically. A speech of refutation begins with anticipation of what the opponent will say. If you research your opponent's side of the proposition as carefully as you research your own, you will seldom be surprised by his or her arguments. The second step of refutation is to take careful notes on your opponent's speech. The key words, phrases, and ideas should be recorded accurately and as nearly as possible in the actual words used. You do not want to run the risk of being accused of distorting what your opponent really said. Divide your note paper in half vertically and outline your opponent's speech in the left-hand column. The right-hand column will be used for noting your line of refutation on each of the particular points.

At this stage you will have anticipated your opponent's preparation and you will have a reasonably accurate account of all that was said. Now, how are you going to reply? You will present refutation based upon the quantity of the data, the quality of the data, and the reasoning from the data.

Quantity of Data

Human beings are notorious for asserting opinions. "It always rains on my birthday" is an assertion, a statement with no visible support. Assertions are not necessarily false. It is just that from an assertion alone, an audience has no way of testing the validity of the reasoning. Speakers are obligated to substantiate their statements. If your opponent asserts with no substantiation, no data, you have the opportunity to refute his or her argument on that basis alone.

Likewise, you can refute an argument if you think that the total data were insufficient. For instance, if a person says, "Food prices are terrible, the price of a dozen eggs has gone up ten cents in the last week," you could question whether the price of eggs is indicative of other products. Perhaps last week eggs were on sale at ten cents below normal prices. Perhaps other food products have actually gone down in price. A single item of data is seldom enough to support a major conclusion.

Attacking quantity of data is the easiest form of refutation. Although students who understand argumentative speaking should not make the mistakes of asserting or using too few data, you may still find the opportunity to refute a speech on that basis.

Quality of Data

A better method of refutation is to attack the quality of the data presented. Quality refers to the substance of the data. Cicero, the great Roman speaker and writer, said, "In my own case when I am collecting arguments . . . I make it my practice not so much to count them as to weigh them."[1] Data are weighed by judging source, recency, and relevancy.

Source of the Data   On a topic of the President's role in determining foreign policy, a statement by a political scientist who has studied executive power would be worth far more than several opinions from athletes, musicians, or politicians who have not studied the subject. Nevertheless, even a qualified source may be biased. For instance, an economist with a conservative view of economic trends might not be expected to give an objective analysis of a new liberal theory. If data come from a poor source, an unreliable

---

[1] Cicero, *De Oratore*, Vol. II, trans. by E. W. Sutton and H. Rackham (Cambridge, Mass.: Harvard University Press, 1959), p. 435.

source, or a biased source, no reliable conclusion can be drawn, and you should refute the argument on the basis of the dubious quality of those data.

Recency of the Data   In our age as never before, products, ideas and other data become obsolete almost as soon as they are produced. You should be very much aware of *when* the particular data were true and *when* they were stated to be true. Five-year-old data may not be true today. In scientific or technological circles, two-year-old data may be obsolete. Furthermore, an article in last month's *Time* may still be using five-year-old data. If all the data used to establish the claim are "old," attack the argument on that ground.

Relevancy of the Data   You may find that the data are true and come from a desirable source but have little to do with the point being presented. This question of relevancy may well lead you into the reasoning process itself.

Reasoning from the Data

What makes argumentative speaking so exciting is the opportunity for exercising the intellect. Even after individuals have learned to use data to support conclusions and to test the quality of those data, they find that reasoning can still be faulty. Reasoning, the process we use to get from data to conclusion, is the source of the greatest number of errors in argumentative speaking. A line of argument on a recent intercollegiate debate proposition illustrates how faulty reasoning can come from useful data. The speaker was trying to prove that "20 percent of all Americans cannot obtain adequate food and shelter." He said, "the federal government has set the threshold of poverty for a family of four at $4,500." This statement was well documented. He continued by saying, "By definition, then, 20 percent of all American citizens are living in poverty." This is sound reasoning from the data. But when he said, "So that proves that 20 percent of all Americans cannot obtain adequate food and shelter," he was making a conclusion that could not be drawn from the data presented. Nothing in the argument showed that an income of less than $4,500 meant a family could not obtain adequate food and shelter. More relevant data would be needed in order to draw this conclusion.

To prepare yourself to judge the reasoning, go back to the explanation of warrants in Chapter 14. For practice, get in the habit of framing warrants for all the arguments you hear. As you listen to your opponent, write your wording of the warrants for all the arguments he or she presents in the right-hand column of your note sheet. Remember, it is unlikely that your opponent will state his warrant. It is up to you to record a warrant and test its logic. Although attacking the reasoning process is difficult, it is by far the best method of refutation. Quantity of data can be increased; quality of data can be upgraded; faulty reasoning cannot be readily repaired.

HOW TO REFUTE

Since this assignment is an exercise in direct refutation, your goal is to examine what your opponent has said, then to deal with each part in a clear direct manner. Although you do not have as long to consider exactly what you are going to say, your refutation must be organized nearly as well as your planned informative and persuasive speaking assignments. If you will think of refutation in terms of units of argument, each of which is organized by following four definite steps, you will learn to prepare and to present refutation effectively:

1. State the argument you are going to refute clearly and concisely. (Or as the advocate replying to refutation, state the argument you are going to rebuild.)

2. State what you will prove; you must tell the audience how you plan to proceed so that they will be able to follow your thinking.

3. Present the proof completely with documentation.

4. Draw a conclusion; do not rely upon the audience to draw the proper conclusion for you. And never go on to another argument before you have drawn your conclusion.

In order to illustrate the process of refutation, let us examine both a small portion of a typical note outline sheet (based upon the speech of conviction presented at the end of Chapter 14) and a short unit of refutation directed to one of her arguments.

Comments

(Thoughts recorded by the opponent as he listens to advocate's speech)

True, but are these necessarily beneficial?

True, but what if you miss a payment?

True, but what if you need money? You can borrow, but you have to pay interest on your own money! Cash settlement results in loss of money benefits.

Outline

(Including one point of advocate's speech):

II. Buying insurance provides a systematic, compulsory savings.
   A. Each month you get a notice. (Banks, etc., don't provide service.)
   B. Once money is invested, it is saved. (You can't get it out at your discretion.)

In the following abbreviated statement, notice how the four steps of refutation (stating the argument, stating what you will prove, presenting proof, and drawing a conclusion) are incorporated. For purposes of analysis, each of the four steps is enumerated.

[1] The speaker has said that buying insurance provides a systematic, compulsory savings. [2] Her assumption is that "systematic, compulsory savings" is a *benefit* of buying insurance while you are young. But I believe that just the opposite is true—I believe that there are at least two serious disadvantages resulting from this. [3] First, the system is *so* compulsory that if you miss a payment you stand to lose your entire savings and all benefits. Most insurance contracts include a clause giving you a thirty-day grace period, after which the policy is canceled . . . [evidence]. Second, if you need money desperately, you have to take a loan on your policy. The end result of such a loan is that you have to pay interest in order to borrow your own money . . . [evidence]. [4] From this analysis, I think you can see that the "systematic, compulsory saving" is more a disadvantage than an advantage for young people who are trying to save money.

Assignment A	**Working with a classmate, select a debatable proposition and clear the wording with your professor. Phrase the proposition so that the first speaker is in favor of the proposal. Speaker A presents a four- to six-minute speech of conviction in support of the proposition. Speaker B presents a four- to six-minute speech of conviction in refutation of the proposal.**
Assignment B	**Working with a classmate, select a debatable proposition and clear the wording with your professor. Phrase the proposition so that the first speaker is in favor of the proposal. Speaker A presents a two- to four-minute speech of conviction in support of the proposal. Speaker B presents a two- to four-minute speech of conviction in refutation of the proposal. Each speaker then gets two minutes to question the opponent, after which each speaker gets two minutes to summarize his or her case.**
Assignment C	**Working with a classmate, select a debatable proposition and clear the wording with your professor. Phrase the proposition so that the first speaker is in favor of the proposal. Speaker A presents a four-minute speech in support of proposal; Speaker B presents a five-minute speech in refutation; Speaker A presents a two-minute speech of summary-refutation.**

Criteria for evaluation will include soundness of argument and skill in refutation.

The Price of Dying: Speech of Conviction

The following two speeches are presented to illustrate the debate format. The first speech is a speech of conviction with two reasons in support of the proposition. The second is a speech of refutation.[2]

Analysis

Speech

After a short introductory statement, the proposition is clearly presented.

Notice how the speaker defines the key term of the proposition.

Here the two reasons in support of the proposition are clearly stated.

In 1963, when Jessica Mitford's exposé of funeral practices, *The American Way of Death*, was published, such a furor was created that some reforms occurred. Now, more than twelve years later, however, most of the same problems that prompted her to write the book still exist. Today I am here to argue the proposition that the Federal government, through each of the fifty states, should set prices for various types of funerals. By "set prices" I mean that each state, in consultation with funeral directors, will determine a fair price for services and materials for a range of funerals running the gamut from simple to elaborate. I base my case on two points: one, there is a need to protect the individual in times of grief and stress; and, two, the individual will benefit from the state setting the prices.

The speaker moves on to statement and development of the first reason.

Notice how source material is cited.

Let's look at the first reason: there is a need to protect the individual in time of grief and stress. This reason has three aspects to it. First, under the status quo, the funeral director can appeal to the guilt of the consumer at a time when he's under great pressure. According to Leroy Bowman, in his book *The American Funeral*, 90 percent of the people are at a loss as to how to proceed—they leave details in the hands of the funeral director. The funeral director is then able to take advantage of the situation to sell a person more than what he wants or needs. By appealing to guilt, the funeral director is able to convince a family that the funeral is an outward sign of the esteem in which the family held their loved one. The guiding statement of the funeral director is "get the money while the tears are still flowing." Such a procedure is not in the best interests of the consumer.

Second, according to *Changing Times*, February 1975, the cost of a funeral is not a set figure that the consumer can weigh and consider but is determined by the family's ability to pay. One major determinant of price is the cost of the casket. What the funeral director doesn't tell the family is that the difference between a $600 funeral and a $10,000 funeral is the casket. According to Jessica Mitford, the better off the family, the more pressure is placed on it to buy the expensive casket. Also, what the funeral director doesn't share with the family is that he is likely to be selling his casket at prices representing a 100 percent markup. Remember, the grieved family cannot shop around—usually, the funeral director already has the body in his possession. A second determinant of price is the

---

[2] These two speeches are based upon a debate between Susan Anthony and Dean Feldmeyer presented at the University of Cincinnati.

Analysis

Speech

funeral director's tendency to convince the family to have an open-casket funeral, requiring embalming and often restoration. The fact is that in many states embalming is not required if the body is not to remain above ground; moreover, few clergy or psychologists recommend the open-casket funeral. According to *Changing Times*, the average cost of a funeral in 1975 is $2,000, or more than double the price of a respectable closed-casket funeral with a modest casket.

The second reason is also clearly stated and developed; however, in this section the speaker provides no documentation for her assertions.

My second reason in support of the proposition is that at least two benefits would accrue from having the state set prices. The immediate benefit is to take pricing out of the hands of the funeral director and put it into the hands of an impartial agency. Second, a person could be assured that no matter where he went in the state, prices would be fair and preconsidered for him.

The state could establish an agency similar to the Civil Aeronautics Board which would oversee funeral prices, much the way the CAB oversees airline ticket prices. Funeral directors could appeal to the board for raises in prices when conditions warranted, but consumer interests would be protected. An individual has a right to honor the dead as simply or as elaborately as he wishes, but his decision should be based upon an analysis of what is available and not under the pressure of a funeral director.

The speaker concludes with a summary of her two arguments.

In conclusion, then, I favor state regulation of funeral prices—one, because there is a need to protect the individual in times of grief and stress and, two, because the consumer would benefit from such a situation.

The Price of Dying: Refutation Speech

Analysis

Speech

The speaker opens by showing his position on the proposition. The speech is a direct refutation of each of his opponent's points.

I agree with my opponent that an unscrupulous funeral director can extort excessive amounts of money from an individual in times of grief and stress. I do not agree with my opponent that the problem is so great that we need to create a new Federal agency to set funeral prices.

Notice how throughout the speech the speaker states the point to be refuted, states his position, and then presents his material.

First, she says there is a need to protect the individual in time of grief and stress. Protect the family from what? I argue that the great majority of funeral directors are doing just what they are supposed to be doing, offering a needed service at prices that the family can afford. Has my opponent shown you that the people are up in arms over some alleged unethical practices? First she tells us that people are at a loss as to how to proceed and thus at the mercy of

Analysis   Speech

unscrupulous funeral directors. Has she shown where people are forced to buy services they don't want or don't need? No. How do people select a funeral director? According to funeral directors themselves, most of their business comes from referrals. When someone has recently had a funeral in the family, someone else asks who they went to and how they were treated. The fact is that most funeral directors are scrupulously honest, for they are in competition. The director who cannot get his share of business will go out of business.

My opponent says that the cost of a funeral is not a set figure but is determined by the family's ability to pay. I have two comments to make on this point. The first is that I applaud the funeral director for considering ability to pay. The fact is that every funeral director must do some funerals for charity; and to make up that they, just like doctors, are likely to charge more for a wealthy family that can afford to pay. But, secondly, I don't see that this is a real problem, for most funeral homes are not "hiding" costs. Although funeral homes, like doctors, do not advertise directly, such places as Moody Funeral Homes and Spring Grove Cemetery encourage people to come in and discuss what they can expect for a given price.

Throughout the speech, the speaker attempts to gain the offensive by challenging his opponent to give more evidence. He is, of course, taking a gamble. If she does give more evidence the line of argument will work against him; but if she does not, he can win the point by showing her failure. Before taking this line of attack, one must be reasonably sure that the opponent cannot provide more material.

In addition, my opponent claims that there is an unfair markup on caskets. I didn't hear any evidence on this point. What I did hear was that the average funeral in 1975 is $2,000. I argue that this *guesstimate* by *Changing Times* is not based upon any facts. The last year that a survey of costs was taken was in 1969; at that time the average cost was $926. Now inflation has undoubtedly raised that price. But more than 100 percent? I challenge my opponent to give me concrete evidence on this point.

She then goes on to say that funeral directors take advantage of grief to convince the family that they should have an open casket. She says that neither psychologists nor clergy suggest this practice (again, if you will notice, with no evidence). In direct contradiction of this conclusion, Dr. Edgar Jackson, in his book *For the Living*, says "the viewing of the body can be a vital part of coming to terms with reality." No, he doesn't advocate open-casket ceremonies, but he does advocate that the immediate family view the remains. The memory picture is no more illogical than the memory itself.

Analysis

Like his opponent, the speaker uses no documentation for this argument.

Speech

I have shown you that there is no need for fee regulation. But even if there were a need, I do not believe that the individual would benefit from having the state set prices. Funerals are just not analogous to airline ticket prices. In every state we have differences between urban and rural areas, large cities and small, rich areas and poor. How is any agency going to establish any meaningful price list that will meet the needs of every community? Second, how can the consumer be assured that the state has sanctioned a service that will meet all the families' needs? A Federal program smacks of a "Here's the choices—take them or leave them" policy. Under the present system, the consumer determines what he wants or needs.

Because of the way he attacks his opponent's arguments directly and supports most of his statements, this is an acceptable speech of refutation.

Because there is no need to protect the individual and because no real benefits would come from asking the state to set prices, I argue against the state setting prices for funerals.

ALTERNATE FORMS

PART FIVE

17

PROBLEM-SOLVING GROUP DISCUSSION

The characteristic American response to problem solving is "Let's form a committee." Despite the many jokes about committees and the often justified impatience with them, the committee system and the group discussion it encourages can and should be an effective way of dealing with common problems. For our purposes, discussion will be defined as a systematic form of speech in which two or more persons meet face to face and interact orally to arrive at a common goal. The goal may be to gain understanding of a topic, it may be for the entertainment of the participants, and in some situations it may be for therapeutic purposes, but in this chapter we will focus on problem-solving discussion. By problem-solving discussion we mean one in which the group meets to accomplish a particular task (for example, recommend whether the group should donate to Easter Seals and if so how much) or to arrive at a solution to a common problem (for example, consider what the group can do to enlarge its membership). In addition to competence in the use of fundamental speech principles, effective problem-solving discussion requires knowledge of the forms of discussion, an understanding of the problem-solving method, and guidelines for leadership and participation in problem-solving discussion.

THE FORMS OF DISCUSSION

Practically speaking, group discussions are either public or private. Since these two basic forms influence goals and procedures, let us examine each to show their characteristics and some of their advantages and disadvantages as well.

Public Discussion

In a public discussion, the group is discussing for the information or enjoyment of a listening audience as much as they are for the satisfaction of the participating members. As such, public discussions have much in common with public speaking. Two prevalent forms of public discussion are the symposium and the panel.

Symposium A symposium is a discussion in which a limited number of participants (usually three to five) present individual speeches of approximately the same length dealing with the same subject area to an audience. After the planned speeches, the participants in the symposium may discuss their reactions with each other or respond to questions from the listening audience. Although the symposium is a common form of public discussion, participation in one is often a dull and frustrating experience. Despite the potential for interaction, a symposium is usually characterized by long, sometimes unrelated individual speeches. Moreover, the part designated for questions is often shortened or deleted because "our time is about up." Discussion implies interaction—a symposium often omits this vital aspect. If the participants make their prepared speeches short enough so that at least half of the available time can be spent on real interaction, a symposium can be interesting and stimulating. So far as meeting the goals of discussion, a good symposium is much more difficult than it appears; however, as a public speaking assignment, the symposium may be very beneficial. Rather than solving a problem, a symposium is more effective in shedding light on or explaining various aspects of a problem.

Panel Discussion A panel discussion is one in which the participants, usually from four to eight, discuss a topic spontaneously, under the direction of a leader and following a planned agenda. After the formal discussion, the audience is often encouraged to question the participants. So the discussion can be seen and heard by the audience, the group is seated in a semicircle, with the person chairing it in the middle, to get a good view of the audience and the panelists. Since the discussion is for an audience, the panelists need to be sure that they meet the requirements of public speaking. Because a panel discussion encourages spontaneity and interaction, it can be very stimulating for both a listening audience and the participants themselves. The panel will work as a form of problem-solving discussion.

Private Discussion

Although your classroom assignment may be in the form of a panel, the majority of discussions that you participate in will be private. Private discussions are ones in which the participants meet to solve a problem or exchange ideas on a particular topic without the presence of an onlooking or participating audience. Committees convened for the purpose of formulating a recommendation to be submitted to the larger legislative body, to another committee, or to the various individuals or agencies authorized to consider such recommendations engage in private discussion. Likewise, individuals who meet informally for the purpose of sharing ideas on topics of mutual interest engage in private discussion. Private discussions are most productive when they are conducted in an atmosphere where all members of the group have equal prominence. The best seating arrangement is a full circle, so that each person can see and talk with everyone else. Sometimes, as a stimulant for study groups, a "resource" person sits in with the group to suggest ideas and to add needed information. Because of the proximity of the participants in private discussion, the group need not be so concerned with public speaking. Furthermore, since no audience is present, the group can adjust its time to meet the needs of the topic. If the question cannot be resolved in one sitting, the group can meet later.

PREPARATION FOR PROBLEM-SOLVING DISCUSSION

For either public or private discussion, preparation requires an understanding of the problem-solving method: phrasing the problem, analyzing the problem, suggesting solutions, and selecting the best solution. This method can be used as both a guideline to preparation and as a basic outline for the discussion itself.

Phrasing the Problem

Although problems for discussion may be drawn from any subject area, they should be (1) of interest to the group, (2) controversial, (3) capable of being discussed within the time available, and (4) written in question form. Participants' interest is a primary test of topic for all forms of speechmaking, including group discussion. Discussion, however, also requires that the topic, the problem, should be controversial. If all discussants have about the same point of view or if the subject matter leaves little room for interpretation, there is really very little need for discussion. "How to make a book" may be a satisfactory topic for an informative speech; for a discussion, however, the problem would generate very little collective reaction. On the other hand, the problem "Should *Catcher in the Rye* be included on the required reading list for tenth-grade English?" would leave room for various viewpoints. Even if a problem is interesting and controversial, it should not be considered for discussion unless it can be discussed within the time available. In an informal social discussion, there is value in coping with a problem regardless of whether consensus can be reached. For most group discussions, however, the resolution of the problem is the reason for meeting, and until or unless a satisfactory conclusion is reached, the discussion is for nought. If the problem is so broad that discussion can only begin to scratch the surface, then a more limited aspect should be considered.

Finally, a discussion problem should be stated in question form. Questions elicit response. Since the goal of discussion is to stimulate group thinking, the problem itself and all of the subheadings are phrased as questions. In phrasing the question, make sure it considers only one subject, that it is impartial, and that the words used can be defined objectively. "Should the United States cut back the foreign aid program and welfare?" considers two different questions; "Should the United States recognize those wretched Palestinians?" would be neither impartial nor definable.

As you consider various phrasings, you will discover that changes in wording affect the kind of response you are seeking. In order to test whether your wording correlates with your intentions, you should understand the implications of questions of fact, questions of value, and questions of policy.

Questions of Fact   These consider the truth or falsity of an assertion. Implied in the question is the theoretical possibility of verifying the answer. For instance, "How much rain fell today?" is a question of fact because rain can be measured and recorded. "Is Smith guilty of robbery?" is also a question of fact. Smith either committed the crime or he did not.

Questions of Value   These consider relative goodness or badness. They are characterized by the inclusion of some evaluative word such as "good," "cool," "reliable," "effective," "worthy." The purpose of the question of value is to compare a subject with one or more members of the same class. "What was the best movie last year?" is a question of value. Although we can set up criteria for "best" and measure our choice against those criteria, there is no way of verifying our findings. The answer is still a matter of judgment, not a matter of fact. "Is socialism superior to capitalism?" "Is a small college education better than a large college education?" are both questions of value.

Questions of Policy   These questions judge whether a future action should be taken. The question is phrased to arrived at a solution or to test a tentative solution to a problem or a felt need. "What should we do to lower the crime rate?" seeks a solution that would best solve the problem of the increase in crime. "Should the University give equal amounts of money to men's and to women's athletics?" provides a tentative solution to the problem of how we can achieve equity in financial support of athletics. The inclusion of the word "should" in all questions of policy makes them the easiest to recognize and the easiest to phrase of all discussion questions.

**Analyzing
the Problem**

Once the group is in agreement about exactly what the problem is, it should move on to the next step, analyzing the problem. Analysis means determining the nature of the problem: its size, its causes, the forces that create or sustain it, the criteria for evaluating solutions. Sometimes analysis can take only a few minutes, at other times it may take longer. Both in preparation and in the discussion itself, analysis is the stage of problem solving that is most easily sloughed off. It is the natural tendency of the researcher or the group to want to move directly to possible solutions. For instance, if your problem is to determine what should be done to solve the campus parking problem, you may be inclined to start by listing possible solutions immediately. And because this procedure sounds as if it is the logical beginning, the tendency is then to pursue these prematurely offered solutions. However, a solution or a plan can work only *if* it solves the problem at hand. Before you can shape a plan you must decide what obstacles the plan must meet, what symptoms the plan must eliminate, and with what other criteria the plan must deal. Before you even begin to suggest a solution, you should check to make sure that the following questions about the problem have been answered:

I. What is its size and scope?

   A. What are its symptoms? (What can we identify that shows that something is wrong or needs to be changed?)

   B. What are its causes? (What forces created it, sustain it, or otherwise keep it from being solved?)

II. What criteria should be used to test the solutions? Specifically, what checklist must the solution meet to best solve this problem? Must the plan eliminate the symptoms, be implemented within present resources, and so on?

**Suggesting Possible
Solutions**

For most problems, there are many possible solutions. Although you need not identify every one of the possibilities, you should not be content with your work until you have considered a wide variety of solutions.

But if you are considering a problem that needs only a single "yes" or "no" solution, your procedure may be altered. Should support for women's sports be increased? This question has only two possible answers. Still, you may need to suggest other solutions for comparison.

How do you come up with solutions? One way is to use brainstorming, stating ideas at random until you have compiled a long list. In a good ten- to fifteen-minute brainstorming session you may think of ten to twenty solutions by yourself. Depending upon the nature of the topic a group may come up with 100 possibilities. Of course, some solutions will come through your reading, your interviews with authorities, or from your observation.

Determining the Best Solution

In your preparation you probably will not want to spend much time trying to figure out the best solution, for the best solution should emerge through the group discussion itself. During actual discussion, if the group has analyzed the problem carefully and has suggested enough solutions, then the final step involves only matching each solution against the criteria. For instance, if you have determined that hiring more patrols, putting in closed-circuit TV, and locking outside doors after 9 P.M. are three possible solutions to the problem of reducing crime on campus, then you begin to measure each against the criteria. The one meeting the most criteria or that meets several criteria most effectively would then be selected.

Now let us put these all together with a sample (and somewhat abbreviated) outline that would help the individual get his own thoughts together and help the group proceed logically. The group is being convened to discuss "meeting the needs of the commuter."

1. State the Problem—Suggested wordings:
   What should be done to improve the commuter's campus life?
   What should be done to increase or enlarge commuter opportunities on campus?
   What should be done to better integrate the commuter into the social, political, and extracurricular aspects of student life on campus?

2. Analyze the Problem of Integrating Commuters

   I. What is size and scope of the problem?
      A. How many commuters are there?
      B. What is ratio between students living on or close by campus and commuters?
      C. How do commuters spend their campus time?
         1. Are commuters involved in social organizations? How many? What ratio?
         2. Are commuters involved in political organizations? How many? What ratio?
         3. Are commuters involved in extracurricular organizations? How many? What ratio?

   II. What are the causes of the problem?
      A. Do commuters want to be involved?
      B. Do on-campus students discriminate against commuters?
      C. Does the commuter's work life or home life inhibit him?
      D. Is commuting time or method a problem?

   E. Are meeting times for groups discriminatory against the commuter?

III. What criteria should be used to test solutions?
   A. Will commuters favor?
   B. Will it cope with discrimination (if discrimination exists)?
   C. Will it interfere with commuter needs (work, travel, and the like)?
   D. Will it fit into commuter's time schedule?

3. State Possible Solutions
(The list can be begun at this point—other possible solutions will be revealed later.)
A commuter information center?
Commuter representation on Social Board? University Student Union Board?
Others to be added as they come to mind.

4. Determine Best Solution
(To be completed during discussion.)

LEADERSHIP IN PROBLEM-SOLVING DISCUSSION

A problem-solving discussion will not work well without effective leadership. Ordinarily we think of an appointed or elected individual acting as leader and all others in the group acting as content contributors. Although that is the way it is often done, it does not have to be that way. A group can be so organized that everyone shares the burden of leadership. Thus, a group can have leadership whether or not it has a designated leader. In order to decide whether your group should vest leadership responsibilities in one person or not, you must understand the advantages and disadvantages of each kind of situation.

When someone is appointed or elected leader, the group looks to him for leadership. If he is a good leader, the group will benefit. Each participant can concentrate on considering the issues being raised, confident that the leader will guide the group justly. Disadvantages are related to inadequacy of the leader: when that person is unsure, the group may ramble about aimlessly; when the leader dominates, participants do not feel free to contribute spontaneously and the discussion follows a path predetermined by the leader; when the leader is unskilled, the group can become frustrated and short-tempered. Good leadership is a necessity. When the appointed leader cannot provide it, the group suffers.

When the group is leaderless, everyone has the right and the obligation to show leadership. Ordinarily, leadership will emerge from one, two, or perhaps three members of the group. Since no one has been given the mantle of leadership, everyone is on equal footing, and the discussion can be more spontaneous. Disadvantages are seen in a group where either no one assumes leadership or where a few compete for leadership. In such situations, the discussion becomes "leadershipless." Depending upon the qualities of the participants, a leaderless discussion can arrive at truly group decisions or it can be a rambling, meaningless collage of fact and opinion. If you have only one round of discussion, I would suggest trying the method that the group would have most confidence in to begin with.

Regardless of whether a leader is appointed or whether several members of the group share leadership, there are certain leadership responsibilities that must be met. In this next section, let us assume that you have or wish to assume the responsibilities of leadership.

Establish a Climate

Your first job is to set up a comfortable physical setting that will encourage interaction. The leader is in charge of such physical matters as heat, light, and seating. Make sure the room is at a good comfortable temperature. Make sure that there is enough lighting, and most important make sure the seating arrangements are conducive to spirited interaction.

Too often, seating is too formal or too informal for the best discussion. By too formal, I mean board-of-directors style. Imagine the long polished oak table with the chairman at the head, leading lieutenants at right and left, and the rest of the people down the line. Since seating may be an indication of status, how the seating is arranged can facilitate or kill real interaction. In the board-of-directors style, a boss-and-subordinates pattern emerges. People are less likely to speak until they are asked to do so. Moreover, no one has a really good view of all the people present. However, an excessively informal seating may also inhibit interaction—especially if people sit together in small groups or behind one another.

The ideal is the circle. Here, everyone can see everyone else. At least physically, everyone has equal status. If the meeting place does not have a round table, you may be better off with either no table at all or a setting of tables that make a square at which the members can come close to the circle arrangement.

Plan the Agenda

A second leader responsibility is to plan the agenda. You should do this alone or in consultation with the group. When possible, the agenda should be in the hands of the group several days before the discussion. How much preparation any individual member will make is based upon many factors, but unless the group has an agenda beforehand, members will not have an opportunity for careful preparation. Too often, when no agenda is planned, the group discussion is a haphazard affair, often frustrating and usually unsatisfying.

What goes in the agenda? Usually a sketch of some of the things that need to be accomplished. In a problem-solving discussion, the agenda should include a suggested procedure for handling the problem. In essence it is an outline form of the steps of problem solving discussed earlier in this chapter. So if you are leading a discussion on what should be done to better integrate the campus commuter into the social, political, and extracurricular aspects of student life, the following would be a satisfactory agenda:

    I. What is the size and the scope of the commuter problem?

    II. What are the causes for commuters not being involved in social, political, and extracurricular activities?

    III. What criteria should be used to test possible solutions to the problem?

    IV. What are some of the possible solutions to the problem?

    V. What one solution or combination of solutions will work best to solve the problem?

Direct the Flow of Discussion

The leader is responsible for directing the flow of discussion. It is in this area that leadership skill is most tested. Let us examine carefully several of the most important elements of this responsibility.

Discussants Should Have Equal Opportunity to Speak Conclusions are valid only when they represent the thinking of the entire group. Yet, in discussions some people are more likely or more willing to express themselves than others. For instance, if a typical eight-man discussion group is left to its own devices, two or three may tend to speak as much as the other five or six together; furthermore, one or two members may contribute little if anything. At the beginning of a discussion, at least, you must operate under the assumption that every member of the group has something to contribute. To ensure opportunity for equal participation, those who tend to dominate must be held somewhat in check, and those who are content to observe must be brought into the discussion more.

Accomplishing this ideal balance is a real test of leadership. If an ordinarily reluctant talker is embarrassed by another member of the group, he may become even more reluctant to participate. Likewise, if a talkative yet valuable member of the group is constantly restrained, he may lose his value.

Let us first consider the handling of the shy or reluctant speaker. Often, apparently reluctant speakers want to talk but cannot get the floor. As leader you may solve this problem by clearing the road for that speaker. For instance, Mary may give visual and verbal clues of her desire to speak; she may come up on the edge of her seat, she may look as if she wants to talk, or she may even start to say something. Because the reluctant speaker in this posture may often relinquish the opportunity if another more aggressive person competes to be heard, you can help considerably with a comment such as "Just a second, Jim, I think Mary has something she wants to say here." Of course, the moment that Mary is sitting back in her chair with a somewhat vacant look is not the time for such a statement. A second method of drawing out the reluctant speaker is to phrase a question that is sure to elicit some answer and then perhaps some discussion. The most appropriate kind of question is one requiring an opinion rather than a fact. For instance, "Mary, what do you think of the validity of this approach to combatting crime?" is much better than "Mary, do you have anything to say here?" Not only is it specific, but also it requires more than a yes or no answer. Furthermore, such an opinion question will not embarrass Mary if she has no factual material to contribute. Tactful handling of the shy or reluctant speaker can pay big dividends. You may get some information that could not have been brought out in any other way; moreover, when Mary contributes a few times, it builds up her confidence, which in turn makes it easier for her to respond later when she has more to say. Of course, there are times when one or more members do not have anything worth saying, because they just are not prepared. Under such circumstances it is best for you to leave him or her alone.

As a leader you must also use tact with the overzealous speaker. Remember that Jim, the talkative person, may be talkative because he has done his homework—he may have more information than any other member of the group. If you turn him off, the group may suffer immensely. After he has finished talking, try statements such as: "Jim, that's a very valuable bit of material; let's see whether we can get some reactions from the other members of the group on this issue." Notice that a statement of this kind does not stop him; it suggests that he should hold off for a while. A difficult kind of participant to deal with is the one who must be heard regardless of whether he has anything to say or not. If subtle reminders are ineffective with this individual, you may have to say, "Jim, I know you want to talk, but you're just not giving anyone else a chance. Would you wait until we've heard everyone else on this point?" Of course, the person who may be the most difficult to control is the leader himself. Leaders often engage in little dialogues with each member of the group. They sometimes exercise so much control that participants believe that they can talk only in response to the leader.

There are three common patterns of group discussion (see Figure 17.1, in which the lines represent the flow of discussion among the eight participants). Discussion A represents a leader-dominated group. The lack of interaction often leads to a rigid, formal, and usually poor discussion. Discussion B represents a more spontaneous group. Since three people dominate and a few are not heard, however, conclusions will not represent group thinking. Discussion C represents something closer to the ideal pattern. It illustrates a great deal of spontaneity, a total group representation, and theoretically at least the greatest possibility for reliable conclusions.

Keep the Discussion on the Topic   Not only must the leader see to it that the key ideas are discussed, but also he or she needs to get maximum value out of each point that is made. The skill that best helps here is appropriate questioning.

Although the members of any group bring a variety of skills, information, and degrees of motivation to the group, they do not always operate at peak efficiency without help from the leader. Perhaps one of the most effective tools of effective leadership is the ability to question appropriately. This skill involves knowing when to ask questions and knowing what kinds of questions to ask.

By and large, the leader should refrain from questions that can be answered yes or no. To ask a group member whether he or she is satisfied with a point that was just made will not lead very far, for after the yes or no answer you must ask another question to draw the person out or you must change the subject. The two most effective types of questions are those that call for supporting information or the completely open-ended question that gives the

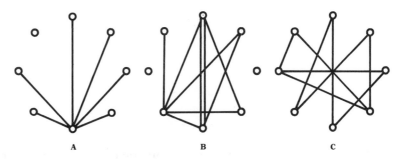

A   B   C

Figure 17.1   Patterns of group discussion.

member complete freedom of response. For instance, rather than asking John whether he has had any professors that were particularly good lecturers, you could say, "John, what are some of the characteristics that made your favorite lecturers particularly effective?" or, "John, from your experience in listening to speakers, what would you select as most important elements of speaker effectiveness?"

When to ask questions is particularly important. Although we could list fifteen to twenty circumstances, let us focus on four purposes of questioning:

1. *To focus the discussion:* Individual statements usually have a point; the statements themselves relate to a larger point being made; and the general discussion relates to an issue or to an agenda item. You can use questions to determine a speaker's point or to determine the relationship of the point to the issue or agenda item; for instance: "Are you saying that the instances of marijuana leading to hard-drug use don't indicate a direct causal relationship?" Or, to what has just been said: "How does that information relate to the point that Mary just made?" Or, to ask about an issue or an agenda item: "In what way does this information relate to whether or not marijuana is a problem?"

2. *To probe for information:* Many statements need to be developed, supported, or in some way dealt with. Yet often members of a group apparently ignore or accept a point without probing it. When the point seems important, the leader should do something with it. For instance, on a question of source, you can say: "Where did you get that information, Jack?" Or, to develop a point: "That seems pretty important, what do we have that corroborates the point?" Or, to test the strength of a point: "Does that statement represent the thinking of the group?" Or, to generate discussion: "That point sounds rather controversial—why should we accept the point as stated?"

3. *To initiate discussion:* During a discussion, there are times when lines of development are apparently ignored, when the group seems ready to agree before sufficient testing has taken place. At these times, it is up to the leader to suggest a starting point for further discussion; for instance: "OK, we seem to have a pretty good grasp of the nature of the problem, but we haven't looked at any causes yet. What are some of the causes?"

4. *To deal with interpersonal problems that develop:* Sometimes the leader can help a member ventilate very personal feel-

ings; for instance: "Ted, I've heard you make some strong statements on this point. Would you care to share them with us?" At times, a group may attack a person instead of the information that is being presented. Here you can say: "I know Charley presented the point, but let's look at the merits of the information presented. Do we have any information that goes counter to this point?"

Questions by themselves are not going to make a discussion. In fact, some questions can hurt the discussion that is taking place. The effective leader uses questions sparingly but decisively.

Summarize Frequently   Often a group talks for a considerable period, then takes a vote on how they feel about the subject. A good problem-solving discussion group should move in an orderly manner toward intermediate conclusions represented by summary statements seeking group consensus. For instance, on the question "What should be done to lower the crime rate on campus?" the group would have to reach consensus on each of the following questions:

What is the problem?

What are the symptoms of the problem? (Draw intermediate conclusion; ask whether group agrees.)

What are the causes? (Draw intermediate conclusion on each cause separately or after all causes have been considered; ask whether group agrees.)

What criteria should be used to test the solutions?

What is one criterion? (Draw conclusions about each criterion.)

What are some of the possible conclusions? (Determine whether all possible solutions have been brought up.)

What is the best solution?

How do each of the solutions meet the criteria? (Discuss each and draw conclusions about each; ask whether group agrees.)

Which solution best meets the criteria? (The conclusion to this final question concludes the discussion; ask whether all agree.)

During the discussion the group might draw six, eight, ten, or even fifteen conclusions before it is able to arrive at the answer to the topic question. The point is that the group should not arrive at the final conclusion until each of the subordinate questions is answered to the satisfaction of the entire group.

It is up to the leader to point up these conclusions by summarizing what has been said and seeking consensus on a conclusion. Everyone in the group should realize when the group has really arrived at some decision. If left to its own devices, a group will discuss a point for a while, then move on to another before a conclusion is drawn. The leader must sense when enough has been said to reach a consensus. Then he must phrase the conclusion, subject it to testing, and move on to another area. You should become familiar with phrases that can be used during the discussion:

"I think most of us are stating the same points. Are we really in agreement that . . ." (State the conclusion.)

"We've been discussing this for a while and I think I sense an agreement. Let me state it, and then we'll see whether it does summarize group feeling." (State the conclusion.)

"Now we're getting on to another area. Let's make sure that we are really agreed on the point we've just finished." (State the conclusion.)

"Are we ready to summarize our feelings on this point?" (State the conclusion.)

Maintain Necessary Control   A leader must maintain control of the discussion. Remember, absence of leadership leads to chaos. Group members need to feel that someone is in charge. If the group has a set of formal rules, be sure that the rules are followed (at times bending is necessary, but total breaking does not help the group). As leader, remember that some members will be playing negative roles in the discussion; do not let them spoil the outcome. You are in charge. You are responsible. You have authority. You will need to exercise it on occasion for the benefit of the group. If John is about to talk for the fortieth time, it is up to you to harness him. If Jack and Mary are constantly sparring with each other, it is up to you to harmonize their differences. If something internal or external threatens the work of the group, it is up to you to deal with it. Also, when the group has solved its problem, end the discussion smoothly. Some discussion groups meet by time instead of by problem. Just because you are scheduled to discuss for an hour does not mean that you cannot stop in forty-five minutes if you have the job done.

RESPONSIBILITIES OF DISCUSSANTS

Even the most successful leader will fail if the members of the discussion group do not fulfill their responsibilities. Good discussion is characterized by responsible contribution, objectivity, and accomplishment of various task and maintenance functions.

Discussants Should Contribute Responsibly

One of the greatest differences between a group discussion and an informal social discussion is in the quality of the developmental material included. Responsible discussion is characterized by documented factual material, careful analysis of every item of information, and sound conclusions and evaluations about and from the factual material. Let us examine each of these characteristics. Since you need documented factual material, your preparation should be extensive. The more material you have sampled, the better knowledge you will have of the subject and the more valuable your contributions will be. As a guideline to quantity of resource material, you should have access to considerably more than you could get into the discussion. It is not uncommon for discussants to be familiar with eight or ten sources. Since, of course, you cannot predict all of the ideas that will be covered in the discussion or when you will be speaking, you cannot prepare your actual contributions ahead of time. Nevertheless, you should be familiar enough with the material that you can find any item you need when you need it. Usually, you will bring your sources with you to the discussion. If you are disallowed the use of the actual sources by your professor, then make note cards containing all the material you are likely to need for the discussion.

A second characteristic of responsible contribution—careful analysis of every item of information—is shown by raising questions about and probing into contributions of others. Your obligation does not end with the reading into the record of items of information. Once an item of data has been submitted, it is the obligation of the membership to determine whether the item is accurate, typical, consistent, and otherwise valid. Suppose that in a discussion on reducing crime, a person mentioned that, according to *U.S. News & World Report*, crime had risen 33 percent in the past five years, the group should not leave this statement until they have explored it fully. What was the specific source of the data? On what were the data based? What years are being referred to? Is this consistent with other material? Is any counter material available? Now, the purpose of these questions is not to debate the data, but to test them. If these data are partly true, questionable, or relevant only to certain kinds of crime, a different conclusion or set of conclusions would be appropriate.

Sound conclusions about and from the factual material, a third characteristic of responsible contribution, refers to the real goal of the discussion itself. Discussants must pool information to provide a basis for conclusions about the topic question. Students sometimes blame the sterility of their discussion on the need to present information responsibly. Yet sterility is a result of poor discussants, not the format. You can still offer opinions, but unlike social sessions in which opinions substitute for data, in discussion, your opinions are based upon the previously tested materials.

Discussion Is Characterized by Objectivity

Discussion is a method of group inquiry. Unlike the debater who seeks to impose his opinions and who desires agreement, acquiescence, or approval, using only the data that will prove his point, discussants seek to ask questions, to share ideas, and to work together toward mutually satisfactory answers utilizing all the data at their disposal. Let us focus on two recommendations for ensuring objectivity of approach. First, report data, don't associate yourself with it. If you reported that crime has risen 33 percent in the past five years, don't feel that because you presented the data that you must defend it. An excellent way of presenting data with a degree of disassociation is illustrated by the following: "According to *U.S. News & World Report*, crime has risen 33 percent in the past five years. That seems like a startling statistic. I wonder whether anyone else found either any substantiating or any contradictory data?" Presenting data in this way tells the group that you want discussion of the data and that, whether it is substantiated or disproven, you have no personal relationship with it. Contrast that disassociative approach with the following statement: "I think crime is going up at a fantastic rate. Why, I found that crime has gone up 33 percent in the past five years, and we just can't put up with that kind of thing." This speaker is taking a position with his data. Since anyone who questions the data or the conclusions is going to have to contend with the speaker, there's a good chance that the discussion that follows will not be the most objective.

A second recommendation for ensuring objectivity is to solicit all viewpoints on every major issue. Suppose you were discussing the question "Should financial support of women's sports be raised?" Suppose that after extensive reading you believed that it should. If in the discussion you spoke only to support your position and you took issue with every bit of contrary material, you would not be responding objectively. Although there is nothing wrong with formulating tentative opinions based upon your research, in the discussion you should present material objectively whether it supports or opposes your tentative claims. If the group draws a conclusion that corresponds to your tentative conclusion, fine. At least all views have had the opportunity to be presented. If the group draws the opposite conclusion, you are not put in a defensive position. By being objective, you may find that during the discussion your views will change many times. Remember, if the best answer to the topic question could be found without discussion, the discussion would not be necessary.

**Discussants Should
Fill Positive Roles**

Everyone in the group has a responsibility for certain functions within the group. These functions are served as participants carry out various roles. A role is a kind of behavior that you determine for yourself or that is determined for you by expectations of the group. Sometimes a person plays one role and one role alone throughout the duration of the discussion. At other times a given person may play several roles simultaneously or alternately, and, of course, more than one person can play a given role in a discussion. In a successful group discussion all the positive roles are usually played sometime during the discussion; an unsuccessful discussion group may be one in which no one plays the positive roles or one in which negative role-playing predominates. Let us examine the most common and most essential positive roles.

Group roles consist of both task and maintenance functions. The *task* function involves doing the job in the best manner; the *maintenance* function involves how the group handles the way they talk about their task, the nature of the interaction, and dealing with the feelings of the group. In a successful group discussion, both functions are usually satisfied. Thus, when we analyze a discussion, we look first to see how and whether they solved the problem; second, we look to see how well the group worked together, whether members like, respect, and understand other members of the group.

Task Roles   In most groups there are at least four major task roles that can be identified.

1. The *information or opinion giver* provides content for the discussion. Actual information provides about 50 percent of what is done in a group. Without information and well-considered opinions, the group will not have the material from which to draw its decisions. Probably everyone in the group plays this role during the discussion. Nevertheless, there are usually one or more persons who have really done their homework. Either as a result of past experience with this or a related problem, long conversations with people who have worked with similar problems, or a great deal of study, these persons are relied upon or called upon to provide the facts. In some groups, there is a designated resource person or consultant called in solely to fulfill the information-giving role. In most groups, one or more persons take it upon themselves to be especially well prepared. The information giver identifies himself by such statements as: "Well, when Jones corporation considered this problem, they found . . ." Or, "That's a good point you made— just the other day I ran across these figures that substantiate your

point." Or, "According to Professor Smith, it doesn't necessarily work that way. He says . . ."

2. The *information seeker*, the opposite of the information giver, is a role played by the member of the group who sees that at a given point the group will need data in order to function. Again, in most groups more than one person will take this role during the discussion, yet one or more are especially perceptive in seeing where more information is needed. The information seeker may be identified by such questions as: "What did we say the base numbers were?" Or, "Have we decided how many people this really affects?" Or, "Well, what functions does this person serve?" Or, "Have we got anything to give us some background on this subject?"

3. The *expediter* is the individual who perceives when the group is going astray. Whether the group is meeting once or is an ongoing group, almost invariably some remarks will tend to sidetrack the group from the central point or issue in front of them. Sometimes apparent digressions are necessary to get background, to enlarge the scope, or even to give a person an opportunity to get something off his chest. Often in a group these momentary digressions lead to tangents that take the group far afield from their assignment. But because tangents are sometimes more fun than the task itself, a tangent often is not realized for what it is and the group discusses it as if it were important to the group decision. The expediter is the person who helps the group stick to its agenda; he helps the group stay with the problem at hand. And when the group has strayed, he helps lead it back to the main stream. This role is revealed by such statements as: "Say, I'm enjoying this, but I can't quite see what it has to do with whether permissiveness is really a cause" Or, "Let's see, aren't we still trying to find out whether these are the only criteria that we should be considering?" Or, "I've got the feeling that this is important to the point we're on now, but I can't quite get hold of the relationship—am I off base?" Or, "Say, time is getting away from us and we've only considered two possible solutions. Aren't there some more?"

4. The *analyzer* is the person who is the master of technique. He knows the problem-solving method inside out. The analyzer knows when the group has skipped a point, has passed over a point too lightly, or has not taken a look at matters they need to. More than just *expediting*, the analyzer helps the group penetrate to the core of the problem they are working on. In addition, the analyzer examines the reasoning of various participants. The tests

he applies may be seen by looking at the explanation of common forms of reasoning discussed on pages 187–191. The analyzer may be recognized from such statements as: "Tom, you're generalizing from only one instance. Can you give us some others?" Or, "Wait a minute, after symptoms, we have to take a look at causes." Or, "I think we're passing over Jones too lightly. There are still criteria we haven't used to measure him by."

Maintenance Roles In most discussion groups there are at least two major maintenance roles that facilitate good working relationships.

1. The *harmonizer* is essential. It is a rare group that can expect to accomplish its task without some minor if not major conflicts. Even when people get along well they are likely to get angry over some inconsequential points in heated discussion. Most groups experience some classic interpersonal conflicts caused by different personality types. The harmonizer is responsible for reducing and reconciling misunderstanding, disagreements, and conflicts. He is good at pouring oil on troubled waters. He encourages objectivity and is especially good as a mediator for hostile, aggressively competing sides. A group cannot avoid some conflict, but if there is no one present to harmonize, participation can become an uncomfortable experience. The harmonizer may be recognized by such statements as: "Bill, I don't think you're giving Mary a chance to make her point." Or, "Tom, Jack, hold it a second. I know you're on opposite sides of this, but let's see where you might have some agreement." Or, "Sue, I get the feeling that something Todd said really bugged you, is that right?" Or, "Hold it, everybody, we're really coming up with some good stuff; let's not lose our momentum by getting into a name-calling thing."

2. The *gatekeeper* is the person who helps to keep communication channels open. If a group has seven people in it, the assumption is that all seven have something to contribute. But if all are to feel comfortable in contributing, those who tend to dominate need to be held in check and those who tend to be reticent need to be encouraged. The gatekeeper is the one who sees that Jane is on the edge of her chair, ready to talk, but just cannot seem to get in, or that Don is rambling a bit and needs to be directed, or that Tom's need to talk so frequently is making Cesar withdraw from the conversation, or that Betty has just lost the thread of discussion. As we said earlier, a characteristic of good group work is interaction. The gatekeeper assumes the responsibility for facilitating

interaction. The gatekeeper may be recognized by such statements as: "Joan, I see you've got something to say here. . ." Or, "You've made a really good point, Todd; I wonder whether we could get some reaction on it. . ." Or, "Bill and Marge, it sounds like you're getting into a dialogue here; let's see what other ideas we have."

Discussants Should Avoid Negative Roles

The following are the four most common negative roles that group discussants should try to avoid.

1. The *aggressor* is the person who works for his own status by criticizing most everything or blaming others when things get rough. His main purpose seems to be to deflate the ego or status of others. One way of dealing with the aggressor is to confront him. Ask him whether he is aware of what he is doing and what effect it is having on the group.

2. The *joker's* behavior is characterized by clowning, mimicking, or generally disrupting by making a joke of everything. He too is usually trying to call attention to himself. He must be the center of attention. A little bit of a joker goes a long way. The group needs to get the joker to consider the problem seriously, or he will constantly be an irritant to other members. One way to proceed is to encourage him when tensions need to be released but to ignore him when there is serious work to be done.

3. The *withdrawer* refuses to be a part of the group. He is a mental dropout. Sometimes he is withdrawing from something that we said; sometimes he is just showing his indifference. Try to draw him out with questions. Find out what he is especially good at and rely on him when his skill is required. Sometimes complimenting him will bring him out.

4. The *monopolizer* needs to talk all the time. Usually he is trying to impress the group that he is well read, knowledgeable, and of value to the group. He should, of course, be encouraged when his comments are helpful. But when he is talking too much or when his comments are not helpful, the leader needs to interrupt him and/or draw others into the discussion.

Group Assignment

Participants select a question of fact, value, or policy for a 20- to 40-minute discussion. Determine method of leadership, and establish an agenda. Criteria for evaluation of the discussion will include quality of participation, quality of leadership, and ability to arrive at group decisions.

SPEECHES FOR SPECIAL OCCASIONS

18

Most of your speaking time in and out of class will be spent exchanging information or persuading. At times, however, you may be called upon to speak under more ceremonial circumstances.

Although no speech can be given by formula, these occasions require at least the knowledge of some conventions expected by many audiences. Of course, speakers should always use their own imagination in developing their thesis; they should never adhere slavishly to those conventions. Still, one should know the conventions before trying to deviate from them.

This chapter gives the basics for accomplishing five common types of special speeches: introductions, presentations, acceptances, welcomings, and tributes.

INTRODUCTIONS

The occasion calls for a short but important speech.

Purpose

The purpose of the introduction is to pave the way for the main speaker. If you make the introduction in such a way that the audience is psychologically ready to listen to the speech, then you have accomplished your purpose.

Procedure

An audience wants to know who the speaker is, what he or she is going to talk about, and why they should listen. Sometime before the speech you will want to consult with the speaker to ask what he or she would like to have told. Ordinarily you want the necessary biographical information that will show who the speaker is and why he or she is qualified to talk on the subject. The better known the person is, the less you need to say. For instance, the introduction of the President is simply, "Ladies and gentlemen, the President of the United States." Ordinarily, you will want enough information to allow you to talk for at least two or three minutes. Only on rare occasions should a speech of introduction last more than three minutes. The audience assembled to hear the speaker, not the introducer. During the first sentence or two, then, you should establish the nature of the occasion. In the body of the speech you should establish the speaker's credibility. In the conclusion you should usually include the name of the speaker and the title of the talk.

Considerations

There are some special considerations concerning the speech of introduction. First, do not overpraise the speaker. If expectations are too high, the speaker will never be able to live up to them. Over-zealous introducers may be inclined to say: "This man is undoubtedly one of the greatest speakers around today. You can look forward to one of the greatest speeches you have ever heard. See whether you don't agree with me." This appears to be paying a compliment, but it is doing the speaker a disservice by emphasizing comparison rather than speech content. A second caution is to be familiar with what you have to say. Audiences question sincerity when an introducer has to read his praise. You may have been present when an introducer said, "And now it is my great pleasure to present that noted authority . . . ," and then had to look down at his notes to recall his name. Third, get your facts straight. The speaker should not have to spend time correcting your mistakes.

Assignment

Prepare a two- to three-minute speech of introduction. Criteria for evaluation will include creativity in establishing speaker credibility and in presenting the name of the speaker and the title of the speech.

PRESENTATIONS

Next to introductions, presentations are the kind of ceremonial speech you are most likely to give.

Purpose

The purpose of a speech of presentation is to present an award, prize, or gift to someone. In most cases, the speech of presentation is a reasonably short, formal recognition of some accomplishment.

Procedure

Your speech usually has two goals: (1) to discuss the nature of the award, including history, donor, and conditions under which it is made; and (2) to discuss the accomplishments of the recipient. If a competition was held, you should describe what the person did in the competition. Under other circumstances, you should discuss how the person has met the criteria for the award.

Obviously, you must learn all you can about the award and about the conditions under which such awards are made. The award may be a certificate, plaque, or trophy. The contest may have a long history and tradition that must be mentioned. Since the audience wants to know what the recipient has done, you should know the criteria that were met. For a competition, you should know the number of contestants and the way the contest was judged. If the person earned the award through years of achievement, you should know the particulars of that achievement.

Ordinarily, the speech is organized to show what the award is for, to give the criteria for winning, and to state how the person met the criteria. If the announcement of the name of the recipient is meant to be a surprise, all that is said should build up to the climax, the naming of the winner.

Considerations

For the speech of presentation there are only two special considerations: (1) Be careful of overpraise during the speech; do not explain everything in such superlatives that the presentation lacks sincerity. (2) In handing the award to the recipient, hold the award in your left hand and present it to the left hand of the recipient; shake the right hand in congratulations. If you practice, you will find that you can present the award and shake the person's hand smoothly and avoid those embarrassing moments when the recipient does not know quite what he is supposed to do.

Assignment

Prepare a three- to five-minute speech of presentation. Criteria for evaluation will include showing what the award is for, criteria for winning, and how the person met the criteria.

ACCEPTANCES

When an award is presented, it must be accepted. This speech is a response to speeches of presentation.

Purpose

The purpose of the speech of acceptance is to give brief thanks for receiving the award.

Procedure

The speech usually has two parts: (1) a brief thanks to the group, agency, or people responsible for giving the award; (2) if the recipient was aided by others, he or she gives thanks to those who share in the honor.

Considerations

Unless the acceptance is the lead-in to a major address, the acceptance should be brief. (A politician accepting a gift from the Chamber of Commerce may launch into a speech on government that the audience was expecting.) Yet, as the Academy Awards program so graphically illustrates, when people are honored the tendency is to give overly long and occasionally inappropriate speeches. The audience expects you to show your gratitude to the presenter of the award; they are not expecting a major address.

Assignment	**This assignment may well go together with the speech of presentation assignment. Prepare a one- to two-minute speech of acceptance in response to another speaker's speech of presentation. Criteria for evaluation will be how imaginatively you can respond in a brief speech.**

WELCOMINGS

Another common ceremonial speech is the welcoming.

Purpose

A speech of welcome expresses your pleasure in greeting a person or organization. In a way, the speech is a double speech of introduction: you introduce the newcomer to the audience, and you introduce the audience to the newcomer.

Procedure

You must be familiar both with the person or organization you are welcoming and with the situation you are welcoming them to. It is surprising how little many members of organizations and communities really know about their community. Although you may not have the knowledge on the tip of your tongue, it is inexcusable not to find the material you need to give an appropriate speech. Likewise, you want accurate information about the person or organization you are welcoming. The speech should be brief, but you need accurate and complete information to draw from.

After expressing pleasure in welcoming the person or organization, tell a little about your guests and give them the information about the place or organization to which they are being welcomed. Usually the conclusion is a brief statement of your hope for a pleasant and profitable visit.

Considerations

Again, the special caution is to make sure the speech is brief and honest. Welcoming guests does not require you to gush about them or their accomplishments. The speech of welcome should be an informative speech of praise.

Assignment	**Prepare a short speech welcoming a person to the community, organization, or institution. Criteria for evaluation will include how well you explain the nature of the institution and how well you introduce the person being welcomed.**

TRIBUTES

The final ceremonial speech we will consider is the tribute.

Purpose

The purpose of a speech of tribute is to praise someone's accomplishments. The occasion may be a birthday, the taking of office, retirement, or death. A formal speech of tribute given in memory of a deceased person is called a eulogy.

Procedure

The key to an effective tribute is sincerity. Although you want the praise to be apparent, you do not want to overdo it.

You must know the biographical information about your subject in depth. Since audiences are primarily interested in new information and specifics that characterize your assertions, you must have a mastery of much detail. You should focus on the person's laudable characteristics and accomplishments. It is especially noteworthy if you find that the person had to overcome some special hardship or meet some particularly trying condition. All in all, you must be prepared to make a sound positive appraisal.

One way of organizing a speech of tribute is to focus on the subject's accomplishments. How detailed you will make the speech will depend upon whether the person is well known or not. If the person is well known, you will be more general in your analysis. If the person is little known, you will have to provide many more details so that the audience can see the reasons for the praise. In the case of very prominent individuals you will be able to show their influence on history.

Considerations

Remember, however, that no one is perfect. Although you need not stress a person's less glowing characteristics or failures, some allusion to this kind of information may make the positive features even more meaningful. Probably the most important guide is for you to keep your objectivity. Overpraise is far worse than understatement. Try to give the subject his or her due, honestly and sincerely.

Assignment

Prepare a four- to six-minute speech of tribute to a person living or dead. Criteria for evaluation will include how well you develop the person's laudable characteristics and accomplishments.

THREE CONTEMPORARY SPEECHES

APPENDIX

THREE CONTEMPORARY SPEECHES

The following speeches, all delivered in 1974, illustrate how three men and women in responsible positions met their challenge of effective speaking. Each was delivered to a different kind of audience, for a different purpose, and under a different set of circumstances. Analyze each of the speeches, using the questions asked on page 19.

Think Strawberries *A speech by James Lavenson, President of the Plaza Hotel, delivered before the American Medical Association, February 7, 1974.*[1]

I came from the balcony of the hotel business. For ten years as a corporate director of Sonesta Hotels with no line responsibility, I had my office in a little building next door to The Plaza. I went to the hotel every day for lunch and often stayed overnight. I was a professional guest. You know nobody knows more about how to run a hotel than a guest. Last year, I suddenly fell out of the corporate balcony and had to put my efforts in the restaurants where my mouth had been, and in the rooms and night club and theater into which I'd been putting my two cents.

In my ten years of kibitzing, all I had really learned about the hotel business was how to use a guest room toilet without removing the strip of paper that's printed "Sanitized for Your Protection." When the hotel staff found out I'd spent my life as a salesman and that I'd never been a hotelier, never been to Cornell Hotel School, and that I wasn't even the son of a waiter, they were in a state of shock. And Paul Sonnabend, President of Sonesta, didn't help their apprehension much when he introduced me to my executive staff with the following kind words: "The Plaza has been losing money the last several years and we've had the best management in the business. Now we're going to try the worst."

Frankly, I think the hotel business has been one of the most backward in the world. There's been very little change in the attitude of room clerks in the 2,000 years since Joseph arrived in

[1] Reprinted from *Vital Speeches*, March 15, 1974, pp. 346–348. By permission.

Bethlehem and was told they'd lost his reservation. Why is it that a sales clerk at Woolworth asks your wife, who points to the panty-hose if she wants three or six pairs—and your wife is all by herself—but the maître d' asks you and your wife, the only human beings within a mile of the restaurant, "How many are you?"

Hotel salesmanship is retailing at its worst. But at the risk of inflicting cardiac arrest on our guests at The Plaza when they first hear shocking expressions like "Good Morning" and "Please" and "Thank you for coming," we started a year ago to see if it was possible to make the 1400 employees of The Plaza into genuine hosts and hostesses. Or should I say "salesmen?"

A tape recorder attached to my phone proved how far we had to go. "What's the difference between your $85 suite and your $125 suite?" I'd ask our reservationist, disguising my voice over the phone. You guessed it: "$40!"

"What's going on in the Persian Room tonight?" I asked the Bell Captain. "Some singer" was his answer. "Man or woman?" I persisted. "I'm not sure" he said, which made me wonder if I'd even be safe going there.

Why is it, I wondered, that the staff of a hotel doesn't act like a family playing hosts to guests whom they've invited to their house? It didn't take too long after becoming a member of the family myself, to understand one of the basic problems. Our 1400 family members didn't even know each other! With that large a staff, working over eighteen floors, six restaurants, a night club, a theater, and three levels of subbasement, including a kitchen, a carpentry shop, plumbing and electrical shops, a full commercial laundry—how would they ever know who was working there, and who was a guest or just a purveyor passing through? Even the old-timers who might recognize a face after a couple of years would have no idea of the name connected to it. It struck me that if our own people couldn't call each other by name, smile at each other's familiar face, say good morning *to each other*, how could they be expected to say amazing things like "Good Morning, Mr. Jones" to a guest? A year ago The Plaza name tag was born. The delivery took place on my lapel. And it's now been on 1,400 lapels for over a year. Everyone, from dishwashers to the General Manager, wears his name where every other employee, and of course every guest, can see it. Believe it or not, our people say hello to each other—by name—when they pass in the halls and the offices. At first our regular guests thought The Plaza was entertaining some gigantic convention, but now even the old-time Plaza regulars are able to call our bellmen and maids by name. We've begun to build an atmosphere of welcome with the most precious commodity in the world—our names. *And* our guests' names.

A number of years ago, I heard Dr. Ernest Dichter, head of the Institute of Motivational Research, talk about restaurant service. He had reached a classic conclusion; when people come to a fine restaurant, they are hungrier for *recognition* than they are for food. It's true. If the maître d' says "We have your table ready, Mr. Lavenson," then as far as I'm concerned the chef can burn the steak and I'll still be happy.

When someone calls you by name and you don't know his, a strange feeling of discomfort comes over you. When he does it twice you *have* to find out *his* name. This we see happening with our Plaza name tags. When a guest calls a waiter by name, the waiter wants to call the guest by name. It will drive him nuts if he doesn't know. He'll ask the maître d', and if he doesn't know he'll ask the bellman, who will ask the front desk . . . calling the guests by name has a big payoff. It's called a *tip*.

At first there was resistance to name tags—mostly from the old-time, formally trained European hoteliers. I secretly suspect they liked being incognito when faced with a guest complaint. We only had one staff member who said he'd resign before having his dignity destroyed with a name tag. For sixteen years he'd worn a rosebud in his lapel and that, he said, was his trademark and everyone knew him by it. His resignation was accepted along with that of the rosebud. Frankly, there are moments when I regret the whole idea myself. When I get on a Plaza elevator and all the passengers see my name tag, they know I work there. Suddenly, I'm the official elevator pilot, the host. I can't hide, so I smile at everybody, say "good morning" to perfect strangers I'd ordinarily ignore. The ones that don't go into shock, smile back. Actually, they seem to mind less the fact that a trip on a Plaza elevator, built in 1907, is the equivalent of commuting to Manhattan from Greenwich.

There are 600 Spanish-speaking employees at The Plaza. They speak Spanish. They don't read English. The employee house magazine was in English. So was the employee bulletin board. So were the signs over the urinals in the locker rooms that suggest cigarette butts don't flush too well. It was a clue as to why some of management's messages weren't getting through. The employee house magazine is now printed one side in English, the other in Spanish. The bulletin board and other staff instructions are in two languages. We have free classes in both languages for departmental supervisors. It's been helping.

With 1,400 people all labeled and smiling we were about ready last June to make salesmen out of them. There was just one more obstacle to overcome before we started suggesting they "ask for the order." They had no idea what the product was they would be selling. Not only didn't they know who was playing in the Persian Room, they didn't know we had movies—full-length feature films without commercials—on the closed-circuit TV in the bedrooms. As a matter of fact, most of them didn't know what a guest room looked like, unless they happened to be a maid or a bellman.

The reason the reservationists thought $40 was the difference between two suites was because they'd never been in one, much less actually slept there. To say our would-be salesmen lacked product knowledge would be as much an understatement as the line credited to President Nixon if he had been the Captain of the Titanic. My son told me that if Nixon had been Captain of the Titanic, he probably would have announced to the passengers there was no cause for alarm—they were just stopping to pick up ice.

Today, if you ask a Plaza bellman who's playing in the Persian Room he'll tell you Ednita Nazzaro. He'll tell you because he's seen her. In the contract of every Persian Room performer, there's now a clause requiring him to first perform for our employees in the cafeteria before he opens in the Persian Room. Our employees see the star first, before the guests.

And if you ask a room clerk or a telephone operator what's on the TV movies, they'll tell you because they've seen it—on the TV sets running the movies continuously in the employees' cafeteria.

Believe me, if you are having your lunch in our cafeteria and watch "Female Response" or "Swedish Fly Girls" on the TV set, you won't forget the film. You might, however, suspect the chef has put Spanish fly in your spaghetti.

Our new room clerks now have a week of orientation. It includes spending a night in the hotel and a tour of our 1,000 guest rooms. They can look out the windows and see the $40 difference in suites, since a view of the Park doesn't even closely resemble the back of the Avon building.

As I mentioned, about six months ago, we decided it was time to take a hard look at our sales effort. I couldn't find it. The Plaza had three men with the title "salesman"—and they were good men. But they were really sales-*service* people who took the orders for functions or groups who came through the doors and sought us out. Nobody, but nobody, ever left the palace, crossed the moat at Fifth Avenue, and went looking for business. We had no one knocking on doors, no one asking for the order. The Plaza was so dignified it seemed demeaning to admit we needed business. If you didn't ask us we wouldn't ask you. So there! Our three sales-service people were terrific once you voluntarily stepped inside our arena. You had to ring our doorbell. We weren't ringing yours or anyone else's.

This condition wasn't unique to our official Sales Department. It seemed to be a philosophy shared by our entire staff—potentially larger sales staff of waiters, room clerks, bellmen, cashiers, and doormen. If you wanted a second drink in the Oak Bar, you got it by tripping the waiter. You asked for it. If you wanted a room you were quoted the minimum rate. If you wanted something better or larger, you had to ask for it. If you wanted to stay at the hotel an extra night, you had to ask. You were never invited. Sometimes I think there's a secret pact among hotelmen. It's a secret oath you take when you graduate from hotel school. It goes like this: "I promise I will never ask for the order."

When you're faced with as old and ingrained tradition as that, halfway countermeasures don't work. We started a program with all our guest contact people using a new secret oath: "Everybody sells!" And we meant everybody—maids, cashiers, waiters, bellmen —the works. We talked to the maids about suggesting room service, to the doormen about mentioning dinner in our restaurants, to cashiers about suggesting return reservations to departing guests. And we talked to waiters about strawberries.

A waiter at The Plaza makes anywhere from $10,000 to $20,000 a year. The difference between those two figures is, of course, tips. When I was in the advertising agency business, I thought I was fast at computing 15 percent. I'm a moron compared to a waiter. Our suggestions for selling strawberries fell on responsive ears when we described a part of the Everybody Sells program for our Oyster Bar restaurant. We figured, with just the same number of customers in the Oyster Bar, that if the waiters would ask every customer if he'd like a second drink, wine, or beer with the meal, and then dessert— given only one out of four takers we'd increase our sales volume by $364,000 a year. The waiters were way ahead of the lecture— they'd already figured out that was another $50,000 in tips! And since there are ten waiters in the Oyster Bar, even I could figure out it meant five grand more per man in tips. It was at that point I had my toughest decision to make since I've been in this job. I had to choose between staying on as President or becoming an Oyster Bar waiter.

But, while the waiters appreciated this automatic raise in theory, they were quick to call out the traditional negatives. "Nobody eats dessert anymore. Everyone's on a diet. If we served our chocolate cheesecake to everybody in the restaurant, half of them would be dead in a week."

"So sell 'em strawberries!" we said. "But sell 'em." And then we wheeled out our answer to gasoline shortages, the dessert cart. We widened the aisles between the tables and had the waiters wheel the cart up to each and every table at dessert time. Not daunted by the diet protestations of the customer, the waiter then went into raptures about the bowl of fresh strawberries. There was even a bowl of whipped cream for the slightly wicked. By the time our waiters finish extolling the virtues of our fresh strawberries flown in that morning from California, or wherever he thinks strawberries come from, you not only have had an abdominal orgasm but one out of two of you order them. In the last six months we show our waiters every week what's happening to strawberry sales. This month they have doubled again. So have second martinis. And believe me, when you get a customer for a second martini you've got a sitting duck for strawberries—with whipped cream. Our waiters are asking for the order.

"Think Strawberries" is The Plaza's new secret weapon. Our reservationists now think strawberries and suggest you'll like a suite overlooking Central Park rather than a twin-bedded room. Our bellmen are thinking strawberries. Each bellman has his own reservation cards, with his name printed as the return addressee, and he asks if you'd like him to make your return reservation as he's checking you out and into your taxi. Our Room Service order takers are thinking strawberries. They suggest the closed-circuit movie on TV ($3.00 will appear on your bill) as long as you're going to eat in your room. Our telephone operators are even thinking strawberries. They suggest a morning Flying Tray breakfast when you ask for a wake-up call. You just want a light breakfast, no ham and eggs? How about some strawberries?

We figure we've added about three hundred salesmen to the three sales-service team we had before. But most important, of course, is that we've added five pure sales people to our Sales Department. Four of them are out on the street calling—mostly cold —on the prospects to whom they're ready to sell anything from a cocktail in the Oak Bar to a Corporate Directors meeting to a Bar Mitzvah. The chewing gum people sell new customers by sampling on street corners. The Plaza has chewing gum licked a mile. Our sales people on the street have one simple objective: get the prospect into the hotel to sample the product. With The Plaza as our product, it isn't too difficult. And once you taste The Plaza, frankly, you're hooked.

In analyzing our business at the hotel we found, much to my surprise, that functions—parties, weddings, charity balls, and the like— are just about three times more profitable than all our six restaurants put together. And functions are twice as profitable as selling all 1000 of our rooms. Before we had this analysis, we were spending all our advertising money on restaurants, our nightclub, and our guest rooms. This year we're spending 80 percent of our advertising money to get function business—weddings instead of honeymoons, banquets instead of meals, annual corporate meetings instead of a clandestine romantic rendezvous for two. We've added a full-time Bridal Consultant who can talk wedding language to nervous brides and talk turkey to their mothers. Retailers like Saks and Bonwit's and Bergdorf's have had bridal consultants for years. Hotels have Banquet Managers. Banquet Managers sell wedding dinners. Bridal Consultants sell strawberries—everything from the bridal shower, the pictures, the ceremony, the reception, the wedding night, to the honeymoon, to the first anniversary.

When you fight a habit as long standing as the hotel inside salesman, you don't just wave a wand and say "Presto: now we have four outside salesmen." We want our new salespeople to know how serious we are about going out after business. We started an Executive Sales Call program as part of our "Everybody Sells" philosophy. About forty of our top and middle-management executives, ones who traditionally don't ever see a prospect, are assigned days on which they make outside calls with our regular salesmen. People like our Personnel Director, our Executive Housekeeper, our Purchasing Director, and our General Manager are on the street every day making calls. Our prospects seem to like it. Our salesmen love it. And our nonsales "salesmen" are getting an education about what's going on in the real world—the one outside the hotel.

As a matter of fact, that's why I'm here today. I made a sales call myself with one of our salespeople. We called on your program chairman and tried to sell him strawberries. He promised that if I showed you a strawberry he'd book your next luncheon at The Plaza. I'm looking forward to waiting on you myself. Thank you very much.

The Hazards of Equality

A speech by Mary Lou Thibeault, Assistant to the President of Hartford College for Women, delivered as Commencement Address at the Hartford College for Women, June 1, 1974.[2]

Fellow celebrants of the graduating class and honored graduates! When you students invited me to be your Commencement speaker, I was surprised, honored, and worried. I was worried because *I* am so informal a speaker and I know that commencement addresses are supposed to be serious, profound, and pontifical.

The first one I ever heard was at my own commencement here at Hartford College seventeen years ago. I do not remember the speaker or anything he had to say (it probably was a "he"), but it was in the familiar and traditional style. (One of our staff members calls such offerings "encouraging noises.") Two years later at Mt. Holyoke the same kind of speech was a little more memorable— perhaps because we had a *woman* speaker. Journalist Pauline Fredericks advised us to be "uncommon women." The choice between being common and uncommon was not a difficult one to make, or so I thought at the time anyway.

I have listened to many commencement speeches since then. Typically, they commend the graduates for what they have accomplished thus far, warn them that there are obstacles ahead, but —the ray of hope—by applying what they have learned at college and facing the future with strength, determination, faith, and courage, they shall win professional and personal fulfillment.

My address will say the same thing.

[2] Reprinted from *Vital Speeches*, July 15, 1974, pp. 588–591. By permission.

I do commend you for what you have accomplished thus far. Working with you during the past year, I identified with many of you and recalled my own struggles, lacking financial and emotional support, to get a college education. I learned in my time, as you have learned in your day, that the president of Hartford College had her own affirmative action program for women long before it was fashionable. I am only one of many products of that program.

I know what some of you have sacrificed for your achievement.

Today, you should feel it was worth it. You now have the intellectual tools with which to continue learning for the rest of your life—tools given you by the finest undergraduate faculty in the country.

My charge, as I took it from you students who wanted a woman to talk about women, is to discuss the opportunities and obstacles that lie ahead.

In what kind of world can you expect to live? A world greatly changed in terms of economic structure and personal relations. Traditional ties will be loosened. Some of you will be married two or three times. This need not be viewed as a deterioration of the social fabric. Rather, it may be seen, as Gloria Steinem contends, as an affirmation of marriage, a conviction that a loveless union should not be falsely maintained as a substitute for the vibrant relationship that a marriage should be.

Many of you will change careers at least twice. You will also change your city and state of residence several times. This new mobility, this new freedom for women, must seem exciting and attractive, especially at your age.

There is an old Spanish proverb: "Take what you will, says God. Take it and pay for it."

Yes, you graduate into a society that has been made more open, with opportunities in fields and positions previously denied to most women. Yet, remember that for decades in this country individual women have forced this kind of equality for themselves. They have become doctors, lawyers, judges, and college presidents. Some have even managed to be wives and mothers en route to their professional success. But not without cost.

Equality has its obvious attractions, but equality also has its hazards.

1. *The Battle of the Sexes* The first, and perhaps the most serious hazard is the temptation to make man the enemy.

When Anita Loos, author of the classic sociosexual analysis, *Gentlemen Prefer Blondes*, was asked about women's liberationists, she replied she was furious with them. "They keep proclaiming women are brighter than men and that's true, of course," says Miss Loos, "but it should be kept quiet or it ruins the whole racket." I'll register my own partial agreement with Miss Loos and the women's liberationists. I do believe that women, in general, are more acute about *some* things than *most* men. And I generally find it advantageous in the company of men to camouflage that superiority. I hope that *you* have learned by now not only that there are some differences between men and women, but also that you can join with me in saying, "Vive la difference." And I speak here not merely of a physical, but also, and most emphatically, of the temperamental, emotional, and psychological differences between men and women. The differences between male and female perceptions create, I believe, constructive tensions and broader dimensions that enhance life for men and women.

Let me warn you, too, against indulging yourself in the blanket accusation that men have oppressed us. Rather, develop an awareness of the socioeconomic and historical reasons for women's assignment to limited or subordinate roles in our social and economic life.

Try to understand as well the not entirely happy role created for a man. He was socially programmed to say, "No wife of mine will ever work," and to see himself as the sole breadwinner for his family. These same social expectations lead this man to work to put his wife into a neocolonial suburban house so that mowing the lawn in the summer, shoveling the driveway of the two-car garage in the winter, and meeting the demands of his job all year long will result in his just reward—an early heart attack.

While the professional man is engaged in the struggle for professional success, his wife finds herself in what Betty Friedan calls "the sexual ghetto," with no one to talk to over three feet tall. So it is no surprise if some men in the world of work treat a woman they meet professionally as they treat their own wives and daughters. Having learned at home that women have little knowledge about anything significant, a man often does not know how to react when a woman at work is competent and forthright in discussing professional problems.

This does not make man the enemy. He is, rather, a victim of the same attitudes that keep some women from exhibiting their competence.

Those of us who have spent any time at a career know one unpleasant fact to keep us from thinking of man as the enemy. You sometimes discover that women can harbor the same attitudes attributed to a male chauvinist. In short, not all male chauvinists are men!

So, misuse of authority is bad, no matter *who* does it, and sexual prejudice is a sin that may be committed by either sex.

For example, I have heard some women say they do not want to work for a woman. Yes, I know they may have had one bad experience and hence condemn all women supervisors. They often say it to a man who may be the one to hire them. Since, in most cases, it is a man who holds the power to hire, promote, give raises and better titles and office space, this attitude is understandable. So, if you should become a supervisor, be prepared for some suspicion or even hostility from some of the women you supervise, and strive to be the kind of supervisor who recognizes talent, ability, and performance regardless of sex.

A final reason why we must not let man become the enemy is that we want to live with him—as a brother, a father, or a husband. "Love thy enemy" may be a valid moral imperative, but who wants to *live* with an enemy?

2. *Why Be a Man?* A second hazard of equality is the risk of becoming like a man. If masculine qualities seem to assure success, it is to be expected that women, seeing this, will imitate those qualities. But such observation is myopic, such logic deficient, and such conduct ludicrous or offensive.

A cynical male observer has remarked that the real purpose of the women's lib movement is to win for women the right to swear like men. If that were so, then our heroines would be Calamity Jane and Tugboat Annie. In rejecting his assertion, however, I cannot ignore that he was given cause for his remark by a few injudicious crusaders.

If a man has a right to smoke on the street, I suppose the Constitution secures for me the same privilege. But I learned at a rather tender age by doing so, that such conduct by a young woman evoked a somewhat surprising, let me say, shocking, conclusion in the mind of a young sailor. (That was quite a learning experience!)

Does it seem too old-fashioned to say that what a man may be free to do is not always proper for even a liberated woman to emulate? I have never viewed the cause of sexual equality as having any significant relation to the use of offensive language, restrictive undergarments, or access to saloons. If the boys at Yale want to hang onto the principle of sexual segregation round "The tables down at Mory's," I say "God have mercy on such as they." I'm not concerned about opening the doors to a bar, but we must be concerned about the bars to the doors of opportunity.

Let me advise you, then, that in seeking your equal rights— political, economic, or social—that you do so—feminists forgive! —as a lady. A woman should have full regard and *honor* for her own nature. Do not try to become a man.

Our society conditions men to inhibit their emotions. Will life be improved if women, too, are so conditioned? If we desire more open, honest relationships, should we not insist that both men and women need to be more loving and trusting and giving? In this instance, at least, can it not be recognized that women's attributes are the better ones?

3. *The Demands of Equality* The third hazard of equality is the unrealistic appraisal of responsibilities.

Now let me confess that I sometimes have difficulty thinking of myself as a militant feminist. When Tony Gallinari needed someone to help out in his grinder shop and was willing to hire a fourteen-year-old high school girl to work afternoons and evenings, pay her twenty-five cents an hour, and teach her to make the best Italian grinders in Bridgton, Maine—no, let me expand a little—the best grinders north of Boston—I did not regard him as a male chauvinist pig exploiting an economically oppressed female. I was not very sophisticated and the term "economically disadvantaged" had not yet been invented, but I knew we were poor and this was a chance to make some money. So I was grateful that Mr. Gallinari was willing to give me a job. I was even more grateful a few months later, when I had proved my skill at making and selling grinders, that Mr. Gallinari gave me a raise of four cents an hour. (Good preparation for a career in education!)

I learned something else at Gallinari's Grinder Shop. I learned how to do a job: to show up on time, to do whatever was needed, to work overtime or double-time when the business required it. And I still take pride in the knowledge that I make a really good grinder.

So I have a special viewpoint about women and the job market. Let me give you an example.

One woman recently convinced an advertising firm to hire her part time instead of hiring a full-time employee. The owner reorganized his office to give her a job which would enable her to learn the business. After three days, she decided she did not want to work anymore. She returned to volunteer activities since they gave her *some* fulfillment and were less demanding. Obviously, that man is not going to hire another woman if he can help it.

Many professional women I talk to complain about feeling like tokens. I am happy to see their perceptions are so accurate. Of course, the first women named to traditionally male roles are tokens, but not necessarily mere window-dressing. In part, they are making a trial run. If one woman can fully meet the demands of the job, others can also.

Before *you* decide upon a professional career, decide upon the strength of your commitment. How much are you willing to give? Are you willing to undertake the necessary studies? Will you have the stamina to put in all the time required to be good in your field? Will you want to leave the office at 4:30 because you have a date or will you understand that being "professional" means that your duties are measured not by a time clock, but the demands of the job? Are you ready to meet those demands?

4. *Equality or Security?*   Finally, the most crucial hazard will be loss of security.

At this critical moment in your life there are, I know, two great questions in your mind. What to do about your future—and what to do about a man. If there is a man in your life, you wonder if you should really get married. If there is not a man, you wonder if you will find someone you can love and who will love you. And this poses a series of questions about your future and your career—if any.

Do you choose marriage, a career, or both? It is easy, of course, to decide you will marry someone and let him earn the ulcers for you—let him be responsible for your future. This is the choice made by most women of earlier generations. Indeed, it was *not really* a *choice!* A young girl was *taught* that her proper future was marriage and children.

Your generation knows that you can choose another kind of future. You need not be tied down with a husband and children. You may reject the security of marriage and choose, instead, the freedom and challenge of a career.

This option is likely to be most attractive if you view yourself as a strong-minded modern woman—as I know you all do. You know where you are going. And you know, "She travels fastest who travels alone," and so forth.

Let me tell you a few of the realities of the single state for a career woman. Many young career women (and some of us not so young) will privately confess—perhaps I should say complain—that we do not have time to take care of our personal lives; such troublesome things as changing the studded snow tires before the May 1st deadline, trying to buy draperies for the living room of a new apartment, or even getting a watch fixed so we'll know what time it is. These are tasks that a wife should whip through in one day. But the professional woman, with no one to do these things for her, must sandwich them into her week along with other mundane tasks like laundry, housecleaning, cooking, and dishes—while also writing reports, preparing budgets, and solving personnel problems on her real job for which she must also shop for clothes so she can look the part of a career woman. Of course, she could find a husband to do these things for her (as men find wives), but would she want the kind of man who was willing to perform such jobs? (Well, I guess she could expect him to take care of the snow tires.)

Somerset Maugham said, "American women hope for a perfection in their husbands that English women expect only in their butlers." Some of our critics charge that we do treat our husbands as butlers.

If you concede the charge, you may speed your professional success by seeking a butler rather than a husband. I do *not* recommend such a course. A husband is less expensive and provides greater rewards.

There are further reasons in favor of marriage for the career woman. When author May Sarton was asked recently how she evaluated living alone, she replied, "The worst part of it is loneliness and the best part of it is solitude."

The "loneliness of the long-distance runner" has already been documented, but to my knowledge, no one has yet considered the loneliness of the unmarried woman executive. Yes, her days are filled. *She needs* to be busy 12 hours a day, but she does not have the reinforcement at home enjoyed by her married male counterpart. There is no one there to share with her the troubles and triumphs of the day.

The loss of support, then, that a woman must endure when she chooses a career rather than marriage, or has it imposed upon her by death or divorce, is something far broader than financial insecurity, although that, too, is no small hazard.

At the end of a hard day of crises and unsolved problems, you will sometimes wonder whether equality of opportunity is worth the effort. I remember a fellow woman-executive saying to me wearily at the end of a trying day, "I don't want to be liberated, I just want someone to take *care* of me."

There are times when we all feel that way.

Does the choice of a professional career preclude the option of marriage? Of course not. But if you choose both marriage and a career, you should be aware of special hazards.

Are you prepared to meet the demands, the reasonable demands, of your job and your home? Or will you neglect one because of the demands of the other?

Does that adoring young man who says he cannot live without you, share *your* ideas about *your* professional future? Can you and he adjust your professional and personal lives so that each of you can fully develop your abilities? If you are offered a great job in Boston and his job is in Hartford, what will you do? Suppose your new job will pay more than he is making now?

These are not easy questions to answer and they probably cannot be answered in the abstract. There is a general question, however, that you both *must* consider. Do you have equal respect for the demands of each other's career? Does he care as much about your success as you care about his? Do you share commitment to each other's professional future? If you both can say "yes" to these general questions, then you may enjoy the challenge of a career as well as the joys and security of married life.

Let me conclude, then, by expressing my own commitment to equality and women's liberation without necessarily associating myself with all of the extravagant rhetoric of some of those who speak for the movement.

Any reasonable man *or* woman *must* agree with the principle that opportunity in education, employment, or *other* public endeavor, must be based not on such irrelevancies as gender—nor other irrelevancies such as race, religion, or ethnicity—but on quality of talent, capability, performance, and diligence.

But agreement on this principle does not solve all of the professional and personal problems that will trouble you. Let me add some personal observations that will support my recommendation that marriage can support a career and a career can reinforce a marriage. But choose your marriage and choose your career so that they will reinforce each other.

I guess what I really want you to understand is the real nature of work and the real nature of love.

There is a song you sing that I sometimes think is the anthem of your generation. "I've got to be me. I've got to be me." Within that anthem is a line that I offer as the text of this sermonic address: "I can't be right for somebody else if I'm not right for me.—I've got to be me."

In giving yourself to a man or a career or a cause, remember that theme: "I can't be right for somebody else if I'm not right for me."

No *worthy* cause demeans its followers. If the cause is worthwhile, it will uplift you. It will call upon your talent, but will not call for you to sacrifice your integrity nor your conscience.

No responsible employer wants your heart or soul or—heaven forfend!—your body. He wants your talent and your ability, your intellect and your energy.

No true lover wants for you less than you want for him. Rather, he wants for you all that you want for yourself. It is in this sharing of your aspirations with one you love and who loves you that you may find true liberation.

The contrast in the perception of courtship and marriage has been expressed most succinctly by Judith Viorst.

> "I saw us walking hand and hand
> through life.
>   But now it's clear we really
> need two cars."

Yes, you need to share, but you also need your own motivation. And Hartford College for Women has given you a beginning: the basic intellectual tools, some awareness of yourself, your strengths, your limits, and your potential. You have learned something about living and working with others, to give them respect and to expect it for yourself.

There are hazards ahead, of course, as well as opportunity. But if you will apply the lessons of your experience and your studies at Hartford College, I am confident that you can surmount those hazards and take full advantage of future opportunity.

**The Black and
Jewish Communities**

A speech by Vernon E. Jordan, Jr., Executive Director, National Urban League, delivered at Annual Meeting, Atlanta Chapter, American Jewish Committee, June 2, 1974.[3]

On a recent visit to this country, Rabbi Ovadia Yossef, Sephardic Chief Rabbi of Israel, stated: "If a Jew is in pain any place in the world, every Jew feels that pain." I would amend that only to read that "every decent human being feels that pain." For the treatment of the world's Jewish minority has historically been the barometer of the extent of decency still alive in the world, just as America's treatment of her black minority has historically been the measure of the maturity and decency of our nation.

Thus all decent people should be concerned about the terrible plight of Jews persecuted in Syria and Iraq, of Jews denied elementary human rights in the Soviet Union, and of Jews elsewhere in the world who still face oppression and discrimination based on their racial origins and religious beliefs.

And so too, must all people who value human life and dignity express their concern for the continued existence of the state of Israel, and for her future safety and security. With you, I pray that the coming talks in Geneva will result in a lasting peace in the Middle East; a just peace that will leave a secure Israel in harmonious relationship with her neighbors.

Contrary to so much ill-informed speculation, I believe this hope is shared by the bulk of the black community. And this hope is buttressed by a perspective grounded in black values, in the black religion, in the black history of oppression, and in the basic principles of coalition with the Jewish community, a coalition that has historically imbued each of the partners with a responsibility to support the other in areas of central concern.

Like just about everyone else, I was profoundly shocked at the terrorist raid that took the lives of more than twenty innocent Israeli children last month, but I saw something that perhaps others did not notice. I saw the pictures of wailing mothers and mourning fathers, as did others. But I also noticed that these victims of terrorism were dark-skinned Jews from North Africa. They were brown people who were also Jews and Israelis. No black American sensitive to racial subtleties can swallow the myth that the Mideast struggle is a conflict between brown-skinned Arabs and white Israelis. The victims of this terror raid, like the majority of Israelis, were dark people who fled to Israel in hope of a better life and with the dream of returning to their ancient homeland. Theirs is a dream black people understand. Theirs is a dream we can support. Theirs is a dream

[3] Reprinted from *Vital Speeches*, August 1, 1974, pp. 629–632. By permission.

that must not be allowed to turn into a nightmare of terrorism and death.

To a great degree, how well Israel fares in the peace negotiations depends upon the firmness of American diplomacy and the stability and respect our government has in the eyes of the world. In these days of deleted expletives, sordid revelations, and "White House horrors" gone public, that is a frail reed. The President is in imminent danger of impeachment and his reaction to that danger is to compromise the prestige of his office and the greater values of our society by a sharp rightward turn that he hopes may win him enough conservative support to escape conviction in the Senate.

This politics of impeachment may be behind his revival of the busing issue, as black people are assigned the role of scapegoats and hostages to the waning fortunes of the Administration. For black people the erosion of belief in the Administration did not start with the revelations about Watergate. It started well before that with the so-called Southern strategy, the Carswell and Haynsworth appointments, the budget cuts, the antiwelfare rhetoric, the economic policies that plunged more black people into poverty, and a whole assortment of policies that appeared to many not only to be inimical to the best interests of black people, but also designed to manipulate racial issues so as to drive a terrible wedge of fear and distrust between whites and blacks.

For those of us who saw so much hope in the Second Reconstruction of the 1960s, the Administration's single biggest moral failure was its failure to maintain the national consensus for civil rights and thus to help, as it had promised, to bring us together again.

When Harry Truman was asked about a President's power, he said that "The biggest power the President has . . . is the power to persuade people to do what they ought to do without having to be persuaded. And if the man who is the President doesn't understand that, if he thinks he's too big to do the necessary persuading, then he's in for big trouble, and so is the country."

Well, the President is in trouble today, and so is the country. And so too are blacks and Jews. Black people are in trouble today because of the unprincipled murder of the Second Reconstruction that ended it after our legal rights were ratified but well before the economic substance basic to exercising those rights was secured. And Jews are in trouble today because the nation has degenerated to a state of economic uncertainty, eroded authority, and fragmented leadership characterized by growing polarization that has traditionally been the social condition precedent to revived anti-Semitism.

Some observers see signs of a new growth of this malignant disease. In their new book titled *The New Anti-Semitism*, Arnold Forster and Benjamin Epstein state that while the "old" anti-Semitism was based on overt discrimination against Jews, the new form is based on insensitivity. They state: "It includes often a callous indifference to Jewish concerns expressed by respectable institutions and persons—people who would be shocked to think themselves or have others think them anti-Semites."

My friends, if you change that statement only to the extent of making black people its subjects, then you have a very accurate picture of the resurgent antiblack feeling in the United States today. It is nothing less than a description of that "benign neglect" that has haunted black aspirations and is, in fact, "malevolent neglect."

It is this "callous indifference to black concerns expressed by respectable institutions and persons" that distinguishes the present antiblack atmosphere today from the violence and the overt hostility of the past.

Because I feel at home with you, because I am among friends, I wish to speak with the bluntness of a true friend; with the honesty that must characterize relations between friends who respect each other and who have each other's interests at heart. To the degree that tensions or misunderstandings exist between Jews and blacks today, some of the responsibility must be laid upon the indifference to issues touching the very core of black interests on the part of some Jews.

The civil rights movement owes a tremendous debt of gratitude to the Jewish community, which stood with us in the darkest days of oppression and marched by our side in the brightest days of the common struggle for justice. And even today, after the harsh strains imposed by the New York teachers' strike, the mindless radical hostility to Israel, scatter-site public housing, the controversies over busing and quotas, and other blows to our coalition, even today, there is far greater support for black people among Jews than among any other group in the population and there is far less anti-Semitism among blacks than among any other group in the population.

We share far too much in terms of historic oppression and in noble values for the coalition between Jews and blacks to be split asunder by isolated occurrences and issues. But it would be mistaken for either of us to deny that there are strains in our relationship and it would be inconceivable for either of us to ignore those strains and to refuse to repair them.

The issue that has most visibly separated the Jewish community from the black community is the issue of affirmative action, or, as most people insist on calling it, the issue of "quotas." The celebrated De Funis case was seen by many people as a black-Jewish confrontation, but it was a good deal more than that.

I should point out too, that while the bulk of Jewish organizations that took a stand in that case were for De Funis, the National Council of Jewish Women and the Union of American Hebrew Congregations joined with the National Urban League and other agencies in filing an amicus curiae brief supporting the university's position.

I believe that many black people understand the basis of the Jewish fear of a quota system, a fear that is rooted not only in the American Jewish experience of being subjected to rigid—and very low—quotas for admission to colleges and professions, but also to the European experience of restriction to the pale and the most limited and controlled access to schools, jobs, and professions.

But black people also know that we too have been subjected to a quota system, a quota system that froze us out of America's universities, out of her professions, and out of the mainstream of her social and economic life. It is because of that quota system that a third of all black people are locked into poverty and another third live on marginal incomes today. It is because of that quota system that black people form less than 2 percent of every profession of significance today. It is because of the heritage of that quota system that so few blacks are to be found in graduate schools and in professional schools today.

And it is because of that quota system that special affirmative action programs must be devised in order to include black people in every major sphere of American life.

This was articulated so well by Lyndon Johnson in his last public appearance before his death when he said: "To be black in white society is not to stand on level and equal ground. While the races may stand side by side, whites stand on history's mountain and blacks stand in history's hollow. We must overcome unequal history before we overcome unequal opportunity."

We have no quarrel with the merit system nor with the concept that rigid numerical quotas that overlook individual differences and attributes are wrong. But we reject the suggestion that a merit system is actually in operation today. Nor do we accept that merit may be accurately measured by tests. Public service jobs are often awarded on the basis of political patronage, not merit. Jobs are based on tests that have no relationship to the job to be performed. University positions are awarded on the basis of the buddy system and the old school tie. Construction industry jobs are often restricted to members of the family of a union member. The extent to which merit determines the allocation of jobs and privilege in our society has been grossly exaggerated. Even Justice Douglas, whose De Funis opinion indicated he felt the University of Washington violated Fourteenth Amendment guarantees of equal protection, indicated just as strongly his belief that the Law School tests were not a positive indication of merit and that other criteria could also be used to determine admission.

It is all too often overlooked that only a mere two or three points on that test separated De Funis from black students who were admitted in preference to him. Must two points on a questionable test forever condemn blacks from reversing the University's past history of bias and discrimination?

I wish the word "quota" could be forever expunged from this discussion. Our position has never been that there should be a rigid, numerical quota of blacks in every field of endeavor. We do not believe that unqualified persons should be made doctors, lawyers, or teachers because of their race. We have no commitment to incompetence.

But we do insist that our society has become rigid in its definitions of appropriate qualifications. Yesterday's elementary school dropout could make a living as a janitor; today he must have a junior college diploma and is called a custodial engineer. Our society has erected paper barriers and unnecessary credentials that exclude too many poor people and minorities from positions they are otherwise qualified to hold. We measure test scores, not individual capability and potential. We say that because someone scored 76 on a law school exam he should be admitted, no matter what. But if a black student overcomes a life of poverty, the pressure of the slums, the prejudice of the society, and retains the ambition and drive to—in spite of everything—finish college and score 74 on that exam, then we say he is unqualified. I say that is wrong. I say that is an immoral waste of human resources. I say that given the refusal of our society to allow blacks into law schools in the past, given the fact that a bare handful of black lawyers are practicing today, then that youngster and others like him should receive some kind of preference until such time as black people may be regarded as having achieved full access to the professions of our society.

What has most alarmed the black community has been the intensity with which affirmative action has been fought. We know, from bitter experience, that unless there are affirmative action plans, unless there are programs devised to consciously erase the discrimination of past and present; unless there are flexible goals and guidelines aimed at including blacks instead of, as in the past, excluding them, then promises of equal opportunity become hollow, empty, and ultimately deceitful exercises in rhetoric.

Now this is something I believe the Jewish community must confront head-on. There is no reason why blacks and Jews must agree on everything, including affirmative action. There will be many Jewish people whose perception of the merit system and of Jewish interests is such that they cannot agree that affirmative action programs should be supported. It may even be that they will insist on calling them quotas and oppose them vigorously while insisting that there are other, better means of providing fair access to black people.

But such a position imposes upon its proponents the obligation to support effective programs that *do* result in admitting blacks to the schools and the jobs so long denied them. This is, I think, at the core of the growing black feeling that some Jewish people are no longer including themselves in the coalition to build a more equal society.

On the many issues on which there is a divergence of opinion between some blacks and some Jews, there is a perception that the opposition to the black viewpoint is held with a greater intensity and commitment than are alternative means to what both groups hold to be the same goals.

For example, the intensity of the public expression of opposition to quotas is not matched by similar intensity and fervor in support of affirmative action programs that do not require numerical goals.

The hostility to a public housing project in Forest Hills was deep and powerful. But support for alternative means of housing poor people was limited.

So, too, was busing. Opposition to busing is very strong, even on the part of people who insist they are for equal educational opportunity. But support for other means of integrating the schools and improving them is held on a much lower scale of intensity.

There is nothing wrong with disagreeing on the methods of reaching goals both of our peoples profess. But there is great disappointment when we see the fervor and intensity restricted to opposing the methods we support without the same degree of fervor and intensity devoted to devising and supporting other methods. This gives rise to suspicion that the goals of black people may not be that important to others. And from that follow the strains and tensions that are in the interests only of those who would prefer to exclude both Jews and blacks from meaningful participation in our national life.

Just as black leadership has an obligation to minimize tactical differences with our allies on behalf of jointly-held goals, so too does Jewish leadership have an obligation to do the same. I was very pleased to join with the American Jewish Committee and with the heads of other minority and Jewish agencies in an appeal to the Secretary of HEW to issue new guidelines in the wake of the De Funis case that will assure, to quote from our letter, "special efforts to recruit persons from previously excluded groups."

I would hope that this positive step which does much to dispel black fears of Jewish abandonment, will be joined by continued vigorous activity to reassert Jewish commitment to the cause of equal rights.

Jews and blacks must not accept artificial structural limitations on the numbers of openings to the professions, the crafts, or other basic institutions. Minorities have been set squabbling among ourselves for scarce resources that should be open to all; for poverty funds, construction jobs or professional positions that our society is wealthy enough to provide in abundance. The real underlying problem is not the quota system or preferential treatment; the real problem is the rigidity of the structure of our society. And the real question facing Jews and blacks alike is what we can do together to open our society up so that each of us may make the best use of his talents and fulfill his highest aspirations.

By and large, American Jewry has finally escaped the poverty and oppression it met in this country for so long. The struggle was a long, searing one and there is a great temptation for some Jewish people to turn to others still engaged in that struggle and suggest: "We made it by our bootstraps; we persevered in the face of brutal obstacles. You, too, must now do the same." But there is no need for minorities in the 1970s to retrace every step made by their predecessors on the urban scene. Black people have paid their dues in the form of slavery, peonage, and exclusion for nearly four hundred years and there is little justification to add another fifty or a hundred years to our passage into equality. Times have changed, too. Our technological economy, the shrinking of traditional stepping-stone jobs, the over-credentialization in the workplace all combine to make it impossible for today's deprived to duplicate the Jewish experience.

The black community, and agencies like the Urban League, is following Herzl's precept that "Whoever would change men must change the conditions of their lives." We are trying to change the conditions that bind men to poverty and joblessness, women to deprivation and dependency, and children to hunger and illiteracy.

I believe the Jewish community, too, is committed to changing our society, to changing "the conditions of men's lives," to secure a newer, better, more just, more equal society.

I believe this because of the historic Jewish commitment to the goals and aspirations of the civil rights movement and to the efforts of black people to win our place in America's sun.

I believe this because of the historic Jewish commitment to justice and decency, a commitment rooted in religious values dating to the very beginning of recorded time, a commitment that also infuses the black church and black beliefs.

I believe it because Jews retain a consciousness of the fragility of minority life, a consciousness reinforced by such constant reminders as the hell of Auschwitz, the horror of Munich, and the terror of Maalot. The Jewish community is always aware that minority status invites persecution and discrimination and thus, whatever the degree of security and prosperity it may enjoy in this nation, it is sympathetic to the plight of other, less favored minorities.

And finally, I believe it because the future of the American Jewish community is tied to the future of our nation. A racially divided society will forever curse our nation with domestic violence and economic unrest, while an open, integrated, pluralistic society will afford to both blacks and Jews, as to the nation at large, the peace and prosperity we all long for.

In this time of division, in this period of doubt, it would be good for both Jews and blacks to reflect on the timeless words of the great Hillel:

> "If I am not for myself, who shall be for me?
> If I am only for myself, what am I?
> If not now, when?"

We must be for ourselves in that we have an obligation to pursue reasonable self-interest. But if we are to retain our humanity, we must also demonstrate our concern for others. And we must not delay constructive action. "If not now, when?" The time is now for blacks and Jews to come together, to reinvigorate our alliance forged from our joint passion for justice and brotherhood.

And the eye hath not seen nor the ear heard that which we can do together, united and unafraid.

INDEX

5 × 7
cards

subject	text-author
pages	

General Purpose - to inform

Central Idea

Specific Purpose: I want my audience to understand

4 stages for planning a speech

① Plan

  a) choose a topic - familiar to you, something you can get enthused about

  b) talk about something that really concerns you

  c) analyze your audience

  d) select a specific purpose

    1) informative - give an understanding

    2) persuasive - convince

  e) research - visual aids

② Organization

  a) central idea - idea entire speech revolves around

  b) Main points

  c) organizing ideas

  d) outline

  e) introduction

  f) conclusion

③ Developing stage

  a) develop main ideas - illustrate, facts, stats, visual aids

  b) develop visual aids

④ Presentation stage

  a) plan style

  b) practice aloud

establish common ground